WORLDS REBORN

DATE DUE			

Cover and title page photographs of Quetzalcoatl,
front and rear views: Lord of Life (cover) and Lord of
Death (title page). Ca. A.D. 1000. Huastec. Mexico.
Brooklyn Museum.

WORLDS REBORN

The Hero in the Modern Spanish American Novel

William L. Siemens

WEST VIRGINIA UNIVERSITY ·PRESS·

Morgantown

863
Silw
130755
Feb. 1985

Dedication

For Dad, who could not tarry to see
the book but who is in it.

Contents

I. Introduction   1

II. Roberto Arlt, *Los siete locos (Seven Madmen)*   12

III. Alejo Carpentier, *Los pasos perdidos*
(The Lost Steps)   35

IV. Juan Rulfo, *Pedro Páramo*   62

V. Julio Cortázar, *Rayuela (Hopscotch)*   82

VI. Gabriel García Márquez, *Cien años de soledad*
(One Hundred Years of Solitude)   109

VII. Guillermo Cabrera Infante, *Tres tristes*
tigres (Three Trapped Tigers)   138

VIII. Mario Vargas Llosa, *Pantaleón y las visitadoras*
(Captain Pantoja and the Special Service)   172

IX. Carlos Fuentes, *Terra nostra*   189

X. Conclusion   222

Notes   227

Bibliography   232

Index   241

Acknowledgment

This study was done in part during a National Endowment for the Humanities Summer Seminar. The author wishes to express his gratitude to the Endowment for its support.

I

Introduction

Jorge Luis Borges once observed, "In the books of old, quests always prospered: the argonauts managed to obtain the Fleece and Galahad the Holy Grail. Now, in contrast, one takes a mysterious pleasure in the concept of an endless quest or the quest of something that, once found, brings on deadly consequences. K, the land-surveyor, fails to enter the castle, and the white whale is the perdition of the one who finds it in the end."[1] Yet in the curiously hero-less twentieth century the Spanish American novel has persistently set before us a hero in the making, one who, viewed in the aggregate, has become increasingly successful at adapting his life to the traditional hero's trajectory. One no longer takes it for granted that the protagonist of one of these novels will, like Demetrio Macías in *Los de abajo*, retrace the epic pattern only to die where he started, with a bullet—real or metaphorical—between the eyes. In our generation it seems acceptable for an author to create a character of more or less worthy motives and at least moderate ability to overcome the obstacles set before him. Such a process demands closer examination, and my intention is to show, by way of representative novels published between 1929 and 1975, how the hero has grown in stature in Spanish American prose fiction.

One can only speculate with regard to the cultural factors that have led to such a change, culminating in Carlos Fuentes' unabashedly metaphysical novel, *Terra nostra*, with its hero who ultimately changes the rules of the cosmos. It is not enough to say that Latin Americans feel an acute *need* for a

1

hero to save the world, for in the first novel considered here, Roberto Arlt's *Los siete locos,* the protagonist himself states that Christ or someone comparable will have to come to save society, but the speaker is a total failure. Nor is it possible to say that conditions in Latin America have given hope that such a hero will appear, for most of the countries in the region are in deep difficulties. Perhaps the answer is to be found in the experience of the Mexican Revolution, when the Porfirio Díaz administration was perceived to be bankrupt in terms of human values despite its technological advances, and the nation set about examining its indigenous roots, including Mayan and Aztec mythologies. The reinstatement of pre-modern ideology as a respectable alternative provides for a belief in the hero, whose story is the focal point of all myth. Clearly, the ongoing industrialization and urbanization of Latin America are accompanied by a persistent fascination with those primordial images that Carl Jung claims exist within the collective unconscious, waiting only to be activated, perhaps by experiences such as that of revolutionary Mexico.

Unquestionably, the standard hero tale for the Western world—the story that sets the pattern for the would-be literary hero—is that of Odysseus. Any lengthy series of trials undergone by a modern protagonist tends to be termed an odyssey. Odysseus' heroic deeds are as normative for the West as the radically different deeds of Gautama Buddha are for the Orient. The salient points of his journey as they apply to the Spanish American novel of the twentieth century are his obsession with returning to the Center of his cosmos, which is threatened by the forces of chaos, to reunite with Penelope in a new *hieros gamos,* the sacred wedding that makes all things new; and the persistent theme of hospitality and communion as over against the boorish hostility and love of isolation seen in characters such as Polyphemus. Civilization begins at the meal shared with a stranger in the process of establishing a friendship, and the noble oafs who violate the principle by invading the king's house to devour his cattle and woo his presumed widow are worthy only of being slaughtered.

The heroic pattern to which I have referred was set over a millennium before the events depicted in *The Odyssey,* and in

2

the earliest extant piece of secular literature it has a rather pessimistic strain. The *Epic of Gilgamesh* refers to events that supposedly took place more than 4,000 years ago. All the major elements listed by students of the hero myth are already present in it: mysterious origins (Gilgamesh is two-thirds immortal), a youthful wildness that must be tamed, the call to adventure, the voyage to the Source, the meeting with the goddess, the slaying of monsters, the triumphant return. The problem faced by this legendary king, however, is that the boon he seeks is personal immortality, exactly what Miguel de Unamuno is preoccupied with in the twentieth century, and it proves as elusive for the legendary king of Uruk as it does for the modern Basque philosopher.

Gilgamesh is offered immortality in various forms along the way, but each time he either rejects it or loses it. True myth always has an undercurrent of humor, and in the *Epic of Gilgamesh* it is present in the hero's brusque refusal to marry the goddess Ishtar, who has offered him immortality into the bargain, because he knows her reputation for fickleness and for performing horrible deeds upon the men of whom she tires. The curious feature of this tale is that the hero stands up in the face of the goddess's vengeance. When Ishtar retaliates by dispatching the Bull of Heaven to wreak havoc on his kingdom, Gilgamesh summarily kills it. The point seems to be that in some cases the price of immortality is too high.

Gilgamesh comes closest to his goal when he obtains a plant with the power of the perpetual regeneration of youth. His information concerning the plant is gained from Utnapishtim, the Sumerian Noah, at the instigation of the ancient one's wife. In the hero tales woman is consistently associated with the origin and renewal of life, a point that takes on considerable importance in the Spanish American novel. When Gilgamesh relaxes his vigilance the serpent emerges from the waters and takes the plant for himself, thus gaining the power to shed his skin and renew his youth. What woman has bestowed has become the property of the serpent, as in Eden, where her name is Eve, meaning "life." In the end the boon obtained by Gilgamesh is not immortality but the realization that the best he can hope for is to rule so well that he will be remembered.

Later this conclusion will be reflected in the frustrated quest of Don Quixote, who, in his failure to enter the mythic world of the immortals, declares in the end that it is after all sufficient to be known to posterity as Alonso Quijano the Good.

According to Lord Raglan, one of the pioneer investigators of the hero theme in the twentieth century, the typical hero is successful in approximately the first half of his career, and then begins an inevitable decline to the point where he is replaced by a younger and more able man. Raglan's list of events in the hero's life is as follows:

1. The hero's mother is a royal virgin;

2. His father is a king, and

3. Often a near relative of his mother, but

4. The circumstances of his conception are unusual, and

5. He is also reputed to be the son of a god.

6. At birth an attempt is made, usually by his father or his maternal grandfather, to kill him, but

7. He is spirited away, and

8. Reared by foster-parents in a far country.

9. We are told nothing of his childhood, but

10. On reaching manhood he returns or goes to his future kingdom.

11. After a victory over the king and/or a giant, dragon or wild beast,

12. He marries a princess, often the daughter of his predecessor, and

13. Becomes king.

14. For a while he reigns uneventfully, and

15. Prescribes laws, but

16. Later he loses favor with the gods and/or his subjects, and

17. Is driven from the throne and city, after which

18. He meets with a mysterious death,

19. Often at the top of a hill.

20. His children, if any, do not succeed him.

21. His body is not buried, but nevertheless

22. He has one or more holy sepulchres.[2]

Standing squarely in time between the purported events portrayed in *The Odyssey* and the actual composition of the poem is the story of Israel's King David, whose rise and decline touch Raglan's outline at several points. His notable attempt to establish the meal taken in common as the basis of a gentler civilization has been too often ignored. Perhaps having understood more fully than most the significance of his nation's beginnings in a communal meal in Egypt, he decrees that his predecessor's last surviving descendant, rather than being executed, shall eat at the king's table for the rest of his life. David's greatest wrath, in contrast, is reserved for the man whose very name has crossed the centuries as "fool," Nabal, the farmer who refuses hungry men his hospitality. There is poignant symbolism in the subsequent marriage union between the king of hospitality and the woman who urged that virtue upon her late husband. As in *The Odyssey,* once the violator of hospitality has been eliminated the sacred wedding may proceed.

Furthermore, the New Testament presents as the "Son of David" the one whose culminating act of his own initiative (as opposed to his submission to crucifixion) was the establishment of the communion meal which was to become the focus of the Church's life and of Christian civilization at its best. David, in Homer's era, had played the dual hero role as both man of words and man of action. Jesus was to reject the warlike hero quest and establish himself as the man of words, albeit precious few even of those. Rejecting also the Far East's tradition of an immobile, contemplative hero, he left behind a story corresponding closely to the archetypal solar and vegetation myths of a divine being bringing salvation by his death and resurrection. The Odyssean hero image has thus been modified

5

for Christendom. The hospitality and communion aspect is well fixed, particularly for the peoples of the North, who were more predisposed to it from the beginning, so that Beowulf's great task is the cleansing of the mead hall, and heaven for the Germanic knight of the Medieval period is feasting with other warriors in Valhalla. The sacred marriage aspect, however, is downplayed.

The Medieval Christian knight, then, is that notable hybrid, an invincible homeric hero with lofty spiritual ideals. His profession is that of cleaving enemies in two with a single blow, or bashing in skulls, but he does it not directly for God but for his lady, variously conceived as the Virgin Mary or as one of her surrogates at court. Mary can offer him immortality for his exploits, like Ishtar with Gilgamesh but without entanglements. In this scenario one may perceive the beginnings of trouble for the modern hero, for as soon as the manichaean division of the world into representatives of good and evil shades off into ambivalence there is self-doubt. Unless each battle is *the* battle in which Michael once again makes the universe safe for goodness by casting Satan out of heaven, in which the White Knight again confronts the Black Knight, the vision of a Christian gentleman—and the Spanish for "gentleman" is still the old word for knight—brutally mauling an enemy becomes intolerable. In the background there is an uneasy combat of two New Testament images of the Christ: he who in one segment of the Johannine writings forgives the enemy who betrays him to death, even offering him the bread and wine of the first communion, and he who in another segment of that Johannine corpus, the Revelation, is seen with his white garments stained with the blood of his enemies. Seemingly he forgives one who is only a tool of the forces of evil, but not those forces themselves.

For the knight it becomes a question of identifying one's personal enemy as an *embodiment* of the forces of evil, so that victory over him becomes not only inevitable but actually an act of Christian piety. In literature the adversary becomes a dragon, an evil giant, or a satanic knight with no redeeming qualities. In practice, of course, it was much more difficult, for the conflict often was either single combat with any knight met by chance on the road in order to increase one's list of glorious victories, or a reasonably bloodless game on the battlefield, an attempt to knock one's cousin from across the channel off his horse and take him as a virtual house guest until the ransom arrived.

No small part of the genius of Cervantes is his keen perception of what such ambivalence was beginning to signify for the modern world. His would-be hero begins his career in his library, where every battle is indeed a rerun of Michael's casting of Satan from heaven, and moves into an arena where everything seems to be in some shade of gray. In the library victims are chained only by evil forces, so when Don Quixote encounters some galley slaves they must be freed. Significantly, one of them, Ginés de Pasamonte, is engaged in writing down his life story, in effect a picaresque novel, a work in which the protagonist's motivation, far from the restoration of the Golden Age, is hunger pure and simple. From this point on the hero will virtually never find it possible to envision himself fully as the representative of the forces of good—if indeed such forces exist—and his foes as Satan's emissaries.

There is another curious innovation in the structure of *Don Quixote,* one which may be as subversive of the value-system of the romances of chivalry as is the narrative itself. Whereas in those romances the action is episodic, each segment describing the overcoming of a threat (*the* threat) to the cosmic order, and thus a closed, cyclical world, *Don Quixote* moves beyond that cyclical structure into a linear one in which such modern features as plot and character development become possible. The result is the modern novel, a wondrous and delightful thing to behold, but one in which the hero is inevitably faced with the possibility of defeat, for a hero who can grow and change, who can think and later change his mind, cannot be too closely identified with the archetype, which is static by its very nature. Such a world is already anticipated when the knight Lancelot, with aspirations of having the purest heart and thus being qualified to retrieve the Holy Grail, commits adultery with the Queen. Don Quixote is able for a while to absorb such aberrations into his overall system, but not many of us after him can do so.

Furthermore, Don Quixote is too socratic to be a real hero of the sort that he wishes to be (Socrates being another type of hero). The work is definitively wrenched away from the Middle Ages and placed in the Renaissance mode when Don Quixote, having remarked with some pique that in his books squires are not allowed to hold conversations with their masters, much less second-guess them, relents and permits Sancho to ride alongside. The movement of the donkey to the side of the nag is fatal to the traditional solar hero system. Odysseus engages in much conversation at the tables of his hosts, but it tends to consist of storytelling (with a generous helping of lies to protect his identity) or of plans for getting home. One cannot imagine his debating with the Phaeacians the pros and cons of his sexual relationship with Calypso, for example. Don Quixote, on the other hand, engages in conversations with Sancho that would do the essays of Montaigne proud.

Out of the tendency to reflect and even doubt the rightness of one's actions there emerges the strange paradox of a hero who is fundamentally a solar figure, and thus identified with the forces of rationality like "clear-thinking Odysseus," yet is incapable of any sort of original speculative thought. It has long been recognized that the typical hero is closely identified with the sun. Like that body he descends into the underworld and emerges at the appointed time as a bearer of enlightenment and new life. In most of the ancient tales he acts more as the agent of the forces of cosmic order than according to his own imagination. He may devise a stratagem to enable him to emerge victorious from some ordeal, but only within the framework of an eternally established set of truths. To the modern reader the old tales of knighthood now being offered in new editions are often unsatisfying in some elusive way, and it may be because there are no *ideas* in them, ideas emerging from the mind of the knight, beyond the occasional flash of insight concerning how to escape from one's chains or save the fair maiden. Don Quixote, though, is full of ideas, some of them brilliant in their anticipation of the modern consciousness. What is modern democracy but the expansion of the experience of the common man Sancho Panza as governor of Barataria, guided by the thoroughly sensible principles of the madman Don Quixote?

8

Still, this madman full of brilliant insights is doomed never to fulfill his goal of being *the* knight, which is to say the incarnation of the archetype. How can one who questions his own values serve as representative of an unchanging value-system in the struggle against the representatives of a threat to that system? He would be in danger of becoming his own enemy.

The novel since *Don Quixote* has tended to be one of dialogue, and as Socrates showed in his exasperating challenge to Euthyphro, the essence of good dialogue is to question all beliefs so that the truth may eventually, gradually, be established. There is no room here for anyone claiming to be a hero standing for all that is true and right and pure. Inevitably, the very ideal of representing what is "good" is called into question, and we find ourselves confronted by those Romantics and their heirs who ask us to affirm the demonic in us, to pluck the flowers of evil, to make beauty of the fallen aspects of life.

In that same Romantic era, whose political ideals were found convenient for bolstering the cause of independence in Latin America, appeared what is generally considered the first true Spanish American novel, *El Periquillo Sarniento,* by José Joaquín Fernández de Lizardi. Significantly, it is of the picaresque type, so that this novel is *not* linear in its development, because if the *pícaro*'s character improves at all it does so in a religious conversion that takes place between the narrated events and the time of narration. If the world changes it negates the thesis of the work, which is that human nature is fallen and unredeemed. There is rather a special kind of cyclical structure, one seemingly based on the Wheel of Fortune concept, so that in each episode Periquillo achieves some relatively high position, only to fall to the depths at its conclusion. In this book, as in the Peninsular picaresque tradition, the grotesque is underscored—not just the grotesqueness of some monster to be overcome, but that of the hero himself and his total situation. Instead of alleviating the suffering of his people, as did the knights of the romances, this protagonist typically *causes* it, both for himself and for others. A case in point is the scene in which Periquillo attempts to pull a woman's tooth and ends up surrounded by enough gore, as he says, to provide a good meal for the cat.

9

On the sentimental side of Romanticism, the hero typically follows the pattern of meeting the woman he is seemingly predestined to marry, overcoming great obstacles to win the right to do so, only to learn that they are brother and sister. (In the oldest myths the couple *must* be brother and sister, but here the more mundane incest taboo has shrouded the primordial symbolism.) One is struck by a sense of *déjà vu* in reading this type of Spanish American novel of the late nineteenth century. In Jorge Isaacs' *María* the theme is only slightly modified, the lovers being siblings by María's adoption, while her death is what prevents their marriage. The point to note for our purposes is the implied doctrine that somewhere in the very nature of reality is an element that will prevent Odysseus' reunion with Penelope, the sacred marriage.

Perhaps the most significant hero-figure of the nineteenth century in this literature, though he appears in a long poem rather than a novel, is José Hernández' creation Martín Fierro. Something of a "noble savage," he is a good gaucho, living out the Argentine Romantic ideal of man in harmony with nature. His story appears to be a parody of *The Odyssey*, in that he lives happily with wife and children until forced away to a war in which he has no interest. He overcomes great obstacles in order to return, fighting with great prowess along the way, but he arrives at home only to learn that home has been destroyed and his wife and children are gone forever. Again the quest is a truncated one, and the *hieros gamos* forbidden.

In this century, when the Spanish American novel comes of age it is with a heavy dependence upon such non-Hispanic sources as the works of Gide, Joyce, Proust, Dos Passos, Faulkner, and Kafka. The would-be hero is an unlikely sort, often cast in an uncomfortable role; yet by fits and by starts it *is* the hero's role that he is attempting to play. The renewed interest in mythology came to the writers whom we shall be considering not only with Joyce's influence, but when the tenacious *costumbrista* tendency matured into a more profound interest in the mythic realities of the indigenous societies of Latin America. Mythology, moreover, implies the presence of what some mythographers term the monomyth, the universal hero tale.

10

The remainder of the story involves the clash between this tentative effort to reestablish the hero as a viable character and the modern age's stubborn refusal to believe in the changeless structures of reality which alone can guarantee his success. As this study will attempt to demonstrate, there has been overall increase in the strength of the hero-figure, culminating in Carlos Fuentes' strange Polo Febo.

Luis Eyzaguirre's *El héroe en la novela hispanoamericana* is helpful in its categorizing of the heroes of a great many novels. The approach that will be taken here is quite different, in that I shall attempt to show the development, in a few representative novels, of what I see as a tendency for the hero to become increasingly successful in his endeavors. I am indebted also to other excellent writers on the novels treated here, many of whose works will appear in the bibliography. My hope is that this study may serve as stimulation for further work on these and the numerous other novels in which the hero's career is an important theme, a prospect made more exciting by the appearance of fine new works every year.

II

Roberto Arlt

Los siete locos

(*Seven Madmen*)

La chair est triste, hélàs,
et j'ai lu tous les livres.
Mallarmé

Spanish American novelists have always attempted to read all
the books, as have many of their protagonists. Frequently the
result has been a faint odor of pastiche, particularly as that
vaguely defined entity known as the vanguard began its production. The beginnings of the psychological orientation of the
novel in Latin America are very evident in *Los siete locos*,
published in 1929, and in other works of its day, since the
literary rumblings in the background are those of all the major
European writers of the nineteenth and early twentieth centuries. Perhaps it is unfortunate that the psychological novel
was not allowed a full development, and that the novel of social
realism overwhelmed the tendency to focus upon the
individual's quest for wholeness. Novels such as this one and
Eduardo Barrios' *El hermano asno* suggest that the genre
would have been worth pursuing to a much greater extent.

    Los siete locos has more question marks in the text than
any other novel I can recall having read, and this is significant.
The traditional hero tale has few questions, simply because the
fundamental structure of reality is set and immovable, so that
answers can virtually be catalogued. Within this context questions tend to request firm information, as in the case of
Odysseus' inquiry of Teiresias concerning the fate of his con-

12

tinued voyage, which is clearly predestined. The questions asked by Augusto Remo Erdosain, on the other hand, tend toward the refrain "What am I making of my life?" and admit no satisfactory answers.

Curiously, the novel is set up in the form of an initiation experience in which a very modern character, representative of early twentieth-century mankind, searches for coherence in his life through some sort of heroic transformation. Here, perhaps more than in any other novels, we shall consider the tension between the primitive and the modern becomes evident. An initiation ceremony by its very nature possesses a rigidly prescribed structure because the reality underlying it is thought to be equally rigid. Such a reality dictates that at a certain age a boy must be guided by his societal group in becoming a man, for all aspects of his childhood are inadequate for the role he must now take on. In Erdosain's case there is also a firm recognition of the fact that if he is ever to function effectively in the bewildering world that surrounds him, some radical alteration of his character will have to take place. Erdosain is fully aware of the fact that the basic problems he faces are internal to him. He makes it clear that the sadness he feels has nothing to do with his circumstances.[1] The term "anguish" recurs frequently in the text, recalling the distinction made by Kierkegaard between fear and *Angst*, the latter representing an interior uneasiness having no definable object.

Whereas the initiate in a primitive society has his meaningless old life transformed within the context of a solid social framework, Erdosain has no solid ground on which to base his initiation. Everything around him is in a state of flux, so that he is faced with the prospect of formulating for himself a means of transformation and then attempting to make it work. One inescapable problem for Arlt's characters in general is what they perceive as the failure of traditional religion. For the most part it is rejected as invalid for them, with the notable exception of the madman Ergueta, who, significantly, progressively loses his mind as he makes a desperate attempt to hold on to and practice his faith. He is a recognizable twentieth-century type, the literalist religious crackpot for whom the Apocalypse is to be internalized and exemplified by the believer. Therefore his

13

attempt to become the hero by pre-modern means involves the emulation of the Old Testament prophet Hosea, who was instructed by Yahweh to marry a prostitute. Ergueta is the character who maintains the reader's awareness of the apocalyptic nature of the times, proclaiming that he and the others are living in the Great Tribulation. Significantly, he, like the principal characters of the later Argentine novel *Rayuela*, ends up in an insane asylum. Only there does he find the transcendental experience for which he has been searching, his face-to-face meeting with God (pp. 217ff.). For him, in R. D. Laing's terms, breakdown certainly has meant breakthrough—for whatever it is worth.

Ergueta has conceived the necessity of the hero's work in traditional religious terms: "A man, an angel will have to come, I guess, I don't know. . . . Yes, it is essential that Christ return. . . . And if he doesn't come, who is going to save us?" (pp. 173-174). From the novelist's viewpoint, this is the bankrupt ideology of modernity. What will be called modern from now on may actually constitute a return to more primitive forms, in which a hero will arise from within society at the close of each temporal cycle to locate, and return with, the power to renew it. The expectation that the single linear unit of time granted to mankind will end with the return of the Christ who initiated it may be considered invalid, and the one who espouses it fit only for a mental institution.

As for society in general, it is "sick with religion." Erdosain himself feels that "the day will come when the people will bring about a revolution, because they lack a God. Men will be on strike until God comes to stand before them" (p. 226). The view of the Astrologer, who is the principal ideological spokesman of the work, is quite different: "The sickness of the age, irreligion, has destroyed our understanding, so that we search outside ourselves for what is within the mystery of our subconscious. We are in need of a religion to save us from that catastrophe which has fallen on our heads. . . . And the most terrible thing is that for us the time for acquiring a belief, a faith, is now past" (p. 78).

In what has the appearance of a paraphrase, before the fact, of the familiar statement that "God died in the nineteenth

14

century and man in the twentieth," Gregorio Barsut declares that "humanity, the multitudes of this vast earth, have lost their religion. . . . So men are going to say, 'What good is life to us?' " (p. 120). His cynical conclusion is that "mankind's happiness can only be upheld by the metaphysical lie. . . . Deprived of that lie it falls into illusions of an economic nature" (p. 121). In line with this sort of thinking, the group of madmen intends to put into practice a revolutionary system based on lies, for what else is to be expected of those who have lost contact with the absolutes— who, in fact, live in a world in which vast numbers of people believe that truth must be created by each person in moving through life. Perhaps inherent in such a relativistic system, however, is the danger that the lie may become incarnate. An ominous example may be seen in Thomas Pynchon's *Gravity's Rainbow*, in which Allied propaganda personnel play upon the supposed racism of the German public by proclaiming that the rocket program is increasingly in the hands of black Africans, only to learn at the end of the war that it is true. A system bent on manipulating the common people by means of a metaphysical lie concerning a God of truth might be destroyed eventually by such a God. Meanwhile, the madmen believe that interior "gods" exist.

The important point is that Erdosain desires transformation: "It suddenly occurs to a person that certain definite things must happen to him in his life . . . so that his life will be transformed and renewed" (p. 49). Yet the hero must go off in search of truth and reality or the quest will prove to be fruitless; the lies are those of that archetypal tyrant that Joseph Campbell calls Holdfast, to the effect that security is to be found only in the status quo. The entire range of solar symbolism associated with the traditional hero speaks of enlightenment, the illumination of dark corners too long left unattended. The very root meaning of "apocalypse" involves taking the wraps off what has been hidden in darkness, as Odysseus is at long last able to break *away* (*apo*) from *Calypso* (darkness) and shore up the battlements of civilization at Ithaca, now threatened by the forces of chaos in the form of men with names often beginning with *melan-*, meaning "black." The entire sense of apocalyptic has to do with the rebirth of light so that it may carry out the work of renovation.

A further point concerning Odysseus that may be instructive involves the description of him, Penelope, and their son Telemachus in terms of "clear thinking." It should be noted that this sort of translation is disputed by Julian Jaynes in *The Origin of Consciousness in the Breakdown of the Bicameral Mind.* Jaynes believes that such translations, implying rational thought, are the result of modern preconceptions. If he is correct, however, my point still stands, for what is at issue is behavior that results from sound mental processes. If in the age in question what is normally translated as "clear thinking" meant obedience to the supposed voice of Athena, there is no difficulty. What the poet means to underline is the contrast between the senseless behavior of such characters as the Suitors and Polyphemus on the one hand, and the civilized behavior of Odysseus and his family on the other.

Arlt's hero, Erdosain, is a madman, characterized, says the narrator, by "a mental incoherence" (p. 160), as are all the principal male characters. Not much can be said in favor of the soundness of mind of the wives of Erdosain and Ergueta either. So the character who is sent onto the stage of the novel to impose order upon the prevailing chaos has a mind that is chaotic as well; no sound-minded Odysseus here. In the strange mind of this author there is a good deal of sympathy for his characters, however mad and vicious they may be. Erdosain, for example, is described at the outset as "a failed inventor and a delinquent on the verge of landing in prison" (p. 10). There is not much for the reader to admire in a crackpot and a thief, to be sure—unless that description happens to belong to Trickster. The typical trickster figure—the one in North American Indian mythology is probably the most familiar—is an inventor, and one who quite often fails at his task. He is also a delinquent at times, yet in spite of this he is venerated by certain tribes as "the Ancient One," specifically the Creator in many origin stories. Erdosain clearly believes he has a god within him, but the reader finds it impossible to view him in a positive light as the trickster whose work is so necessary to his society. The difference lies in the fact that Trickster is the being who breaks the order of things before Holdfast can gain too firm a foothold to be easily dislodged, opening the people up by way of laughter to new possibilities

16

that must be considered if the vitality of the tribe is to be maintained. He too asks himself how well he has performed in his life, but it is because he is conscious of having been sent by the highest powers for the express purpose of doing away with hindrances to the lives of people. Then he repents of his foolish tricks and carries out his basic mission.[2] Erdosain, in contrast, has no such consciousness, his total orientation being in the direction of the murder of a man and collaboration in the establishment of a society even more oppressive than the one in which he lives. There is not much hope of creative action here, or even of laughter.

So there is the desire for a transformation, one that will lead to some sort of coherence, even if it be of a criminal sort. Not long after this, Albert Camus was to state that a person's identity is constituted by that person's actions without regard to any set of standards by which those actions might be judged right or wrong. As the character known as the Melancholy Pimp expresses it, "Since life has no meaning, it makes no difference which current you follow" (p. 42). Within such an existentialist framework, strictly interpreted, it might be legitimate to say, as Erdosain does, "[I want] to see what I am like by committing a crime. Only crime can affirm my existence" (p. 223), or "Killing Barsut was a previous condition for existence" (p. 100). There may be an initiation, then, but it may well be one similar to the Garden of Eden experience. There Adam and Eve are initiated out of a primitive, innocent state of being into one in which they are "like God" (or "like gods"), but only in their experience of the difference between good and evil. Furthermore, the initiation process is guided by the snake, a virtually universal symbol of chaos, so that the initiates end in sin, which even Erdosain considers "an act by which man breaks the slender thread that has kept him united to God" (p. 204). In the context in which he makes the statement, Erdosain also reveals that he feels there is no hope of reestablishing the relationship. Indeed, he sounds as if the hero he is about to imitate is Cain, on the verge of murdering his brother to found a new but already contaminated world. The imagery of the passage seems to indicate that history has repeated itself: humanity has reproduced the Fall and this time definitively broken that slender thread, so that the murder of a brother is fully appropriate.

Several of the stages normally found in initiation cere-
monies are evident in Erdosain's trajectory through the work.
One of the most obvious is the requisite stripping away of the
old identity so that a new one may be imposed, one indicative of
the power now in the possession of the hero. Erdosain's two
given names are significant in this regard. The first is Augusto,
that of the greatest of Roman emperors; the second is Remo
(Remus), which also relates him to that empire which was built
on great military organization, magnificent engineering feats,
and sound principles of government. This is worthy of note,
since Erdosain becomes involved in a project the aim of which is
to establish something of an empire, to be based on overwhelming military force, modern technology, and iron-handed
government. Still, there is something amiss, for of the two
founding brothers of Rome, the one who gave his name to the
city and subsequently the empire was Romulus, who built the
walls. The brother called Remus leapt over those walls and was
killed by the other for his trouble. There may be a warning,
then, in the hero's name; even if he is able to maintain his
delusions of grandeur concerning his potential as another
Augustus, he is not likely to make it as far as founding a new
empire. Instead of the great builder presumably required by a
new Rome, he is destined to be the loser who only leaps the
walls built by others. He will never replace the existing Argentine society with one born of his own feverish imagination; all he
can do is break its laws and be destroyed in the act. The goddess
Athena, protectress of heroes, is specifically the goddess of the
defensive warfare that repels those who assault the city.

Nor is either the positive or the negative name replaced in
any sense in the course of the novel. All that Erdosain accom-
plishes, basically, is the removal of his existing name into temporary oblivion; at one point he does not know if he is Augusto
Remo Erdosain. Eventually it is stated that "he was Erdosain.
Now he recognized himself" (p. 61), as he awakens in the
darkness. If, as Emerson has it, "the hero is he who is immovably centred,"[3] what are we to make of one who states, "I
myself am de-centered, I am not who I am, and nevertheless I
need to do something to become conscious of my existence, to
affirm it" (p. 72)? Only in a dream does he find himself in the

18

role of an adventurer, possessing a new name and speaking English. "Perhaps my life will be rebuilt," he says (p. 105).

The ubiquitous question marks are signs of a morbid introspection that might reflect a positive aspect of a certain type of initiation ceremony, but ultimately fails to do so here. From various parts of the world comes the story that in the process of initiation, particularly that of a shaman, a man must watch as his own body is dismembered by demons, who may even boil all the flesh off his bones. The point of the process is that a wholly new person must be constructed from the bare essentials of his bones. Erdosain's monitoring of what happens to him is not this sort of ceremony, though it seems he would like to believe it is. He says, "I am my own spectator. Some day there will be a huge explosion inside of me and I will be converted into another man" (p. 54). Yet there appears to be no force operating in his cosmos that would be capable of producing such an "explosion": "He did nothing but examine himself, analyze what was happening within him, as if the sum total of details could provide him with the certainty that he was alive" (p. 69). Unfortunately, a sum total provides no coherence. Truly, the unexamined life is not worth living, but neither is the overly examined life, particularly if the examination serves only to prove that it makes no sense.

Erdosain possesses the first faint stirrings of a consciousness that the way to heroism is through the reproduction of the character (*i.e.*, the deeds) of a heroic figure. Curiously, he has a tendency to choose models whose lives are anything but exemplary, or, even if he begins with those whose deeds a civilized society would approve, to move gradually down to the reprehensible. He has been deeply influenced by Nietzsche, at least in part through the influence of his friend the Astrologer, and he asks himself whatever became of the life of power (p. 161). The Astrologer wants "to create a haughty, handsome, inexorable man who will dominate the multitudes" (p. 37), and Erdosain, echoing his sentiments, thinks to himself, "One must be strong, that is the only truth. And show no pity" (p. 84). The ideological basis for action, then, leads him to think a great deal about Dostoyevsky's Raskolnikoff and Andre Gide's Lafcadio as possible models. Both of these, significantly, are guilty of

19

murder in a new style: cold and detached. Erdosain speaks of the concept, born in Lafcadio, of "gratuitous criminality" (p. 163). Moreover, "he experienced idle hours in which he would have been capable of committing a crime of any sort, without having on that account the slightest notion of his responsibility for it" (p. 9). Barsut is moved to ask, "What kind of life is this if we commit some sort of barbaric act and don't feel anything?" (p. 64), and perhaps for this reason Erdosain views him as an extension of himself to be done away with if he is to be reborn as a powerful and ruthless person. Mad though he may be, he still represents the last vestiges of the conscience that impedes the full realization of an immoral plan.

In addition to Nietzsche's Übermensch, Raskolnikoff, and Lafcadio, Erdosain is impressed by a number of others whom he feels he has the potential of imitating: "Heroes of all the ages survived in him. Ulysses, Demetrius, Hannibal, Loyola, Napoleon, Lenin, Mussolini" (p. 231). Loyola is a religious hero, belonging to a category rejected by Erdosain except as a means of cynically manipulating the masses. Napoleon betrayed the ideals of the French Revolution by proclaiming himself emperor, and thus serves as a questionable model for the altruistic potential hero, but a perfect one for Erdosain, who intends to bring down the existing government and replace it with his own tyrannical structure. Laborers in this system will work or be shot. Lenin and Mussolini are at the opposite extremes of communism and fascism, neither of them at all admirable in his choice of means for improving the lot of the common person. It is a bit chilling to realize that this book appeared only four years before Hitler came to power. What becomes evident in the list of those heroes Erdosain feels still live in him is that the single aspect of heroism that interests him is power. He feels full of these heroes just when—and because—he has a large sum of money in his possession. Money is power, and power corrupts. The latter part of Lord Raglan's list of events in the hero's life is testimony to the corruption of power, and the Greek tragedy is founded upon it. *Hybris*, after all, is essentially an overblown assessment of the power with which one has returned from the Source, which does run down after a time. The difference in Erdosain's case is that he is corrupted by the very

20

thought of power before he has even completed the top portion of Raglan's list.

The Call to Adventure is often issued by a person corresponding to Jung's Wise Old Man archetype, and this procedure too is twisted in *Los siete locos*. Assuming that role is the Astrologer, who, on the face of it, might be the appropriate one to do so in a search for the primitive roots of human thought. Astrology is based on an extremely ancient belief that earthly events are precise reflections of those in the heavens, so that the skill to read the latter is equivalent to an ability to understand and even predict the former. Even in the Bible, which is generally set in its opposition to astrology, one discovers traces of such beliefs. "A star has stepped out of Jacob" (Numbers 24.17), for example, means that a significant heavenly body is to enter that division of the sky corresponding to the nation of Jacob, or Israel, on earth.[4] Some scholars believe that the story of the "wise men," or astrologers, associated with Jesus' birth, is based on the fact that in the portion of the heavens pertaining to the Jewish nation there appeared in 6 B.C. a conjunction of the planets symbolizing the House of David and kingship (Jupiter and Saturn, respectively).[5] Astrological doctrine still maintains a tenacious hold on the popular imagination.

My comments on astrology are meant to underscore the fact that an astrologer's appearance in a novel coming to grips with a dangerous technological world may signal the advent of a radical change in ideological emphasis. The fact is that astrology and astrologers are relatively prominent in several of these novels; only with the last of them, however, does there appear a serious astronomer, and that paradoxically in an epoch of history characterized by what may be the most backward, superstitious adherence to the tenets of astrology since the ancient Babylonian empire. In terms of a return to pre-modern thought forms, the appearance of an astrologer should signify the possibility of the beginnings of an imposition upon the material world of an order characteristic of the higher spiritual realm of the heavens. The astrologer himself should be something of a hero, Master of the Two Worlds, arrived to serve as link between them, although this does not prove to be the case.

21

Arlt's Astrologer fits better in the category reserved by Eric Hoffer in his *The True Believer* for the intellectual who spurs a mass movement into action than in the category of the Wise Old Man of dream and myth. Hoffer's theory is that every mass movement must have its ideological foundations laid by a "man of words," who in fact may not even be capable of carrying out any of the actions he prescribes as being absolutely necessary.[6] Karl Marx was probably incapable of being a revolutionary activist, and Friedrich Nietzsche was hardly his own superman in practice. It remained for Lenin and Hitler, respectively, to serve as the "men of action." An even more striking case is that of the French writers of the eighteenth century, whose ideas were put into practice by the Americans and only later by the men of action among their countrymen. While Arlt's Astrologer also serves as organizer, his basic function within the strange revolutionary movement is to serve as something of a focal point for its fundamental doctrines and to inspire his followers, including Erdosain.

As the intellectual behind a proposed mass movement, the Astrologer proclaims that "extraordinary times . . ., new times" are on the way (p. 116), and that he and his followers are the ones who will both provoke and take advantage of them. The worker, the exploited underdog, but also the criminal element, will carry out the revolution: "Who are those who must make the social revolution but the confidence men, the downtrodden, the murderers, the phonies, all the rabble suffering in the gutter without any hope of any kind?" (p. 19). He and the so-called Melancholy Pimp have elaborate plans to mold such people into a vast organization, one with as much power and influence as the Ku Klux Klan that they admire so much. The Gold Seeker tells Erdosain, "What the Astrologer proposes is the salvation of the souls of those men worn out by the mechanization of our civilization" (p. 149), and "We young people will create a new life" (p. 150).

All of this sounds very much like typical twentieth-century revolutionary rhetoric shouted by a person of more or less sincerity, except for the suspicious declaration of his intention to make use specifically of the criminal element. This is a clue to the cynicism of the man, whose plan calls for nothing less than the inauguration of "the empire of the Lie" (p. 85), again in anticipation of Hitler: "He who discovers the lie that the crowd needs will be the King of the World" (p. 131). In this entire passage the Astrologer sounds disconcertingly like a Nazi propaganda chief before the fact, particularly since he even uses lies to manipulate his own followers into aiding in the establishment of the empire of the Lie. The use of illusion is the key to controlling the masses, and again good use is to be made of the advances of modern technology, since the cinematographic element will be important in the group's propaganda campaign.

In fact, it will be necessary to make good use of the propensity of people for religious belief as an "industrial mysticism" is created (p. 37). With this statement we have arrived at the key to the power that is always sought by the hero—the power of renewal in society. It is sought when a society suffers from what Julio Cortázar calls a "resolute entropy"[7] and the attendant chaos begins making life unbearable. The power should reestablish order, reasonable behavior, and civilized life. Moreover, it must come from an unchanging and immovable source, from some manifestation of the realm of Being. Perhaps the key to the utter failure of the hero's quest in this novel lies in the fact that the nearest the characters are able to come to that eternal, immaculate Source is the world of the industrialist: "A Ford or an Edison has a thousand times more chance of provoking a revolution than a politician" (p. 37). Henry Ford in particular is viewed as possessing power even over extraterrestrial affairs, since with his wealth he could arrange to blow up the moon if he so desired; thus the reign of the superman has begun (p. 120). The Astrologer's goal is "to create one who will be able to control the masses and show them a future based on science" (p. 37). It is worthy of note that the word "ciencia" in Spanish is used first of all to designate knowledge in general, and only in a derivative sense for what the English word "science" signifies. An astrologer true to his ancient profession would no doubt have used this word in the older sense, but this indidual, with his roots in one of the oldest systems of knowledge in the world, is prepared to throw it all over in favor of the more restricted kind of science—more accurately, the amoral variety of technology—and its cynical use to manipulate humanity.

23

That science, with its related technology, will provide the means of controlling the multitudes, for the Astrologer envisions a vast police state with a massive military organization, complete with well-stocked arsenals and even bombers. His idea of an effective organization is found in the Ku Klux Klan of the 1920s, one that will prove capable of uniting all the malcontents. All those involved will make money from the venture, for money is the element that transforms a man into a god. Now it becomes evident that the ancient relationship of power to transformation has become, in this society of madmen, a very specific thing: a person can leave an empty, meaningless existence behind and become a god, and the power to realize the transformation is money. One recalls that heroes of all ages live within Erdosain when he is in temporary possession of a large amount of cash, and that obtained through the kidnapping of Barsut.

Clearly, then, the initiation process will be successful only if enough money can be raised, by whatever means, to enable the madmen to exercise a great deal of power. Since they believe that "men are only moved by hunger, lust and money" (p. 195), the most logical business for a quick profit is prostitution: "The firmest foundation for the economic segment of our society will be the whorehouse" (p. 141). It seems obvious that this plan constitutes another gross violation of traditional standards of the hero quest and the order that is supposed to result from it, just as obvious as it is in the case of Vargas Llosa's Pantaleón Pantoja, an army officer forced to organize a prostitution service. Within any society an even more fundamental unit than the tribe is the family, and prostitution has always represented a distinct threat to it. The only possible exception is the closely controlled ritual prostitution of the pagan temples, which is quite a different matter, since an act symbolizing union with the goddess of fertility could hardly be farther removed from the offering of a body for money. The significance of prostitution as a force in opposition to divine order can be clearly seen in Odysseus' hanging of the servant girls who disported themselves with the Suitors, as well as the appearance of Rome as the Great Prostitute in the Apocalypse, in contrast to the New Jerusalem, which is portrayed as the Bride of Christ.

The money to be gained from the great chain of brothels is to be used to finance the group's entry into serious industry, the gains from which in turn are to be employed in the service of the revolution. This is where Erdosain enters the picture, for although he has been described at the outset as a failed inventor, he is to contrive the schemes that will bring in large quantities of money.

For his part, the Astrologer wants to be a "manager of madmen" (p. 129), for he has no illusions concerning the sort of person he is dealing with, feeling perhaps that only madmen could ever carry out a scheme of this nature and scope. His theory may not be so far-fetched when one recalls what Hitler had to do to the German mentality to set his scheme in motion, or what any number of cult leaders have accomplished in our generation. What are they, indeed, but "managers of madmen"? Like Hitler, the Astrologer intends to bring out the superman in his followers: "You know something? Many of us bear a superman within us. The superman is the will in its maximum expression." Then, "It is up to us to inaugurate the age of the innocent monster" (p. 233). The curious part of all this is that in a book in which the principal characters all fall clearly into the lowest category of Northrup Frye's division of fictional heroes, the Ironic Mode, the reader should be confronted with so much discussion of the superman, who certainly would appear in the High Mimetic Mode or higher yet. Perhaps the active fantasy life eventually produces a mythology that works, but only where a mentally healthy person is involved.

To summarize what has been said concerning the role of the Astrologer: the potential hero Erdosain's call to adventure is issued by a gross caricature of the traditional Wise Old Man, whose concept of the nature of the power of transformation and its expected results in the reorganization of society represents a parody of any healthy system. No wonder that Erdosain should say, "It was not in my hands to be a good man. Other dark forces twisted me . . ., threw me down" (p. 194).

A quest with such an inauspicious beginning is, of course, doomed to dismal failure. There must be the requisite separation from the world of human existence, and this too is planted in grotesque parodic terms. The hero's "descent into Hades" is provoked by his wife's abandoning him to live with a military man. Immediately the following hero-related events take place within him: (1) time ceases to exist for him, as it often does for the hero who has penetrated to the realm of timelessness; (2) he feels as if he is falling into a bottomless pit, a common experience for the hero who descends to the Source of power; (3) he holds within him all the suffering of the world, as a hero who represents—even embodies—his people must do; and (4) he becomes more and more isolated from the world of human beings (pp. 57-58). It is all an internal, psychological experience, as is typical of the novels of this era which have not gone to the social realist camp, and it corresponds quite well to the traditional hero pattern. But the value of the experience, the hope of bringing back the power of renovation from it, is vitiated entirely by its having been provoked by another violation of the principle of order, which is adultery. Whereas the force that motivates Odysseus to overcome the most formidable obstacles, and even to leave a goddess who he finds more sexually desirable than Penelope, is the firmness of his belief in the importance of a strong house held in serenity, in Erdosain's case the mock hero quest is brought about by nothing less than the breakup of that house.

One of the goals of the transformation Erdosain expects to take place in his life is that he will be made worthy of serving as a founder of the new society. As if on cue, Arlt provides the reader with his version of the theme of the two brothers which is so often associated with such a founding. Erdosain's brother-figure is Gregorio Barsut, who has already been mentioned in several connections. Erdosain intends to kill Barsut, but on one occasion he offers to kill himself for Ergueta's wife's pleasure. In contrast, Barsut says, in a speech vaguely reminiscent of the already mad Don Quixote's rationally planning to lose his mind in order to become a better knight, "How remarkable it would be if I were to go mad, kill you all by shooting you and then commit suicide!" (p. 21). It is stated that "Erdosain perceived him, when he was in the vicinity, not as a man, but precisely as a double" (p. 67). It is noteworthy that in *Rayuela*, the other Argentine novel considered in this study, an author who is very aware of the work of Arlt should also set up his hero's problem in part as the task of dealing with his double.

Barsut seems to represent for Erdosain something very close to what Jung terms the shadow, the embodiment of those negative personality factors that a person wishes to repress. In Jungian psychology wholeness is a result of incorporating the shadow, accepting it as an aspect of one's personality, rather than rejecting it and projecting its characteristics upon some other person. It becomes evident early in the novel that the qualities in Barsut that tend to irritate Erdosain are some of his own worst traits, but instead of accepting himself as he is and subsequently growing to maturity, he intends to kill the unacceptable characteristics in the person of Barsut. Through this crime he intends to affirm his own being, to begin to live.

There is a sacrificial quality to the proposed murder. The Astrologer tells Erdosain that he should read Plutarch's *Lives*, for in it he will learn that a "human life is worth less than that of a dog if, in order to impose a new direction on society, one must destroy that life" (p. 115). Presumably he has reference to those who become worthy of inclusion in Plutarch's work about great men by murdering others. Therefore, by implication Erdosain can follow some worthy examples and become a hero by carrying out this murder. Furthermore, there is a sort of boon involved in the killing, for the money belonging to the dead brother will then be available for the surviving brother to use in the act of founding a new world. The act is analogous to the slaying of the dragon that guards the treasure.

The progress of the plan to murder Barsut leads Erdosain ever deeper into introspection as he contemplates the enormity of putting an end to the life of a human being and wonders what it will mean to him, the perpetrator of the crime if not the one actually soiling his hands with it. What he expects is a sort of rebirth, but he is unable to avoid the feeling that the weight of the human life laid to his charge is tremendous, a fact which totally contradicts his expressed opinion that life is worthless, and particularly that of this man he is about to kill. Incredibly, he is able to deal with his guilt feelings before the act by convincing himself that the resultant happiness will absolve him: "Joy is the essential thing. And also loving someone" (p. 85).

The question is what sort of transformation can be wrought through such a twisted process. Erdosain's feelings concerning himself are highly ambivalent. At the outset the author informs his reader that Erdosain "was the husk of a man moved by the automatism of habit" (p. 9), and again there emerges the theme of the lack of rationality or the will to change either himself or the world in any meaningful way. When he does move, he does so to promote death rather than life. The traditional hero serves as something of an incarnation of life and Being, but Erdosain says of himself, "As far as everyone else is concerned, I'm the negation of life. I'm something sort of like nonbeing." He sees himself as "nothingness for everyone." He asks, like the existentialists, whether it is possible to exist in spite of not being (pp. 72-73). The answer given by the pre-modern world would be no, as long as one fails to reproduce the archetypal deeds of a hero, and that of the radical existentialist would presumably be yes, if by existing he means acting, for action constitutes essence. Erdosain's confused soliloquy at this point, however, underscores the fact that he belongs in neither camp.

The ambivalence he feels towards himself is well illustrated by his impression at one point that if all the worthless accretions were removed from the core of his life—what Jung terms the Self—there would be found within him "a splendid man, strong as one of the first gods who brought the creation to life" (p. 73), which is quite a far cry from the narrator's comment about his being a mere husk, precluding any sort of core whatever. The point is underscored by the fact that this particular fantasy of Erdosain's concerning his resemblance to the gods who originated life comes in the midst of a soliloquy about killing a man.

The reader should recognize, nevertheless, that Erdosain has unwittingly hit upon a very primitive concept. As Lord Raglan puts it, "The idea of deity and the idea of power are and always have been inseparably connected."[8] Another way of stating the same thing is that the essential point about a god is his possession of great power, or even that he is a personification of power, without reference to the moral attributes inherent in ethical monotheism. Oversimplified though it may be, the concept aids us in seeing how the polytheistic mind functions, recognizing diverse kinds of power in nature and molding each of them into a manageable shape, that of a personal being. The major consideration for our purposes, though, is that Erdosain, having lost contact with traditional religion, appears instinctively to make the radical association between deity and power. If there is within him the potential of great power, there is perforce a god within him. In the context of a discussion concerning his power over the money extorted from Barsut— "Everything depends on my criminal trustworthiness" (p. 202) —he tells Ergueta's wife Hipólita that certain considerations, in this case presumably involving the power inherent in money, transform a man into a god, and then admits that he has been resolved for some time to commit suicide (p. 202). Yet later he has moved away from the idea of suicide and, on the basis of the thought that he can invent a death ray, he envisions himself as "Master of the Universe" (p. 231).

The hero is often thought of as not only representing, but actually embodying, his world. By realizing this the reader of the Oedipus myth understands how the contamination of the hero-king, however unintentional on his part, pollutes the entire kingdom, land and people alike. The transformation of the hero, then, is tantamount to the transformation or re-creation of nature. Therefore, when Erdosain, whose concept of revolution involves such a gross perversion of natural processes, deals with nature, the results reflect that perversion. His place in the industrial scheme is to put into production certain concepts that he as inventor has developed. The principal one involves the copper plating of roses. Beyond the fact that the ordinary person's sensibilities are offered by the covering up of a flower's beauty in metal, there are metaphorical considerations as well. The rose has long been a symbol of love, and the advent of an industrial process involving its envelopment in copper is reflective of the obscuring of human relationships resulting from the overall dehumanization of life in a technologically oriented world. Erdosain's secondary idea has to do with the dyeing of dogs in whatever artificial colors are desired by the customer. The revolution is to be brought about by means of lies, cinematic propaganda, the simulation of love (in the brothels), and the conversion of nature into an artificial fabrication. All is illusion, and that not even the *maya* of India, a form of illusion which at least has its roots in fundamental reality, but the sort that springs from the minds of madmen.

In the work the reader notes a general tendency towards dehumanization, based in part on the remnants of naturalism in the novel of this period, and in part on the author's perception of humanity's decreasing self-esteem in a machine-dominated age. The naturalistic tendencies emerge in Arlt's habit, especially near the beginning of the novel, of describing persons by reference to animals. Curiously, in the second paragraph Erdosain's director on the job is described as having the head of a wild boar (p. 7), which may represent a reflection of Erdosain's status as a would-be solar hero, since a common feature of mythology has the hero being killed, or at least wounded in his youth, by a boar. Erdosain is in a position to be seriously harmed by way of imprisonment at the hands of this man, whose pupils, incidentally, are like those of a fish. The accountant who is present, by the same token, has the neck of a bull, while Barsut, later, has the face of a tiger (p. 100). As is so often the case in twentieth-century art, the grotesque is important in the work, especially in the description of the characters. The madman who carries out the supposed murder, for example, is known only as "The Man Who Saw the Midwife," twisted and hopelessly deranged from birth by that mysterious occurrence. In general, the narrator speaks of the "certainty that the life of a man is of no value" (p. 208), and his handling of descriptive material serves to underscore that point.

In spite of this, as noted earlier, Erdosain feels that the essential things in life are to experience joy and love someone. It would appear that the former would depend on the latter, which never happens in this work. In Erdosain's case it is not a matter of his violation of the sanctity of the marriage bond through promiscuous behavior, least of all in his youth. He is described as having been extremely puritanical as a young man, possessed of something reminiscent of the ideals of courtly love. Perhaps significantly, two other major figures of the novels under consideration in this study possess similar ideals as young men: Pantaleón Pantoja and the second El Señor of *Terra nostra*. In this there may be a faint echo of the dedication that Odysseus exhibits to Penelope; his sexual adventures on the way home partake more of the character of ritual union with the goddess than conventional adultery. On the other hand, in all three of the cases of full chastity noted in these novels, the earlier principles are grossly violated in some way.

Erdosain's quest does at times take on the proportions of a search for the Goddess—that is, the ideal Woman, "that arbitrary woman, kneaded from the flesh of all the women he had not been able to possess" (p. 98). His wife, who says she would have preferred to remain unmarried and simply take a lover, eventually leaves Erdosain to do just that, and the narrator reveals that she has previously denied her husband sexually. His search even leads him to a meaningless encounter with the wife of the institutionalized Ergueta, an ex-prostitute according to whom the life of a whore is a liberation from the body. Here Erdosain announces his intention to commit suicide, offering to do so if she wants him to, in what again may be a pale reflection of the self-emasculation of the ancient devotees of lunar goddesses such as Cybele. Clearly this is his meeting with the prostitute-aspect of the Great Goddess, whom he perceives as the devouring female. With her cold hands along with the offer of her body, she is in fact both death and life to him.

Erdosain has a tendency to project his anima onto certain females, a procedure that Jung warns is dangerous in that it reflects a failure on the part of a man to integrate his own feminine qualities into the psyche. Thus Erdosain, who in his developing plans for murder and ruthless exploitation is increasingly far removed from such characteristics as tenderness, compassion, and trust, recalls an incident involving a sentimental encounter with a schoolgirl of perhaps fifteen. As he imagines it, "he is another man, and through the mere fact of having thought about the child who in a railroad car had rested her head on his shoulder" (pp. 86-87). He is emphatically not a new man; in a few moments he has awakened from his reverie, and the narrator states, "He would like to violate something—violate common sense" (p. 87). In fact, the word "violar" may be translated as "rape."

What is signified by all this is the failure of any representation of the sacred wedding, the *hieros gamos,* to take place. Social stability throughout recorded history has been

31

symbolized by a man and a woman uniting to produce new life, and that in turn has meant that the continued life of the cosmos at large is assured. Even Ergueta, the madman who retains the closest connections with traditional beliefs, misreads his Bible, for the story of Hosea's marrying a prostitute to symbolize Israel's abandonment of her symbolic marriage of Yahweh by "committing adultery" with foreign gods is in the Old Testament, while in the New Testament Apocalypse those who have dealings with the "Great Prostitute" perish with her so that the Christian version of the *hieros gamos* can take place: the marriage of the Lamb who is Christ to his bride, the Church. Even Ergueta misses the point of the sacred marriage.

More serious is the fact that the new society is to be *based* on prostitution. In this, incidentally, Arlt anticipates Giraudoux's *La Folle de Chaillot,* which appeared in 1945, in portraying capitalist exploiters as pimps. Prostitution is an insistent theme in the Spanish American novel, from Federico Gamboa's *Santa* through Jorge Edwards Bello's *El roto* and Arlt's work to several of the novels of Mario Vargas Llosa. Taken as a whole, the phenomenon has to mean that even the most intimate and meaningful of personal relationships has been lowered to the level of commerce in the modern world, and in terms of traditional mythology it signifies the emphatic denial of the *hieros gamos,* in which opposites unite on all levels from the microcosmic to the macrocosmic to achieve the full union from which a rich new life is to emerge. In *Los siete locos* prostitution, not the family, is to serve as the foundation stone of a new world.

In place of the legitimate offspring of multiple unions of male and female, the Astrologer proposes what amounts to a parody of the fruit of the sacred wedding: "to raise a child of exceptional beauty and train him to play the role of a god." Admitting that he himself is a cross between a cynic and a madman, the Astrologer says that the child must be a cross between Krishnamurti and Rudolph Valentino (pp. 125-26). That is, pop religion is to be wedded to the cinematic nature of the propaganda that he intends to employ. Thus, he both recognizes and feels he knows how to exploit the masses' need for religious belief. The theme of a child god (or at least a saint and martyr,

32

which in the popular imagination may represent the same phenomenon) recurs in *Pantaleón y las visitadoras.*

This is the only one of the eight novels here considered in which a position of any significance is conceded to a meal taken together, with the possible exception of Bustrofedon's combination Mad Hatter's tea party and Last Supper in *Tres tristes tigres.* At the end of *Los siete locos,* after Erdosain has calmly watched the mock murder of Barsut, thinking it to be real, there is a meal based on the "death" of Barsut as the original Last Supper is based on that of Christ. But whereas the great deal of eating in *The Odyssey,* as well as the Last Supper of Jesus and the twelve, signifies the communion that binds persons together in a life-enhancing civilized bond of friendship, loyalty, and mutual trust, the dinner given by the Astrologer is based on a murder that is a lie, and seals a bond of falsehood and exploitation.

An initiation ceremony often ends in a significant time of sleeping and dreaming from which the initiate awakens with a new identity. A Plains Indian boy, for example, is taught his true name in his Vision Quest, which involves just such a period of ceremonial sleep.[9] After the meal Erdosain, relieved that the ordeal of the killing is over, sleeps for twenty-eight hours, and the Astrologer tells him that he appeared to be dead when asleep. He is to buy some new clothes, also symbolic of the transformed person back from the dead, in a motif seen also in *Cien años de soledad.*

The reader is warned long before the conclusion that at the time of writing Erdosain is already dead of tuberculosis, not suicide or a wound suffered in some revolutionary battle. This too is a theme of a number of works considered in this study: the hero's difficulty with breathing. Considering that breath and spirit are identical in so many languages and systems of thought, it would appear that there is reflected here a serious flaw in the spirit of many potential heroes. José Lezama Lima's *Paradiso,* which cannot be dealt with at length here, actually opens with an asthmatic crisis of the young Jose Cemí, which is implicitly set over against the biblical representation of another Paradise, in which the Creator bends down to provide the first man with the breath of life directly from his own spiritual being.

The point travels well from the recent Cuban novel back to

the Argentine work of 1929. The lack of belief in that entire realm of origins underlying the book of Genesis not only frustrates Erdosain in his desire for a transformation from an empty husk into a god, but sends him breathless to his grave. The success of the hero's quest in this novel is denied by the distance between the mythic *aspirations* and his inability to make any contact with what I have termed the realm of Being. Arlt seems to imply that if the world of his novel is the only one there is, humanity is condemned to something worse than an existence as so many automatons. Even an attempt to be reborn is inevitably fated to reverse all the values of the myths and fairy tales by which the world has lived.

III

Alejo Carpentier
Los pasos perdidos
(*The Lost Steps*)

*Can we creep back into the past when we are summoned to a
new future?*
—Hans Küng

Woman is born free and we find her everywhere a jailer.
—Guillermo Cabrera Infante,
*La Habana Para Un Infante
Diefunto*

Alejo Carpentier's interest in mythology and the pre-modern as
novelistic themes goes back at least to 1933 and the publication
of *Ecué-Yamba-O,* which concerns the extended initiation process undergone by a young Afro-Cuban. It is paradoxical that this
should be the case with the writer who is perhaps the most consistently cerebral of the prominent Spanish American novelists
and whose works invite the reader to go through them with a
dictionary in hand.

Carpentier had an ongoing fascination with archaic concep-
tions of time, ranging from his worthy attempt to match the
tempo and tone of the story "El acoso" to those of Beethoven's
Eroica (the hero's destiny linked to a deterministic order) to the
somewhat disconcerting reversal of time in "Viaje a la semilla"
and the depressing circularity of revolution and tyranny in *El
reino de este mundo* and *El siglo de las luces.* This cyclical concept is clearly recognizable as the "orthodox" primitive view of
time, while the theory of its possible reversal appears to have its
roots in Plato, who, in speaking of the nature of the cosmic

process, says, "Once its revolutions have attained the duration which befits this universe . . . it then begins to turn in the opposite direction, of its own motion,"[1] which means horrendous cataclysms but also a final regeneration in which people begin to grow young again. The process is often called enantiodromia, and we shall have occasion to return to it in this study.

Los pasos perdidos represents an experiment with time reversal. Whereas in "Viaje a la semilla" time itself begins to run backward, in the novel the historical time experienced by the narrator depends upon his location in space, since the more remote regions of South America tend to be farther and farther removed from modern civilization in more than a spatial sense. The traditional quest often involves the hero's discovery of a Center of the cosmos where one may descend to the Source, at which point ordinary time is abolished. Upon returning, the hero often learns that years have passed in the outside world while in the realm of Being he has experienced only a few days.[2] In Carpentier's novel, in contrast, the narrator experiences a subjective cessation of time at the Source, indicated by the disappearance of dates from the chapter sections as he penetrates the territory upriver.

The novel represents an advance over *Los siete locos* in that the hero no longer wallows in existential *Angst* and debilitating intellectual exercises but actually engages in something like a traditional quest. The stages outlined in the works of such mythographers as make outlines are adhered to fairly closely for the most part. The combination of realism and the pre-modern mythic mode is noteworthy in itself. In order to make it work, Carpentier has employed a process used many centuries earlier by the poet Pindar, who, when composing works in praise of winning athletes, avoided simply describing surface reality, choosing instead to use the occasion to relate men and deeds to mythic patterns, thereby elevating them to the status of heroes and guaranteeing them immortality. Another Cuban novelist, José Lezama Lima, has made a striking use of the process in *Paradiso,* and a curious point is that his baroque style serves as the means of elevating ordinary deeds to heroic levels, embellishing them by comparisons to archetypal heroic acts, while Carpentier's character quickly rejects the baroque—at least in its traditional meaning—as a grotesque example of overcivilization.

The author who invents the quest and the narrator who lives it are fully conscious of the latter's assimilation to the identity of the collective hero of the monomyth as he approximates the archetypal deeds of the past, especially those of *The Odyssey*. The ultimate failure of the quest, leaving the narrator not as Master of the Two Worlds but an alien to both, rests upon his total lack of willingness and ability to serve as representative of his world, without which indispensable element the hero quest is doomed to inevitable failure. One of the most important aspects of any initiation, and the one which gives the word its most common meaning in modern society, is the subject's integration into the proper social group. Carpentier's protagonist, in contrast, desires only to escape that group.

The hero whose work Carpentier's hero reproduces most faithfully is Narcissus, so intent upon viewing his own image in the waters of renewal that they become the waters of death for him. One generalization that might be made, in fact, is that the candidates for hero status in the Spanish American novel more often than not end up by imitating the wrong mythic figures, those who fail even before achieving the initial cycle of renewal.

Another paradox arises in the manner in which the call to adventure is issued in Carpentier's work, coming as it does from the very heart of the civilization that must be renewed, the museum which places the dead past in forms meaningful to the present. Yet the museum's interest in primitive musical instruments may represent the subversive penetration of the realm of Being into that of existence in order to issue the call. In fact, the very modern—though not original—impulse to obtain a paid vacation at public expense, by falsifying the voyage and the primitive instruments he is sent to find, finally moves the adventurer; hardly an auspicious beginning, but one predictive of the terminal narcissism which finally dooms the transformation process.

Nevertheless, the narrator's growing rejection of the forms of modern civilization in the end moves him to complete the quest as originally proposed (and in fact to go far beyond its original intentions). Declaring that "certain themes of 'modernity' struck me as intolerable,"[3] he visits the museum and feels that he has "gotten to the borders of humanity, to that limitation of the possible that could have been, according to certain primitive cosmographers" (p. 39). If that is true, then a new temporal cycle must be about to begin, and some hero must travel to the Source for the power to bring about the transformation.

Significantly, the narrator's wife is quite successful in modern terms; she is in the cast of a long-running Civil War drama. The salient point in this regard is that in part the role-playing tendencies of the modern world prevent the normal functioning of more basic human relationships. Involved in the illusory portrayal on stage of a modern conflict between brothers, she is unable to concentrate on the formation of a genuine existence. Her husband is terrified "at how difficult it is to become human again once a person has ceased being human" (pp. 26-27), for "we had fallen into the net of the Wasp-Man, Noman, in which souls were sold not to the Devil, but to Accounting or the main office" (p. 15).

Art proceeds, seemingly, from the most basic instincts of mankind, for it emerges simultaneously with other aspects of civilization and order. The narrator, however, is in advertising, which he views as the debasement of art characteristic of an overcivilized world. As he reflects on this concept he begins to feel himself to be "a horse of a different color" (pp. 30-35). This should signal the emergence of the hero, for, although an embodiment of his society, he is by virtue of that very fact distinct from the other individuals that comprise it. The hero is unique, and he is always alone at the critical point of transformation. For this reason the narrator goes away, leaving behind the unworthy exploitation of art in the service of gold, to search for the musical instruments that represent the true and worthy beginnings of art in the service of aesthetic considerations alone. Later he remarks at what has become the Source for him that gold is meaningless here—gold is for those who are going back—and thereby provides the reader with one more of several announcements of his imminent refusal to return, which is also ironically to be botched by him.

Each new temporal cycle must begin in a primordial unity that signifies peace, for there has not yet arisen the diversity in which two or more entities may be in conflict. Thus war is necessarily viewed as belonging to the entropic chaos of the end of the temporal cycle, when civilization has overextended itself and is in the process of self-destruction. Accordingly, the break between the narrator and his wife is provoked by her involvement in a play depicting a particularly barbaric violation of the stated norms of Western civilization, the slaughter of brother by brother, and that over the question of whether human beings should remain enslaved in the modern world. The narrator mentions also that "the war" (presumably World War II) interrupted his ambitious cantata on *Prometheus Unbound,* and that when he returned from that war he was a changed man (pp. 23-24). The meaning is obvious: modern technological warfare is the end result of the hero Prometheus' theft of fire from the gods for the use of humanity. Since the destructive rather than the beneficial aspect of fire has prevailed, Prometheus shall not be released from his punishment; the birds of war continue to consume his vital organs daily.

The third mention of warfare in the text is in the episode of the revolution which surprises the narrator and his paramour, Mouche, in the Latin American capital. Its importance, aside from the demonstration of how rapidly nature recovers its former territory once chaos puts an end to mankind's vigilance, lies largely in its character as an expression of the final disintegration of order. A representative of harmony known as the *Kapellmeister,* aloof to the personalities and issues of the revolution, is killed by a stray bullet. The man of artistic order is destroyed by the senseless randomness of the cataclysm.

Before the quest described in the novel's present time, the narrator has undertaken a pilgrimage of far less import in an attempt to discover and recover his spiritual underpinnings. His father, also a musician, left him a meager inheritance. In order to discover his origins he travels from the United States to Europe, abandoned long ago by his father as that "rotten old continent." Whereas the older man had been drawn to North America by the pervasive myth of a new Garden of Eden, the younger one has now discovered that the Fall has taken place there as well, though he continues to nurture the hope that the values of the past may still exist in the Old World and be recoverable. His method is to go about "undertaking long voyages through time" in museums in search of what he terms "the Apollonian soul," that firm European dedication to the ideals of reason, order, and the arts. He finds nothing of the sort, and ends by believing that his father was correct in the first instance (pp. 92-97). Both men's quests have failed, but the father's has come closer to success, and it remains for the son to redeem them both by penetrating more deeply into the third continent, the one where he was born, this time in search of roots far deeper than those of Apollonian Europe. In fact, a sort of Atonement with the Father takes place in the course of his basic quest, provoked by a hearing of Beethoven's Ninth Symphony, and the narrator feels that a positive encounter with his trumpeter father has occurred in it.

Another minor motif having to do with his European ancestry involves his family's Huguenot background. That background constitutes one element in his resistance to what he considers an attempt on the part of the priest of the expedition to contaminate Paradise with outworn Medieval European customs. For example, he dismisses the clergyman's urgings that he make peace with the Church by formalizing his relationship with Rosario. This would be ironic, he feels, since his family has not been at peace with that Church for 400 years. Thus, he finds it much simpler to return from his modern North American reality all the way to that of the most primitive peoples without being detained along the way by any Latin American Roman Catholic ties.

As in the case of *Los siete locos,* an astrologer intervenes in the process. She is Mouche, who remarks that the newly painted astrological signs on her wall constitute proof that the voyage is predestined. The signs in question are Hydra, Argo Navis, Sagittarius, and Coma Berenices (p. 29). What Mouche has in mind is never explained, but it would appear that the Hydra, whose heads multiply when severed one at a time, so that they all must be cut off with one stroke, may represent the civilized world, whose debilitating features must all be excised at once, since their complexity only increases if they are con-

40

fronted individually. In the end the narrator's desire to preserve just one civilized custom aborts his quest. Argo Navis is the vehicle of Jason's great adventure with many other heroes, and the narrator's voyage is largely by boat; moreover, he is identified with Jason at one point (p. 275). Sagittarius is the Archer, and as such is related to Apollo, patron of Europe's alleged "apollonian soul." His presence hovers over Homer's *Odyssey*, and his deeds are reproduced by Odysseus as he kills the representatives of chaos with bow and arrows. Carpentier's narrator, in contrast, is unable to fire a gun at the representative of chaos at the Center. The locks of Berenice are those sacrificed by her to ensure her husband's safe return, and herein lies the irony of the case, for not only the narrator's wife, Ruth, but the entire civilization not quite rejected by him finally draws him back. Clearly, whatever may be in the mind of Mouche, who in any case is quite deficient as an astrologer, the course of the voyage is indeed inscribed on the wall.

Eventually the narrator is unable to resist the call, as he is more and more captivated by the potential adventure lying before him: "When we emerged from the opalescent fog that was growing green with the dawn, there would begin for me a kind of Discovery" (p. 84.). Then, "The night before our departure . . . I have invoked the well-known *desire for evasion*, endowing the great word *adventure* with all its implications of 'invitation to the voyage,' flight from the everyday world, fortuitous encounters, a hallucinating poet's vision of Incredible Floridas" (pp. 128-29). Since the transformation has not yet taken place, he persists in imagining the adventure in traditional European terms, and specifically in terms of the Spanish search for wealth in the New World. He fantasizes that he and the others whom he joins later are "Conquistadors going off in search of the Kingdom of Manoa" (p. 165). It is hardly an established, already civilized empire that he is to encounter, however, but a newly founded city. As for the fabled gold of Manoa, he later decides that it is for those who are going back.

Carpentier's narrator in this work is very much the heir of the romantics, and nature plays a major role in the call by progressively drawing him to itself. Its great staying power, as opposed to the relative weakness of humanity's artificially

41

contrived and maintained structures, is first seen in the fact that when the hotel staff leaves to join the revolution, insects almost immediately begin to overrun the building. Later the narrator remarks, "What astonished me the most was the never-ending mimetism of virgin nature. Here everything appeared to be some other thing, creating for itself a world of appearances that hid reality, placing many truths under interdict" (p. 172). Nature is as much creator as created, recalling Plato's *Timaeus,* which "showed that the entire cosmos must, by virtue of its order and harmony, possess intelligence and be 'in truth a living creature with soul and reason.' "[4]

Specifically, the jungle is viewed as being in that state just before creation, when there is no time as yet; this is "a dateless landscape" (p. 175). Yet it is not the chaotic *massa confusa* of the medieval alchemists, for there is what the narrator calls "an Order" (p. 203) to it, one that shall serve as antidote to the illusory order of the modern city.

This is the only one of the eight novels here considered in which nature itself, in the sense of the primeval forest with its corresponding life-forms, is conceived as the embodiment of the power of Being. There is a great deal of distance between this novel of 1953 and Arlt's *Los siete locos,* which appeared in 1929, still saturated with the brooding, urbane philosophies of nineteenth- and early twentieth-century Europe. In the only other one of the novels in which nature, so conceived, plays a role, *Pantaleón y las visitadoras,* that role is negative and destructive.

In his exaltation of the purity and creativity of nature over the corruption of civilization in a setting that Carpentier admits is Venezuela, he is reversing the values set forth by Romulo Gallegos in his celebrated *Doña Bárbara,* in which the hero represents the civilization of Caracas and the villain is the barbarity of the interior. Therefore *Los pasos perdidos* constitutes something of a return to a romantic attitude, but it should be stressed that this is on the part of the narrator, not the author.

The novel opens with a minor regression in time, back from modern architecture to a house with white columns, and the narrator has "the almost painful sensation that time had reversed itself" (p. 9). While this statement sets the tone for the total experience of the work, an even more important signal regarding its philosophy is given in the same paragraph: "Time again coincided with the date," an allusion to the fact that neither in Einstein's universe nor in that of psychology is there any such thing as an absolute, uniform present time, a single fixed instant to which all points in the cosmos might correspond at once. The only important time is that being experienced by the hero, regardless of what any calendar might indicate. These temporal clues are spatial from the outset; the correspondence, or lack of it, between calendar time and existential time is dependent upon the narrator's location.

When the full regression of time has taken place, the protagonist reflects on the fact that, whereas it took the human race fifty-eight centuries to move from the fourth chapter of Genesis to the present, he would be able to cross the same time span in three hours, simply by boarding an airplane and traveling in it from jungle to capital. The hero often experiences time differently from people in general, but this seems to be a new departure. In mythological terms the distance between the two temporo-spatial realms is that between the worlds of Genesis and Revelation. In the general current of pre-modern thought, the events of Revelation normally should lead full circle back into the creation of Genesis; as a true apocalypse, Revelation itself indicates this, in that chapters 21 and 22 present a modified version of Eden, complete with the hitherto forbidden Tree of Life. One is struck, then, by the fact that instead of moving forward in time with the apocalyptic events of his time, the narrator chooses (or is chosen) to retrace the steps of civilization, going backward, according to Plato's doctrine, in order to arrive at Genesis. The boon is lost when he does indeed choose to cross those many centuries in a few hours in order to return to the world of Revelation, not to save it by revealing to it the way back to Genesis, but, like Lot's wife, in order to salvage a glimpse of the condemned city.

The basis of our measurement of time is the sun in its regular motions, and significantly, as the narrator returns to the continent of his origins, even the sun seems new. The periodic rebirth of the sun is in fact an important motif in the pre-Columbian mythologies of Latin America and appears as the key event in *Terra nostra*. In Carpentier's work it represents a prefiguration of what is potentially the rebirth of the hero. The spatial aspect is dependent upon a river voyage, which would seem appropriate, since the flow of a river between its source and the sea often symbolizes the flow of the time of a human life—or the human race—between its origins and its death. To go upriver, then, to go against the current, is to go against the normal flow of time.

In his travels the narrator enters the Valley of Flames, perhaps representative of humanity in the stage of advance towards technology, and then the Land of the Horse, indicative of a stage of development in which useful work animals have been domesticated. The Land of the Dog speaks of that remote age when mankind had barely begun to live with its first animal companion. Eventually he arrives in the Land of the Bird, not only the first land animal according to the Genesis creation account, but a perpetual symbol of freedom and spiritual aspirations. García Márquez was later to use birds as a symbol of timelessness, for the advent of measured time in Macondo is marked by the freeing of the songbirds from their cages and their replacement by chiming clocks.

On the way to this territory various devices have aided the narrator in disentangling himself from the twentieth century. One of them is Father Pedro's skill in storytelling. In archaic societies the official storyteller achieves success by reproducing the exact words of a hallowed myth or folktale with such skill that the hearer is made to live *in illo tempore,* in the Great Time in which all events worthy of recall and emulation took place—or, from the pre-modern point of view, perpetually take place. For Father Pedro and his listeners it is much like this when he weaves his tales, and more so in the mass. As he tells the stories of saints and martyrs it is "as if it had happened yesterday; as if he had the power to pass forward and backward through time" (p. 175). In the mass offered in thanksgiving for the salvation of the travelers in a storm, the priest speaks in an "accent that causes time to cease, so that other times may become assimilated to the present." The narrator feels himself to be contemporary with the days of the Spanish conquest in 1540, and even with the day when the disciples called upon Jesus to still the storm.

But the essentially medieval character of the mass is not enough, and the hero passes all the way into the paleolithic era and finally into the spacetime of some primitive food-gatherers. Believing that he has arrived at the beginnings of the human race, he is astonished to find that this tribe holds some even more primitive beings captive in a pit. Beyond that he can only arrive in the land that looks like the earth before the creation of the human race, the world of the beginning in Genesis. Not long after leaving the capital he has seen a prefiguration of this in the form of a motionless deer, which appears to him "like the mythical ancestor of men about to be born" (p. 116).

His regression in time is divided into stages by the women who accompany him. His wife Ruth is above all the actress, so immersed in the modern world that she never really ceases her role-playing. She comes to embody the entanglements of civilization that prevent the potential hero from venturing off in search of the power of renewal. Ruth is identified by the narrator as Penelope, but he recognizes that this too is a performance. In that role she pulls the levers of modern civilization that bring him back and make it impossible for him to return to the primitive world. There are internal factors attracting him, but the actual means of his return is provided by her: "I was being kidnapped by a woman mysteriously forewarned that only extreme measures would provide her with one last opportunity to have me on her ground" (p. 279). Upon his arrival at home he remarks, "The city won't let me go" (p. 266), but by this time Ruth *is* the city. Eventually he loses everything in a divorce settlement with her, in what has become as complete a negation of the sacred marriage exemplified by the reunion of Odysseus and Penelope as is the proposed chain of brothels in *Los siete locos.*

The second woman involved is his mistress, the astrologer Mouche, who is unable to locate in the actual heavens the constellations whose supposed influence is the basis of her livelihood. As Eugene R. Skinner says, "Mouche . . . comes to represent the artificial forms imposed upon life."[5] Once again, as in *Los siete locos,* we are presented with the spectacle of a person

45

ostensibly representing the oldest of sciences, in touch with the heavens and their influence on earth, which is the essence of the *hieros gamos,* but who in fact is among the most superficial persons in an artificial world. Her nickname means "fly," and places her in comic opposition to the "Lands of the Bird." She is the one who proposes to the narrator that he falsify the trip and the musical instruments. As he becomes increasingly captivated by the genuine quest in which he becomes involved almost in spite of himself (a typical characteristic of heroes), he begins experiencing "a sort of return," while she is bored (p. 73).

Some Spanish American writers, including Carlos Fuentes, have a tendency to use women more as incarnations of the archetype than as subjects for full character development, and this is the case with *Los pasos perdidos.* Each major female figure corresponds to one portion of the story, and Mouche simply does not belong in a non-European context. The three women, in fact, correspond to the three continents to which the narrator relates, and Mouche is something like the soul of Europe to him, something to which he is still attached despite the disappointment of his pilgrimage to the Old World. She is French, and for the narrator the capital of France is the height of overcivilization, precisely the opposite of its meaning for Fuentes in *Terra nostra,* where it is the "Source of all Wisdom" and "Capital of the Third Age of Mankind."

The narrator speaks of Mouche's "incapacity to tear herself away, in the face of any sort of reality, from the commonplaces of her generation," and of the fact that "she was becoming terribly foreign" to him (p. 112). She is hopelessly bourgeois, he decides, and to his consternation her beauty fades when she has no access to makeup. She becomes a Gorgon head to him, in part because her disheveled hair suggests snakes, and this image is readily recognizable as being closely related to the Hydra which she herself had painted on her wall. Of the Gorgons, moreover, the one named Medusa was able to turn men to stone when her head was contemplated. It seems that if the narrator continues to occupy himself with Mouche he will be turned to stone—be depersonalized as well as immobilized in his desire for renewal.

The second chapter of the novel ends with the narrator's

46

determination to break Mouche's hold over him and enter the jungle. In a sense she is a Calypso-figure, the very image of darkness holding the solar hero. The difference is that whereas Calypso holds back Odysseus from ending his adventure in a reunion with Penelope, Mouche holds back the narrator from beginning his adventure and uniting with Rosario. That difference is instructive, for the key to failure in this book is the hero's ambivalence concerning which direction is home, and to which woman he belongs.

In another symbolic move, Mouche ends up in the company of the Greek diamond hunter, the crude descendant of the people in whose long-past days of glory are planted the roots of the culture she represents. Perhaps a worn-out Greece is as far as Europe is able to go in search of its roots. As a diamond hunter the man is drawn to the same location as the narrator, but only to retrieve a boon representing contemporary European values; the only possible renewal involved is that of his financial standing.

The meeting with the goddess takes place in the narrator's encounter with Rosario, and, as has been noted by Eugene Skinner, the scene has overtones of a fairy tale rather than an authentic mythic feel. First he notes that "the trip from the capital to Los Altos had been, for me, a kind of regression in time to the days of my childhood" (p. 83). At an extremely high altitude Rosario is discovered, almost dead from the lack of oxygen. Meeting a woman on the heights when one has already sensed a return to his infancy strongly suggests that she is a mother-figure. This conclusion is confirmed later when, in the midst of the great storm, he clings to her "no longer with the gestures of a lover, but those of a child who holds onto his mother's neck" (p. 176).

Still, she is young, and she also appears to be a mixture of the three major racial groups of the world. This qualifies her not only to be viewed as an Earth Mother-figure, but also to be the lover of a hero whose life is involved with that of three continents and whose universality is underscored by his bearing no name. Furthermore, in accordance with one of the dominant themes of the work, "she was dressed . . . outside of time" (p. 89). The fairy tale aspect enters when Rosario awakens and

47

immediately seems to recognize the narrator, as if on some level they belonged to one another. She takes hold of him and begs him not to let her "die again." In Skinner's words, she is the enchanted princess, "the companion that lay buried, in this case frozen, within the psyche of the hero" ("Archetypal Patterns," p. 138). In the context of having succumbed to a lack of oxygen, the inability to maintain the breath of life, her request to him is tantamount to asking of the prince the kiss that surely signifies the union of his life with that of the princess. As for his viewpoint on the matter, "her mystery was the emanation of a remote world, whose light and whose time were familiar to me" (p. 180). When, in the presence of a Gorgon-headed Mouche, delirious with malaria, he unites sexually with Rosario, it is "as if our bodies had sealed a pact that was the beginning of a new way of living" (p. 157). Whereas one of the women present is capable of turning him to stone, the other provides him with new life.

The narrator has discovered and united with a mother goddess and positive anima-figure, and he means to remain with her, which would be the same as if Odysseus had chosen to remain with Circe or Calypso. Homer indicates, with no lack of humorous intent, that Calypso is better in bed than Penelope, and Odysseus might have had a highly pleasant existence with her in place of the series of disasters. One is inclined to suspect, however, that in addition to his near-obsession with returning to house, wife, and kingdom, he has in the back of his mind another reason for not remaining with Calypso, one directly expressed in the tale of Gilgamesh. Offered marriage to the supreme goddess Ishtar, Gilgamesh refuses simply because she, like the moon she represents, is fickle. Adding insult to injury, he slays the Bull of Heaven, her sacred animal. The narrator of Carpentier's novel, who spends so much time in *The Odyssey* and knows of Gilgamesh, should have been forewarned about the dangers inherent in giving oneself too fully to what he perceives as a goddess, for goddesses tend to be lunar in character, possessing a dark side that is destructive of their lovers.

The Odyssey becomes a book of increasing importance to

the narrator as he progresses in his quest, and his violation of its intent is what causes his failure, his exile from both the primitive and the modern worlds. At the beginning he says, "I felt like buying that *Odyssey*" (p. 17). The demonstrative adjective employed is "aquella," indicating remoteness, although some force within him compels him to look into a tale whose action symbolizes the processes involved in cosmic renewal. When he becomes acquainted with Yannes, the Greek diamond hunter, he finds himself living in a "Hellenistic atmosphere" (p. 145), one created by the presence of a group of Greek miners "united by the ancestral need to know the fire is alive in the night" (p. 147). That is, even in the degeneracy of the modern world, of which they partake to a great degree, they instinctively desire the light and warmth which are symbolic of civilization. The major expression of this is precisely in Yannes' attachment to *The Odyssey*, about which he speaks to the narrator as the river voyage is underway. Eventually it seems that Yannes is transformed into Eumaeus, Odysseus' faithful swineherd (p. 161). There is even a bulldog known as Polyphemus with the group. The narrator's consciousness of *The Odyssey* culminates in Yannes' giving him his own copy of the work.

The Hellenistic element in the protagonist's cultural background pursues him to such an extent that, even as he has embarked upon his voyage to far more remote origins in his union with Rosario, he still cherishes the notion of writing a piece of music on the theme of the evocation of the dead by means of sacrifice in *The Odyssey*: "I had allowed myself to be impressed by slogans concerning a 'return to order,' the necessity of purity, geometry, asepsis" (p. 228). All these are features of the ancient Greek concept of periodic renewal, which he will eventually abandon, in part because he is attracted to even more primitive concepts and in part because he is unwilling to bear the responsibility to family and society and their renewal which is implicit in the Homeric work.

One of the more intriguing facets of the influence of classical mythology on the career of this hero is the manner in which his quest *parallels* that of Odysseus without ever matching it. In one tradition Odysseus is the son of Sisyphus, and it almost appears that Carpentier's narrator is another, destined not to break the ceaseless round of punishment of the father, but to repeat it. It should be stressed that punishment was visited upon Sisyphus because he was "fraudulent and avaricious,"[6] which squares very well with the narrator's image of himself as a musician in advertising. Early on in the narrative he describes himself as carrying out the travails of Sisyphus, and later, in a passage in which he speaks of a boundless desire to insert himself into the world of Genesis, a "longing for the womb," he balances that with a declaration: "I am going to extricate myself from the destiny of Sisyphus" (p. 206). The return of the womb, if successful, liberates Prometheus and Sisyphus from their punishment, but it fails to function correctly in this case, and the novel's penultimate paragraph ends with the words, "Today Sisyphus' vacation has come to an end" (p. 286).

In Carpentier's mad little novel entitled *Concierto barroco,* the statement is made that "where no Troy is available one is, in the proportion of things, Achilles in Bayamo or Achilles in Coyoacán, according to the noteworthiness of one's deeds" (pp. 24-25). This represents a more poetic expression of Mircea Eliade's basic theory: "By virtue of . . . paradigmatic models revealed to men in mythic times the Cosmos and society are periodically regenerated" (*Eternal Return,* p. xiv). It is all well and good when the model after whom one's quest is patterned is Odysseus or Achilles, but what is to be expected when the hero instead follows Sisyphus into the disorderly conduct that threatens the very structure of civilization? Then he is condemned to be *Sisyphus* in Bayamo, the jungles of Latin America, or a North American city. The fact is that the narrator extricates himself from one manifestation of the sin of Sisyphus—the misuse of a certain amount of power in the world of the Apocalypse—but not from its essence, for in going in search of the power of Genesis he never has in mind a return to use it for the benefit of the society he represents, or even to rebuild a meaningful life for himself and his wife in the place where he properly belongs.

The narrator decides he wants to write a *threnos,* or threnody, a song of lamentation. In so doing he is still in the Greek mode. He wishes to compose it on the theme of Odysseus' descent into Hades, and specifically on his evocation of the dead there. (Therein is another meeting with the mother.) His coming to terms with death is in fact of some importance to his career as hero, since all radical renewal is predicated on the concept of a return from death. His principal encounter with death comes about when he attends the funeral rites for Rosario's father. On the day of the burial, the sun seems not to appear because a thick cloud of butterflies prevents its being seen. The butterfly is often a symbol of the immortal soul arising from death; here the departure of a great soul obscures the light of day. The rites themselves are from the ancient past, which fascinates the narrator, but he is most impressed by the concomitant sexuality of the proceedings, the game "that makes us hunger for living flesh in the presence of that flesh that will never live again" (p. 138). A point made by Mircea Eliade concerning pre-modern orgies may be instructive: "Even the most extravagant behavior on the part of the primitive world . . . corresponds to a desperate effort not to lose contact with *being*" (*Eternal Return*, p. 92). One must adjust one's behavior to the cyclical character of time, in which the end is identical with the beginning. At the end of a human life one is inexorably attracted to that process which originated it, the act of intercourse. The scabrous character of the Greek comedies, growing from the rites of Dionysian worship, springs from the same desire to maintain contact with the process by which life is periodically renewed.

Although he appears not to remember it specifically, the narrator has already played that game in making love to Mouche while the slaughter involved in the revolution was taking place outside. The theme is also presented by Octavio Paz in *Piedra de Sol* as his version of the sacred marriage that overcomes the death attendant upon the Apocalypse; in that novel two lovers are united even as the carnage of the Spanish Civil War is going on in the city below. In a much more formalized manner, much more conscious of the fulfillment of certain mysterious cosmic processes, this also takes place at the climax of *Terra nostra*, in the union of Polo Febo and Celestina to form the androgyne.

The narrator is conscious of the fact that the hero must successfully pass through a certain number of foreordained ordeals; in Spanish the word for them is simply "proofs" or "trials." The first, in his view, relates symbolically to his return from the womb, as, having found the appropriate mark on a tree indicating the direction in which the group should go, the adventurers pass through a narrow tunnel in the jungle, after which the narrator remarks, "I had passed through the First Ordeal" (p. 170). Lord Raglan points out that "the usual setting for a ritual drama is a doorway or gateway."[7] The Second Ordeal involves a violent baptismal experience to correspond to the new birth imagery of the first, in his passing through the great storm and awakening, like the typical initiate, in a new world. The succeeding trials are indicative of the ultimate futility of his quest, for back in the world of the Apocalypse he says, "I have passed through new Ordeals" (p. 275). Upon his attempt to return to Rosario and the world she represents, and finding that the waters of time have hidden the guiding mark from him, he describes the decisive ordeal as that of the temptation to return. These last, far from being the traditional tests that demonstrate the candidate to be the true, predestined hero, worthy of receiving the power of renewal, are proofs to him that he is unworthy of handling that power.

The quest is strongly conditioned by the fact that the narrator is a musician, actually a composer. He is inextricably attached to symmetry, even geometry, and in large measure he owes his failure to man's tampering with these features of the natural cosmos. He is compelled by that portion of himself which has not been reborn to return to the city for the paper on which he may be able to create his own sort of order rather than submitting to that which already exists around him. When he finally realizes that the composition of music is "a profession of the end of the race" (p. 286), it is too late.

Implicit in his concept of cosmic order and music seems to be the Pythagorean doctrine of the harmony of the spheres, based on the idea of geometry as the primary expression of the structure of reality. David Maclagan says that in Pythagorean/Orphic thought, "number, the cosmic 'law,' is seen as the interface between . . . infinite and finite," but adding zest to the theme is his statement in the same article that the highly influential physicist Werner Heisenberg "suggests that 'for modern natural science there is no longer in the beginning the material object, but form, mathematical symmetry' " (*Creation Myths*, p. 7). Once again the thought of those in the forefront of science has come full circle and stands face to face with that of the ancient world. Heisenberg, in fact, often mentions his fascination with the fact that Plato already saw elementary particles as having the nature of geometric forms rather than "things." Given this sort of presupposition, the hero must reject material objects such as gold and diamonds and search for the more fundamental symmetry behind them. His fatal error lies in his inability to resist the temptation to create order instead of simply accepting it, to impose the order of existence upon that of essence.

His view of the composer's role is revealing. Those of the past, though now dead, "maintained their property rights over time" (pp. 19-20). He himself is a "maniacal measurer of time" who nevertheless has for a while been able to cease thinking about it in his newly discovered "timeless plain" (p. 117). He is deeply disturbed by the atonalism of modern music and learns that it has come even to the Latin American capital, although he is relieved when a musician from the back country arrives and performs music characterized by "a true primitivism" (p. 79). To him, atonalism is the ultimate expression of the fact that a society has lost touch with the underlying geometric structure of reality and the harmony of the spheres inherent in it. As a hero who is a pathological measurer of time he must seek to reestablish that interface between the infinite, the world of Being, and the finite world of existence. This is simply another form of the sacred marriage of heaven and earth. The voyage from atonality back to harmony is viewed as "this symphony that we are reading in reverse" (p. 188), implying that something in the nature of reality has programmed his passage back to the Source.

On the way back he finds the instruments for which he was sent and feels like a pilgrim who has arrived. This is the boon, and it makes him feel as if he is entering upon a new cycle of his existence. Yet in the final analysis these objects are only objects, the material things that *express* primitive musical structures with their roots in ontological harmony. He has yet to arrive at the Source. Significantly, this occurs immediately following his encounter with the archetypal Mother for whom he appears to have been searching all along. This meeting with the Goddess takes the form of his examination of a clay figure of the Earth Mother, the source of all things upon the earth—in fact, another interface between the two realms. At this point "the Word bursts forth"—that is, the Word by which the cosmos comes into being—and in the funeral ceremony he is attending he listens to a strange incantation and remarks, "I have just attended the Birth of Music" (p. 191).

The threnody, whose form attracts him as one that may be suitable for his original project of setting Shelley's *Prometheus Unbound* to music, is appropriate, he feels, because "it was a magical chant with the object of bringing the dead back to life" (p. 225). He views the release of Prometheus as a kind of resurrection associated with his escape from the modern world. In the composition "he was seeking . . . a musical expression that would spring forth from the naked word, from the word previous to music. . . . That would be like a verbogenesis" (p. 222). Drawing nearer to the sacred marriage implicit in the human perception, by way of numbers or heavenly order, he intends to use masculine and feminine elements in the chorus, a synthesis of concerted "masculo-feminine" forms in a "sort of reinvention of music" (p. 223). This concept follows hard on his realization that perhaps "the superior forms of esthetic emotion . . . consisted, simply, of a supreme understanding of the created" (p. 219). In this contradiction between merely perceiving the harmony of nature and reshaping it according to the predilections of a human mind lies the key to his insoluble problem, which is another form of *hybris*. Having returned to the origins of the human race, a timeless place, he wishes to continue to practice a profession that he himself has described as belonging to the end of that race.

In associating music with the creative Word he has intuitively penetrated to the heart of many a cosmogonic myth, for many speak of the creation of the world by means of the Word. Significantly, the narrator first returns to his native language, the one through which he first viewed and interpreted the world. For her part, Rosario feels that what is written is by virtue of that fact true, and she has reference particularly to the preposterous adventures of her prized Gothic novels. The narrator notes in this context that the (true) past is imaginable only to one who is familiar with all the trappings of history, but one suspects that for Rosario it is more a matter of the events emerging from the words as she reads them than of any very firm belief that they actually took place in the past and were written down because they did. The ironic point is that her view on the subject is similar to that of Fuentes' El Señor in *Terra nostra*, who is a quite different character, to say the least.

One problem facing the narrator is that in the modern world "myths had been replaced by lectures" (p. 97). Considering myth as, in Malinowsky's words, "the re-arising of primordial reality in narrative form,"[8] what would appear to be needed is a return first to silence, which traditionally precedes creation. As he begins his journey away from the capital the narrator says even the word "silence" "would take on the sound of creation" (p. 115). When he arrives in the world where creation is actually taking place, what he has said far earlier takes on meaning: that the only task that struck him as appropriate would be that of Adam naming things. Of course, one must not take this as simply the placing of labels on things for the sake of convenience in handling them, for in primitive thought to name an object not only signifies taking possession of it but completing its creation. As a matter of fact, this may be the true meaning of the "image of God" in which Adam is created in the Genesis account. The gift of the Word with which Yahweh has brought everything into existence is itself the very image of God, communicated as he breathes his spirit into Adam, so that when Adam names the animals he is cooperating with God, bringing his creation to completion by the use of the Deity's most formidable power. As Stella Kramrisch expresses it, "Whatever is Name (nama) is indeed Form."[9]

When new domestic animals are brought into the community of Santa Mónica, the Indians must invent names for them, but throughout the trip the people with whom the narrator associates tend to have only generic names: the *Kapellmeister*, the Carpenter, and so on. Rosario, in contrast, has a proper name, containing that of Santa Rosa, patron saint of Latin

America, with whom the narrator comes into contact quite by chance in a book, and who becomes a point of fascination for him. This is consistent with Rosario's status as something like the soul of the South American continent. A rosary, moreover, is a natural symbol of circular time in a novel deeply concerned with the possibility of an escape from the linear. Eliade remarks, "In the last analysis, what we discover in all these rites and all these attitudes is the will to devaluate time" (*Eternal Return*, p. 85).

The narrator himself is kept as nameless as his companions in order that the archetypal character of the voyage may be maintained, and when Rosario pronounces his name (whatever it is), it seems to have been newly created, as if *he* had just been created. Once more this is Woman in the role of Mother. The narrator is virtually brought into his new existence by Rosario's pronouncing his name, which becomes the familiar "new name" of the initiation proceedings. Following his union with her—modern man with the Earth Mother—and his recovery of the coveted primitive musical instruments, he feels that something inside him has matured tremendously. The point is that in spite of his periodic feeling that he has become a new person, the full transformation has not yet taken place, nor will it; it is only *something in him* that has matured. This follows the experience of the storm, in which he is knocked unconscious and awakens to find himself in what he perceives as a fabulous new city, and he feels like Noah reborn from the waters onto a reborn earth: "We are here on the Mount Ararat of this vast world" (p. 212). Noah is not the only one in view here; he also mentions Utnapishtim, Noah's Sumerian counterpart, who appears in the Gilgamesh epic and is immortal. But the narrator is not; he is not even fully transformed as a mortal must be.

The Governor is a new creation, however. In the very act of founding his city, "the first city," he finds that his interest has turned from gold to land (pp. 197-98). Again a comment of Eliade is to the point: "Settlement in a new, unknown, uncultivated country is equivalent to an act of creation" (*Eternal Return*, p. 10). He is in the process of creating what is pointedly termed a *polis* (p. 217), which is inevitable but not necessarily good from the narrator's standpoint, for it means that the process of diversification that must inevitably end back in his apocalyptic city has begun again. He watches as the role of founder gives way to that of lawgiver, so that soon even capital punishment is called for. The supreme irony lies in the choice of a name for the community, Santa Monica. Its namesake is the mother of St. Augustine, whose *City of God* is one of the foundation stones of the massive Roman Catholic system which is so distasteful to the narrator. The name constitutes an announcement of the fact that a new time cycle has been set in motion and must move essentially into the same forms as the previous one. Still the narrator is able to say, "In the presence of the Governor I have come to understand that the greatest work of which a human being is capable is that of forging a destiny for himself" (pp. 263-64).

Unfortunately for him as something of a "son" of the Founder, there is also another son, Marcos. Out of this situation grows this novel's version of the theme of the two brothers, one of whom must be done away with in some manner. In this case, as in many others, what is at stake is the love of a woman, one who represents the very soul and spirit of the territory in which the Center is established. Upon their arrival in the city, Rosario is already set in her status as the narrator's woman. There is tension, however, between her primitive concept of the permanence of such a union and his, which is based on the subversive norms which survive in him despite his double adultery. For her the union is a firm one only so long as he is unreservedly committed to her and the land with which she is so closely identified. She is, after all, a lunar being, and as such subject to periodic changes. The dangers of the hero's expecting too much from such a goddess-figure are already evident in Gilgamesh's explanation of his refusal to marry Ishtar.

The narrator's weakness is pointed up and symbolized by the incident of the sexually perverted leper, whose vicious sexual assault of an eight-year-old girl represents the loss of innocence of this Edenic cosmos. Contamination is inherent in the inevitable forward motion of time from primordial unity into dynamic diversity. Furthermore, the leper and his act also exemplify something personal in the hero, namely the remnant of his attachment to the world of the Apocalypse even within his

57

commitment to that of Genesis. In Eliade's terms, history must be periodically abolished, and nothing that has belonged to it may be borne into the next cycle. The Wise Old Man still asks the emerging hero, as Samuel asks Saul, "What then is this bleating of sheep in my ears?" (I Samuel 15:14). The decisive moment for the two "brothers" occurs when it becomes necessary to execute the rapist by shooting, and the narrator is unable to do so, while Marcos fires with seeming ease. The former has proven himself incapable not only of fulfilling the necessities of the new world, but of symbolically purifying himself of the corruption still binding him to modern society. Not long afterward, the demands of his "profession of the end of the race" draw him back to his starting point, and his betrayal of Genesis bars him from returning to Santa Mónica, first by hiding the signs by which it may be found and then by delivering the woman to the brother who has been able to kill without pity that which has polluted his Paradise. The sacred marriage then belongs not to the supposed hero of the work, who has now disqualified himself—as if playing the role of one of the Suitors unable to string Odysseus' bow and thereby unworthy of the bride—but to another founder. The slayer of the sacred wedding's violator is the only one qualified to fulfill that wedding, and the woman's definitive break with the narrator is made by her pregnancy.

Yannes, the spokesman for classical civilization in the work, conveys the news to the narrator with the comment, "She not Penelope" (p. 285). According to the pattern established in *The Odyssey,* the goddesses encountered along the way serve their purpose, but Calypso is not Penelope, whose function is radically different. Calypso, however desirable, is the darkness that holds the sun in its power for a predetermined season, until the hour appointed for him to continue on his way to cosmic renewal in his reunion with the other lunar weaver of destiny, Penelope. Circe, on the other hand, is the guide to the underworld, and she too must be handled with care, for there is always the danger that she may overpower the hero and bind him in that place by converting him into her sacred animal, the pig.

A return to Ruth, however, is never an open option for the

narrator once he encounters the cosmic figure who seems to recognize him. Penelope is an accomplished actress with the Suitors, in her weaving and unweaving of Laertes' shroud, but Ruth the actress plays destructive roles in the narrator's presence, as he sees it. And whereas Odysseus is the great deceiver in his obsession with returning to Penelope, the narrator deceives her and the public with regard to such a return, while in fact he feels that he belongs in Santa Monica. The deceivers of *The Odyssey* employ illusion so that reality may ultimately be established; those of *Los pasos perdidos* do so to the detriment of reality.

The fact is that the quest is vitiated by the narrator's failure to realize which direction is home. He has in effect understood the desirability of a return to the womb, yet without the realization that one must emerge permanently from that womb as a totally new person prepared to come to grips with a world in need of renewal. This hero emerges from it only to retrieve something from his old life, in the hope of returning to that womb again. When he speaks of his limitless desire to become integrated into the primitive world, he means to tie himself to its physical presence in such a manner that he cannot be extricated from it—once he has his music paper in hand. Thus, rather than emerging as Master of the Two Worlds, he reveals that he belongs to neither of them. He has recalled early on that eating the lotus causes men not to want to return, but he fails to mention the fact that Odysseus refuses to eat it. He never mentions either that Odysseus has himself bound to the mast, symbol of the masculine purposefulness that will carry him back, so that he may hear the song of the sirens without succumbing to its fatal attraction.

Still, he does return. The title of the novel seems to allude to that of the surrealist André Breton's 1924 book of essays, *Les Pas Perdus,* in which the author uses the phrase "le souvenir du futur," echoed as "memories of the future" in this novel. The phrase serves as a sort of premonition, to the reader at least, of what is to become of the quest. Only the knight with the purest heart may find the grail, and the narrator's heart is never fully cleansed of the corruption symbolized by the leper. As he retraces his steps to the past, his memories of what is future to that primordial world draw him back to it. At first it is simple enough: a drink of *aguardiente* awakens his dormant desire for liquor and cigarettes. Even then he determines that all he really needs from that other world is paper and ink. The refusal to return is a common feature of the conventional hero's career, one that is normally overcome by his obligation ultimately to follow a predestined course. Here the refusal is overcome by the hero's desire to return only to retrieve some symbols of civilization, and then to establish himself permanently at the Source—which, of course, he would only succeed in contaminating. There is writing in Santa Monica already, but (1) it is limited to the essential laws and records of the community, (2) it is viewed with suspicion, and (3) the Governor becomes increasingly indignant at the narrator's use of his paper for advanced artistic purposes.

If he is to play the hero role successfully, the narrator must return to impose the power of Genesis upon the world of Revelation. This is never in his mind, as he intends rather to salvage a part of the Apocalypse for his life in Genesis. As he returns, his having given himself to the other world in his affair with one of its women discredits him as the returned hero and results in the cancellation of all possibility of his accomplishing any sort of sacred marriage with his Penelope-figure, leaving him an alien to the world whose representative he had become. All he can think of is ending his obligations to it and returning to the jungle. As he attempts to do so, he finds that the marks on the trees that had guided him in the first instance are now under water, and refers to "the definitive ordeal: the temptation to return" (p. 279).

Even though Yannes reveals that he would be capable of "opening the gate" without seeing the mark, he also establishes the futility of it by noting that Rosario is pregnant by Marcos. No one is born again twice. The narrator realizes that "the people in this remote area never have believed in me. I was a being on loan. Rosario herself must have looked upon me as a Visitor, incapable of remaining indefinitely in the Valley of the Cessation of Time" (p. 285). Here he realizes that he now belongs to neither world, having wished to keep something of each of them without fully committing himself to either. In contrast to "the man of archaic cultures [who] tolerates 'history' with difficulty and attempts periodically to abolish it" (Eliade, *Eternal Return,* p. 36), the narrator tends to feel uncomfortable without history, and thus his "memories of the future" ultimately destroy him.

Of all the arts, music may be the one most likely to preserve an age as a living entity, for its performance is the incarnation of the order—or lack thereof—of an era. Therein lies the special poignancy of the narrator's comment that "the only race of humans which is forbidden to release itself from dates is the race of those who make art" (p. 286). More than incidentally, there may be something of the soul of the literary artist Alejo Carpentier in this as well. Each hero quest involves an attempt to bring about a new order where there is only a stagnant order or outright chaos. In the narrator's world there is some of each, an intolerably overcivilized order, but one whose atonal musical expression prophesies its imminent decay into disorder. As a composer, he naturally views the potential new order in musical terms; his error is in failing to see that what is needed is a return all the way to the harmony inherent in the fundamental, changeless structure of Being itself, of primordial reality. Early in his quest he feels "a sharp expectancy of the instant in which time would cease to convey incoherent sound to find itself framed, organized, submitted to a previous human will" (p. 19), just as the orchestra he hears tuning up its instruments will soon produce harmonious sounds under the conductor's guidance.

The narrator never loses the profound belief that music is "time subjected to human will" (Skinner, p. 119), and the need for paper that draws him inexorably back to the world of advanced human organization is a symptom of that. He has missed his own point that "new worlds must be lived before they can be explained" (p. 285), and failed to go beyond that to the realization that they must *only* be experienced and not organized according to artificial human notions of order. The music of the spheres is to be heard and absorbed into one's being, not rewritten as Theme and Variations.

IV
Juan Rulfo
Pedro Páramo

There is more nothingness than being.
　　　　　　—Arsenio Cue in *Tres tristes tigres*

*The real movement is not from death to any rebirth. It is
from death to death-transfigured.*
　　　　　　—Walter Rathenau, from the grave,
　　　　　　in *Gravity's Rainbow*

When Odysseus stops to question Circe on his way to Hades,
she makes it clear that only a rare man can go there and
return—that in effect he will die twice, the second time
definitively. The case of Juan Preciado in *Pedro Páramo* is
strange, then, for while there are indications that he too is a
hero in the mold of Odysseus, his first descent into Hades is
his last. Even his name seems appropriate for a hero. "Juan"
recalls the John who, as author of the Apocalypse, was called to
heaven to retrieve a revelation for the people, and "Preciado"
means "highly prized." Seemingly he is destined to engage in
some heroic quest, yet it soon becomes evident that everything
is askew. Nothing is as it should be according to our distillation
of the hero pattern from the mythologies of the world, and the
question that ultimately arises is who has issued the call to
adventure.

The quest is set as a typical search for the Father, and
Margaret Lester feels that all indications point to the typical
replacement of the decrepit ruler by a young hero, recalling that
in Hesiod the tyrant father Cronus, who devours his own
children, as Pedro Páramo certainly does in another sense, is
confronted and defeated by Zeus and his mother Rhea. Even

earlier, Cronus had replaced Uranus with his mother's aid.[1] We might recall as well the biblical story in which Jacob and his mother join forces to effect the replacement of Jacob's father, Isaac, but, as Lester points out, in *Pedro Páramo* there is no thought on the part of either Juan or his mother of his replacing the *caudillo*.

The original call is issued from her deathbed by Juan's mother who believes that Pedro Páramo owes them a great deal, having sent mother and child away and forgotten them altogether through the years. The hero, as it turns out, has the mysterious origins so common to the traditional hero and so rare among the protagonists of these novels. Upon his arrival in Comala, Eduviges Dyada informs him that she was to have taken his mother's place on the latter's wedding night, because "the moon was wild," but that Dolores went to Pedro's bed in spite of it. Juan Preciado (who, however, was not conceived that night) should have been the child of Eduviges, according to her. He has the qualifications, the call, even the traditional refusal of the call, for he attempts to forget even the promise made to his mother as she was dying. Yet at the opening of his narration, something—he knows not what—is drawing him to Comala, his father's town. He will indeed go to the Father, but the Father is dead, and going to him means that the son too must die. For that matter, the name "Comala" is ominous enough in itself, for it contains "coma" (a living death) and *mala*, "bad."

Lord Raglan feels that underlying all myth is ritual, and specifically the ceremonial replacement of an older king by a young man, generally his son. Other students of mythology feel that this is an overstatement of the case, but agree that often a father-figure must be defeated by the son in order that the latter may somehow come into his own. Joseph Campbell terms it the Atonement with the Father, even though that term does not properly denote a defeat. Those inclined to a more or less Freudian interpretation of the phenomenon speak of slaying the ogre-father or dragon-father in order to come to maturity. In *Pedro Páramo* the young hero is to go and, although the reader is never told how, force the Father to give him a great deal of money, in spite of the fact that Dolores knows full well that the man is greedy and ruthless to an astonishing degree. He

63

married her, in fact, only in order not to have to pay off a debt to her family.

Even before he arrives, Juan is informed that the Father is dead—informed of that fact by what turns out to be the ghost of his father's murderer. All that remains alive is the hatred that surrounded him. This is the Father, proper provider of the boon, the *caudillo* who is a sort of petty feudal king embodying the polluted land as the young hero embodies the people in their quest for renewal. Paul Tillich has defined love as the longing for reunion of that which has been separated.[2] Insofar as this is valid, it would appear that love is deeply involved in the act of drawing the hero back to the realm of Being from which he sprang. Yet in the present case the hero is drawn back only to a dead father who paradoxically exists only as a living hatred. Is it hate that draws him to this inverted world and to dissolution rather than reunion? After all, the corollary of Tillich's definition should be that hate is the power that divides what has been unified.

Furthermore, the realm of Being is that changeless source of power out of which existence emerges. Could that realm produce a powerful man, almost a deity within his context (for divinity is fundamentally a power concept), and then allow him to die and draw the last of his sons to union with him only in death? One is tempted into the frightening conclusion that within this novel Being is not changeless, is dormant at best, and has no visible prospect of revival. Presumably, though, Being is not dead, because from the traditional point of view existence grows out of it, and even in Comala there is a form of that. Or, from the existentialist point of view, that same existence signifies Being, having created it.

Therein may lie a clue, for in the existentialist world view the existence by which essence is created is specifically an action based on a personal choice, and Pedro Páramo's key act in the work is the choice *not* to act, but rather to cross his arms and allow the region he embodies to die. In existentialist terms, to will not to act is to permit the invasion of nothingness, of nonbeing. This is exactly what Juan Preciado finds in the ghost town of his birth: the meager existence of the dead, which is nonbeing itself. Rather than being drawn into the eternal source of life and fitted for a return with power, he is trapped forever in the living death decreed by his father.

In his *Corriente alterna* Octavio Paz expounds a provocative theory concerning the case: "Only after dying can we return to the Eden of our birth. But Rulfo's character returns to a calcified garden, a lunar landscape, the true hell. The theme of the return is transformed into that of damnation; the voyage to the patriarchal home of Pedro Páramo is a new version of the pilgrimage of the soul in torment. There is symbolism, conscious or not, in the title: Pedro, the founder, the stone, the origin, the father, guardian and lord of the paradise, has died; Páramo (a desert) is his former garden, today a dry plain, thirst and drought, the whispering of shades and eternal non-communication. The Garden of the Lord: Pedro's *Páramo*."[3]

It will be necessary to understand the nature of Pedro Páramo's deficiency in order to reconstruct what has happened to Comala and Juan Preciado. The problem is announced in his very name, which, as noted by Paz, speaks of a rock and a desert, whereas "Pedro" should by rights mark him as an avatar of the founder of a dynamic Christian community. Hardness and dryness are traditionally associated with the masculine principle, as in the Yang of Taoist thought, but the circle is a full one only if the moist, passive Yin is in full union with Yang. As the story of Pedro Páramo's life is developed, he should properly unite with Susana San Juan, and yet neither of them is capable of such a union.

The reader's first view of Pedro Páramo is as a boy, sitting in the bathroom, thinking about Susana and, though it is not directly stated, obviously masturbating. Later Vargas Llosa's Pantaleón Pantoja is to apply to that act the familiar designation "the solitary vice," and therein lies its importance as the character is introduced. The reader's first image of him is as a person mimicking the act of love, as if it were being carried out with his lover. In this fantasy he recalls their flying a kite, symbol of their aspirations together. The word is, "Let out more string," but the string breaks and the kite falls,[4] as an indication of the course their relationship is to follow: it can rise to a certain height, but then all is lost.

Susana is described in terms of moistness. In fact she

65

contains within herself the characteristics of both of the most important symbols of the feminine, the moon and the sea. To Pedro Páramo she has eyes like sea water. He even enters the sea naked with her when they are very young, as if they were god and goddess. She is embraced by the sea to which she belongs, but not by Pedro, who is alone even when naked with her. He fails even to understand her love of bathing in the sea. For her it is a return to her element, a renewal and a purification, while he remains essentially hard and dry even while in her presence and surrounded by the waters symbolic of rebirth.

When Susana arrives at the ranch a soft rain falls instead of the destructive cloudbursts that have often attacked the region. Moreover, even in the act of dying, Pedro conjures a vision of her presence when "there was a great moon in the middle of the world," and its rays fall in her face so that she is "soft, washed by the moon" (p. 128). Yet she has never fully become one with him, sexually or otherwise. At best it has been a courtly love experience in which the knight refuses to close the distance between him and his lady, since she belongs to the pure Platonic realm of Forms. Yet as the situation develops, or rather deteriorates, what comes to the fore is Pedro's inability to unite with her, not any unwillingness to do so.

The oak tree is often associated with the hero, but Pedro is described as a hardwood trunk rotting inside. Yet the hardness and dryness in themselves need not cause this; rather, they cry out for the complementary feminine elements. In her mad hallucinations Susana has deeply fulfilling experiences with a certain Florencio, who to her mind is "dry as the driest earth" (p. 104), just as Pedro Páramo is; But when she says, "We have spent a very happy time together" (p. 105), it becomes clear that a union has taken place between the man of dryness and the moistness incarnate in Susana that makes him worthy of a name suggestive of fertility and blossoms. Evidently, Florencio is Pedro Páramo as he should be. There is nothing in his firm masculinity *per se* to prevent his union with her, yet he seems condemned to solitude as surely as the characters of *Cien años de soledad.*

He moves heaven and earth to bring her into his presence, but is unable to bring her fully into his life. Even if he were able

66

to do so, however, it is doubtful that she would be capable of the union, for she is hopelessly mad, and beyond that fact, within her story are several allusions to myths and traditions that reinforce the difficulties. The name Susana relates her to the Hebrew character renowned for both her beauty and her chastity, particularly as she was desired by men who saw her bathing. Her name itself, then, bears an indication of her destiny. Her servant Justina calls her "mint candy," and her fate in what is becoming the land of death is portended by the fact that Mintho was a nymph beloved by Hades—lord of the land of death—and metamorphosed by Persephone into mint.[5] Eventually everyone in this novel belongs to Hades.

Susana has lived with her father at a ranch known as La Andrómeda, and this too may be significant, for Andromeda is another woman of extreme beauty. Sir William Smith says, "Her mother boasted that the beauty of her daughter surpassed that of the Nereids, and Poseidon sent a sea-monster to lay waste the country. The oracle of Ammon promised deliverance if Andromeda was given up to the monster; and Cepheus was obliged to chain his daughter to a rock" (*Classical Dictionary*, p. 25). It would appear that in this case the monster responsible for laying waste the country bears the name of the rock to which the beauty will be chained. Pedro Páramo takes this lunar figure to a ranch known as the Half Moon, and that indeed is to remain its status, for life and fertility are never to be achieved there.

Pedro Páramo finally comes to the realization that Susana San Juan, like García Márquez' Remedios the Beauty, is not a creature of this world; but in contrast to the devouring female of *Cien años de soledad,* who ascends to heaven with the bedsheets, she has a destiny only in Hades. She announces to Justina that she believes only in hell, not in heaven. Yet Pedro Páramo has placed her in the heavens: "Hundreds of meters away, above all the clouds, far, far beyond everything, you are hidden, Susana. Hidden in the immensity of God, behind his Divine Providence, where I can't reach you or see you, where even my words can't climb" (p. 17). He is wrong, of course, for far from being hidden in God's immensity, she is destined to play the role of Mintho as the beloved of Hades. She lies inaccessible to him there, not in the heavens.

In her youth it was Susana's lot to descend into Hades in a mirror image of Juan Preciado's later experience in coming to Comala. Whereas he is bidden by his mother to go to a location described in terms of Hades and attempt to obtain a boon from his father, Susana is forced by her father to descend into a deep grave in search of a boon from what seems to be her mother. In both cases the boon involves money from the dead and proves to be illusory. For her the experience is a terrifying one, intensified as it is by her father's repeated urging that she go deeper. Eventually she encounters a disintegrating corpse, which horrifies her even more, but her father insists that there must be a cache of gold coins there. This is her awakening to the fact that at the Source, where the power of life paradoxically arises out of death, there is nothing but death in its most revolting form. There are no riches, no coins, nothing of that metal thought by her Mexican ancestors to have come from the sun itself, source of life—tears of the sun god in the round form that signifies psychic wholeness. Her last name, that of the author of the Apocalypse, who ascends to heaven for his visions, is ironic, for her lot is only the cataclysmic aspect of that book, with nothing of its ultimate return to Paradise. Only the elect manage to avoid the Pit reserved for the devil and his angels, and the citizens of Comala are emphatically not among the elect—not even Juan Preciado, who is mysteriously summoned there by some power beyond his ken.

Susana's death takes place near Christmas, which is the birthday of the sun in Mithraism, adopted by Christendom as the date on which the birth of the Savior to the Virgin would be celebrated. At this time, then, the goddess should rightly give birth to a solar hero, and in fact this does happen in *Terra nostra*, but in *Pedro Páramo* the goddess herself dies. The priest, Father Rentería, exerts himself to the fullest to bring her to his concept of salvation. He is as bewildered as his semi-pagan flock at the disintegration of life, love and the relationships growing naturally from them. But Susana is beyond his reach, desiring another unfulfilled and unfulfillable relationship, that of a meaningful sexual union, much like the young Mexican woman in Buñuel's film *Nazarín*, who rejects the priest in favor of her lover as she dies of the plague.

Susana is totally unconcerned for the salvation of her soul (she does not believe in heaven), yet she still makes a desperate attempt to achieve something at least vaguely resembling the sacred marriage, which seemingly should have been her mission in life. She is an Eve-figure, convinced, in an extreme reading of the doctrine of original sin, that merely having been born constitutes a sin, so that one spends one's life paying for it. The supreme cultural hero of a supposedly Roman Catholic community such as Comala should be Jesus Christ. The implication of Susana's beliefs, however, is that this hero too has failed. Eve has sinned and fallen, but her name is not changed even in her expulsion from the Garden; it still means "life." In spite of the Fall, all humanity proceeds from her, and ultimately too the Redeemer of that race from the Fall. Yet this avatar of Eve is spiritually sterile in her madness, and furthermore, the male in the role of her mate is incapable of the profound, whole-souled union which is the indispensable element in the sacred wedding. "Adam" means something like "red earth," but "Pedro Páramo" stands not for that fertility but for the impermeability of the desert that will never admit abundant life.

At Susana's death Pedro Páramo, as *caudillo*, is able to command that all the bells of the region be rung incessantly, as is appropriate at the death of what in his mind had been a goddess. Much the same atmosphere prevails in García Márquez' story, "Los funerales de la Mamá Grande," whose title character is something of an Earth Mother whose importance needs no explanation to the reader, and whose services are attended even by the Pope. In Comala, people are deafened and eventually rendered unable to think clearly by the non-stop ringing, and when outsiders are drawn in, thinking the bells are announcing some sort of great celebration, it turns into just that. Here is another case of Plato's enantiodromia, in which an extreme case of mourning is converted into its opposite, a celebration of life. Ironically, what the supposed goddess was unable to accomplish as a living being, she has achieved in death, although there is precious little life to celebrate under the rule of Pedro Páramo. In fact, this will be their last occasion to celebrate life, for the indignant *caudillo* who embodies his territory declares, "I will cross my arms and Comala will starve to death" (p. 121). One need have no deep knowledge of the secrets of body language to perceive that the gesture he chooses is one excluding other beings from one's breast—the locking-out of meaningful relationships. Still, the gesture does no more than confirm him in the solitary mode of being to which he has been condemned from birth.

Even in his marriage—which blocks him from formally sealing his relationship with Susana—there is a gross, cynical violation of the principles of the sacred wedding. Upon assuming control of the ranch at his father's death he learns that he owes a large debt to the Preciado sisters. His means of dealing with it is to marry the one named Dolores, in what amounts to another form of the prostitution that contaminates the *hieros gamos* in nearly all those works. A falsification of love for material gain goes contrary to all that is productive of life. Pedro Páramo's life, in fact, seems to consist of an endless series of nights with nearly all the women in and around Comala.

Curiously, there are two badly mutilated hermaphrodite-figures in the work. The first to appear is Eduviges Dyada, to whose rooming house Juan is first directed as he enters Comala. A dyad is two units considered as one, and in a strange way this is what she has been in the eyes of the public. Having many children by any number of men of the town, who always refuse to recognize them, she says each time, "In that case I am also its father, even though I happen to have been its mother" (p. 34). Therefore she too fulfills the destiny indicated by her name: she is male and female in one, the androgyne, but not the one that signifies the primordial unity out of which cosmic renewal springs forth.

Perhaps even stranger is the case of Dorotea, whom Juan calls Doroteo when he first meets her in the grave. As she says, "It makes no difference. My name is Dorotea, though. But it makes no difference" (p. 62). That is, one's sex is irrelevant beyond death, for no sexual activity is possible in this version of Hades. There is irony, then, in the fact that there should be another mock-hermaphrodite situation, one arising precisely when the circumstances that should produce the true androgyne are forever negated. The two vaguely hermaphroditic figures in the work achieve such status only on the basis of promiscuity and death.

70

Bartolomé San Juan, before Susana goes to live with Pedro Páramo, asks her, "Why has our soul rotted on us?" (p. 88), for even at this stage of the story of Comala it is abundantly clear that things are drying up, morally as well as physically, to match the soul of Pedro Páramo. Much later, when Juan Preciado arrives, he finds a land in stark contrast to the green and productive farming region described by his mother. Abundio's comment is "It's the times" (p. 8). Eduviges also tells the hero, "The times have changed" (p. 19). The territory from which Juan began his quest is not the one in such a state of chaos; the place which by the norms of the universal hero tale should be the unchanging source for him, the place *to* which he is called, is chaotic. A situation analogous to it is discovered by Don Quixote in the Cave of Montesinos, where all the myths of chivalry should by rights be alive and well in an eternal present, but where instead the knights are sarcastic, the women have aged, and Dulcinea behaves in an undignified manner and asks for a loan. Such a revelation concerning the bankruptcy of the source of the power of renewal soon wrecks Don Quixote's ability to sustain his illusion, as it leaves Juan Preciado abandoned in the grave.

One distressing feature of Comala's reality after Pedro Páramo takes power is that, whereas in a normal society a chain of life is passed on from generation to generation, here there is a chain of deaths, each one dragging the next with it, the process having begun symbolically with Pedro Páramo's reaction to the death of Susana. It culminates—though the murderer and a few others have yet to die—in the death of Pedro himself, which is provoked by the death of Abundio's wife. Abundio, in order to escape his grief, drinks a huge quantity of straight alcohol and initiates a mini-quest in search of a boon from his father, which both anticipates and nullifies that of his legitimate half-brother, Juan Preciado. All he asks of the already dying man is the money to bury his wife, and when refused he stabs him to death. The last words of the novel are, "He struck the ground a dry blow and began crumbling as if he were a pile of stones." That force of cohesion which is an extension of Tillich's definition of love is now lacking not only between Pedro Páramo and those of his land, but within the man himself.

Hades as the land of the dead and at the same time the inexhaustible source of new life is a paradox, one growing, perhaps, out of the earliest observations of human beings as they entered the age of agriculture: a grain of corn is buried in the earth, and after a time there emerges a living plant with many more grains. In a society such as that of the pre-Columbian Indians of Mexico, in which the *Popol Vuh* states that humanity was formed from maize, the analogy would be a natural one to make. One who is made of corn and sustains his life with it must have the same destiny as corn—to enter the earth in death so that new human life may arise from it. The persistent Levantine cult of Tammuz, fought so unsuccessfully by the Hebrew prophets, portrays the god as an extension of the vegetation whose life he ensures; or, to state it another way, he embodies the power that renews the life of the cosmos through burial in the earth and ressurection from it.

Not coincidentally, then, Juan Preciado finds a land described from the outset in terms of "the very mouth of hell" (p. 9) instead of the Paradise portrayed in the words of his mother. He must travel to Hades to retrieve new life, yet here the paradox is not that of life arising from death, but that of a synthesis of life and death, a land of the living dead much like the Hades visited by Odysseus, where the disembodied spirits seem to hover without substance, but with one great difference. In the Hades of *The Odyssey* the hero encounters not only his mother, but a manifestation of the Wise Old Man archetype, Teiresias, and receives from him the boon of knowledge indispensable for the successful completion of his voyage and the consequent renewal of the cosmos. In Comala there is no Wise Old Man, there is no life worthy of the name, there is no way to return. Even the total cessation of being which is feared by so many would be better than the lot of these dead, for Juan wonders why instead of just death there must be this tender music from the past.

The answer lying on the surface for the taking is that the solar figure who embodied the region is dead, as is the lunar figure who could have complemented his life, and they never achieved the necessary union. The incessant murmurs, a pale reflection of the creative Word, must be a desperate attempt to

72

maintain some contact between this world and that of Being. Pedro and Susana failed to achieve the necessary union because there were forces internal to each which prevented it: in him the vicious circle of a hard dryness that impeded him from reaching outside himself for the relationship capable of ending such a deficiency; in her a mental derangement presumably curable through union with the solar rationality of the male, yet a madness standing in the way of her doing so.

At a still deeper level lies the question *why* there should be such an incapacity on the part of the two of them. The sociologically oriented critic replies that the *caudillo* system itself has made some regions of Mexico sterile, but that does not explain how such a system could come about and maintain control of the people after death. Rulfo is pointing to something highly sinister within the very metaphysical structure of the reality being lived by Mexico. The fact is that the hero myth implies that the hero and the goddess or other female figure with whom he must unite are extensions of the source of life itself, which does not so much call him *out* as call him *back* to itself. It must be so in the very nature of pre-modern thought, if the most fundamental aspect of divinity is power. The source of the power of Being is divinely ordained, and the hero, who is generally described in ancient texts as being at least partially divine, belongs to that realm by nature. He is not only the appropriate one to return to the Source, but the only one who may do so, for he is by nature a bearer of power. For this reason he seems to be recognized when he arrives, and there are tests along the way that only the one elect being is able to pass.

Perhaps the best and most familiar illustration of this point lies in the gospel presentation of Jesus Christ. The changeless, eternal Ground of Being is Yahweh, whose very name comes from the Hebrew verb "to be." When the time is ripe for the renewal of the cosmos the one sent by him is the Word who was active in the creation process at the beginning. Virgin-born, engendered by the divine Spirit, viewed as the being who orders life-structures, he is both divine and human.

We return from that construction to the one in which the potential father-hero and the goddess lack both the force of Being and that of bare existence. If all is dead in their world, then again the question arises, who or what issues the call to the young hero to come and take power from his father, only to be trapped in death?

The reader is confronted here with the startling fact that, in effect, nonbeing, instead of playing its normal role of eroding all structures, actually appears to be occupying the throne of Being and mimicking its activities, having usurped its power. This is quite a different matter from the common situation in which the Tyrant Holdfast sets up his reign of nonbeing in the realm of existence. Here the supposed Paradise to which the hero is called out is the one held by nothingness. Thus, the familiar call to adventure is actually a call to death, or more precisely, to nonbeing, for the situation in Comala, while not partaking of the nature of life, is not really death, in the sense of total nonbeing, either. The hero turns out not to be the son of Being by way of the *hieros gamos,* but the son of nonbeing by way of a union based on cynical exploitation, of a man named Stone and a woman named Sorrows. If love is the longing for reunion of that which has been separated, hate must be the force that tears apart that which would be bound together, and Pedro Páramo, a "living hate," is the embodiment of this Center of nonbeing which denies any new beginnings to the cosmos.

The reality behind the fictional situation is that of certain villages that, according to Rulfo, are virtually dedicated to the cult of death, a sort of ancestor worship.[6] It would appear that such an orientation towards nonbeing (for these people feel deeply that their dead dwell among them) might well stifle the operation of the most basic forms of renewal. In such an atmosphere, how could one grasp the concept of complementary male and female figures as veritable projections of the source of Being, for the entire spiritual atmosphere is permeated with nonbeing? Here one may easily imagine a woman of unearthly beauty being born and growing up, seemingly destined to be married to a heroic man and produce a beautiful child who will do great things for the land, but who instead is forced to live the perpetual presence of death exemplified by Susana's descent into her mother's grave. She might be expected to think of life as payment for the sin of having been born, and then go mad, for her destiny is only to hover around those semi-living creatures among whom she now moves. That is to say that if life itself is denied by the pervasiveness of death, then being born, which is an affirmation of the principle of Being, surely is a sin, not against God but against his usurper.

In our discussion of *Los siete locos* and *Los pasos perdidos* we have touched on the question of how simplistic is the idea that the hero's task is to impose order on chaos, and the time has come, with the discussion of *Pedro Páramo,* for a frontal attack on it. Much to the contrary of what is generally supposed, the hero of the modern novel does not normally confront a world in chaos, at least not in the normal sense. While his life and that of his peers may be fragmented and meaningless, they are so precisely because of the massive *structures* of the society in which he lives. Even what Alejo Carpentier's narrator perceives as the world of the Apocalypse is terminal simply because it is overly structured. His inability to tear himself loose from that structure is what ultimately destroys him. Arlt's Astrologer too only wants to substitute one evil order for another, an industrial order so powerful that it overwhelms human values. The chaos is in the individual; the fear is that the threatening structure will prevail. Even in the biblical Apocalypse the problem to be solved by the Lamb is not a disorderly cosmos, but the deadening order of a false lamb, the Antichrist with his anti-structure. The chaos in the Apocalypse, one must remember, is provoked by God in judgment on the order of Babylon to the end that it may be replaced by a New Jerusalem.

Applying all this to the situation in Comala, we find that the chaos there consists only of the bewilderment of the hero, who finds himself in the clutches of a rather clearly defined structure, that of nonbeing. What he must confront is the order of the neatly maintained cemetery. Stated another way, Comala is the little empire of the tyrant Holdfast, the ogre aspect of the Father, the order which is no order because it callously mimics the dynamic structures of Being while populating the cosmos with creatures who, while alive in a certain sense, have their roots firmly fixed in nonbeing. Existence has the property of affirming Being on the one hand and acknowledging nonbeing on the other. Only if we accept the extreme type of existentialism, in which there is no unchanging structure of Being, but only a being that is created anew with each individual act of existence, can this be denied. The non-cosmos created by Pedro Páramo, whose secret name is Holdfast, is ultimately the paradox of a chaotic structure, for souls disintegrate within it.

Nevertheless, when all this is said and done, the novel *Pedro Páramo* has still slipped through our fingers, for if the Father truly is just another form of Holdfast, and the hero is called forth to make an end of his kingdom, this should take place without any serious difficulty. We have not yet dealt with one essential fact: in the traditional myth the hero is called out *from* the kingdom of Holdfast *to* the Center of Being, for the express purpose of being outfitted to go *back* and confront the tyrant. In this novel we again have the question faced by the narrator of *Los pasos perdidos:* Which way is home? The quest is patently not set up as one in which Juan Preciado will go off with power from somewhere else to confront his father, as for example Moses returns from his encounter with Yahweh in the desert to defeat Pharoah. The quest is presented as that of a poor young man who is to go to a prosperous area in search of wealth to renew his life in Guadalajara or wherever he departs from.

Only on his arrival does he learn that the land is a desert, the people are dead, the Father who was to represent the Source as giver of the boon has been murdered, and he himself is destined to die immediately. This is not the story of a quest in which the would-be hero proves incapable of marshaling the necessary power to overcome the ogre in his home territory. It is not even the story of a young man who cannot overcome the giants and monsters blocking the way to the Source where the real test awaits him. This journey is one to the Source to learn that the Source is dead. In traditional mythology the treasure may be guarded by a formidable dragon, but the dragon is alive until the hero arrives, and, far more importantly, the treasure is there, for it is the gift of life from the realm of Being to the realm of existence through the instrumentality of the hero.

A central point of Tillichian thought is that, while existence is surrounded and menaced by nonbeing, Being is not. For this reason Being can always serve as a source of the renewal of life. *Pedro Páramo* stands as a denial of that doctrine, for in it Holdfast, which is to say the power of nonbeing, has not just invaded the realm of existence but has overwhelmed Being itself. Nonbeing issues the call to Juan Preciado, first through his mother, who is described as being deeply immersed in witchcraft, and then in some mysterious manner through his own unconscious processes. Perhaps significantly, she issues the call only on her deathbed, when she is in the hands of death. The call, which is ostensibly one to provide the elect hero with the power of life, appears in truth to be a summons to the last of the sons of Pedro Páramo and Comala to come and die so that their number may be complete. In fact, he cannot succeed in a positive quest because he is not the son of a god who is a bearer of the power of Being. He is, rather, the offspring of that representative of nonbeing who has usurped the throne of Being itself, and a victim of his. Thus, he is a nonentity in the fullest sense. His name, Preciado, does not mean highly prized, but alludes to the fact that his mother was married for the price of her property.

Everything associated with life is gone before Juan arrives. As he does, he crosses a bridge, which according to Jung symbolizes the passage into a new stage of existence. At the house of Eduviges he passes through a corridor which seems to be a series of rooms, a common dream symbol of the passage of the soul towards death which appears also in *Cien años de soledad.* Eduviges, who ironically does not seem to realize that she is dead, pointedly tells Juan that the most important thing is to die when one wills it and not when God wills it. Juan's mother has seemingly accomplished this by means of the voodoo trick of punching holes in her own portrait. However, Juan does *not* die when he wills it, but quite unexpectedly, while in search of the boon of an enhanced life.

Juan does achieve a sort of meeting with the Goddess, an event which under ordinary circumstances is productive of life. Even if the goddess is Calypso, she is a pleasant enough companion, and in the order of things the solar hero must soon be released from the darkness she represents. But in this case she is a goddess of the underworld itself, seemingly a composite figure, and at all events a projection of Juan Preciado's anima. At first she seems to have some positive characteristics, but when her dark sister, obviously the negative anima who signifies death,

77

arrives, all is lost. Although Juan's companion possesses the moistness so lacking in the life of Comala, in his arms she dissolves in her own perspiration. She is "made of earth" and represents the Earth Mother calling him back to herself.

While this is occurring there are two indications that an order of heroism may actually be in operation. One is that Juan's arrival releases an Adonis-figure from the hold of the goddess of the underworld. His name, in fact, is Donis. Adonis is the beautiful youth who is sent to Hades by the attack of a wild boar, symbolic of both the moon and Hades in much of the world. He is so beloved of Aphrodite, however, that he is allowed to spend a part of each year on the earth above with her. When Donis is gone and Juan is dying as the woman symbolic of his life-force dissolves, there appears in the sky the second indication, a conjunction of the moon and Venus, seemingly representing the struggle between the boar-force which is the moon and Hades, and Aphrodite (or Venus), for possession of the god of vegetation. Thus, it would appear that the woman lying with Juan is at least to be identified with the death-dealing aspect of the moon, which, though unable to keep Donis from the grasp of Aphrodite, does manage to hold Juan Preciado.

She is also something of a Persephone-figure, and her very failure to fulfill the role completely may be instructive. She describes Donis as her brother, and this fits in nicely with the fact that Persephone too is a vegetation deity, daughter of Demeter, who is carried off to Hades as the earth opens, being accompanied in her descent by a herd of swine, which are related to the boar that sends Adonis to Hades. So Adonis and Persephone truly are twin figures in what they represent as well as in their actual stories. The point at which the woman in *Pedro Páramo* fails to fit the pattern is in her failure to ascend to the surface like the grain she symbolizes, to spend nine months of the year there. It appears that in her attachment to the cosmos of Pedro Páramo, and specifically to his son Juan Preciado, she too is under the control of death instead of life. She is a mythical expression of the fact that the earth has become sterile under the rule of the *caudillo*. The fact that she *dissolves* should mean that vegetation is to be no more.

Not quite so, for Donis has been released, apparently by

78

means of the age-old principle of a sacrificial death allowing life to go on. Donis, although he fails to remember why, has asked the woman to awaken him at sunrise, which is indeed when a vegetation deity should begin his ascent. He finally does leave at noon in search of a calf, another animal associated with the moon, this time in her fertility aspect. He fails and returns to make another attempt at night, when presumably the moon has more power. The woman says the calf was only a pretext, as it should be for Adonis, who is going to the presence of Venus, not the moon. He does return, but only after the woman has dissolved in perspiration and Juan is dead.

The question whether Donis' hero voyage on the basis of a release from Hades is a successful one is important because if it were it would indicate that somewhere life is surging forth from the land of death which is Comala. But it must be kept in mind that Donis returns, not after a period of months, but the morning after his departure. There is no indication of his having located the calf, pretext or not, or of having accomplished anything worthwhile. Evidently all he is doing is attempting to fulfill his destiny, but without locating the power to do so.

We have encountered the curious theme of the shortage of air in both the novels considered previously: Erdosain's death from tuberculosis and Rosario's symbolic death from lack of oxygen at a high altitude. The theme also appears more or less prominently in several of the other works studied here, as well as in Lezama Lima's *Paradiso.* Taken as a whole, the theme may well represent the diminution of modern man's spirit, vouchsafed him as the very breath of God in the Genesis narrative. In *Pedro Páramo* a major effect of the ban on vitality placed on the region by its *caudillo* is the lack of air. This is first mentioned as Juan enters what appear to be the gates of hell: "nothing but airless heat" (p. 9). The cry of the man executed long before in Juan's room in Eduviges' house—"Oh life, you are unworthy of me!"—produces a silence "as if the earth had been emptied of its air" (p. 36). The key point is that time and air have ceased to exist in Comala with the death of Pedro Páramo. At the exact center of the text Juan Preciado's death takes this form: "There was no air. I had to suck in the same air that was coming out of my mouth, detaining it with my hands before it could get away. I sensed it going and coming, less of it with each breath, until it became so thin that it filtered through my fingers forever. I mean forever" (p. 61).

In the realm controlled by nonbeing the breath of life given to humanity in Genesis by the Ground of Being is withdrawn, never to appear again. Replacing it are the breathless murmurs of the living dead, and Juan concludes that those are what killed him. As in the case of the narrator of *Los pasos perdidos*, who needs recognition of his regeneration by Rosario as mother-figure, deficient as that regeneration turns out to be, Juan's death is confirmed by the fact that his mother says, "No, son, I don't see you" (p. 60).

Nevertheless, in his death he does achieve another sort of meeting with the Goddess, as the living dead find him wandering the streets and bury him in the arms of Dorotea, in what must be nonbeing's ironic counterpart of the sacred marriage. Each of them could be construed as the partner that the other never found in life. For her part, the great curse of her life has been her failure to bear a child. In a dream her womb is discovered to resemble a nutshell. Having failed to "realize the absolute," to particularize the principle of the sacred wedding, she goes to the opposite extreme of working in prostitution, serving as go-between for Pedro Páramo. The circumstances experienced now by her and the hero constitute a bitter denial of Andrew Marvell's lines: "The grave's a fine and private place,/ But none I think do there embrace."

There is in the novel a strange twist on the theme of the two brothers—in this case two brothers, only one legitimate, who come on the scene only after a third one, illegitimate but the only one recognized by the father, is dead. In the normal order of things Miguel Páramo, who for some unknown reason is accepted from the arms of Father Rentería and raised on the ranch, should be the successor, as Odysseus succeeds Laertes and Telemachus is to succeed Odysseus. His name, meaning "Who is like God?," is that of an archangel and indicates that he should be a bearer of power. He is not, however; rather he is nonbeing's equivalent of an archangel. While many heroes of myth and history have been wild and unruly in their childhood, until the power they possess is brought under control and properly channeled, Miguel is destroyed outright by it. He is described as being just like his father, which is ominous enough in itself, and as being so much at one with his horse that they seem to form a centaur. It might be noted that the father of the centaurs was Ixion, a man who, like Pedro Páramo, killed his father-in-law. The centaurs are said to have led a "wild and savage life" (*Classical Dictionary,* pp. 78, 163), for the horse is often an image of chaos and often stands for coarse, brutal masculinity. In Miguel's case it is both, and the horse ultimately kills him as they leap a wall.

The two remaining brothers of any importance to the narrative, then, are Abundio (whose name is grossly ironic) and Juan Preciado. Eduviges tells Juan that Abundio, although ostensibly a breaker of horses—which would symbolize the bringing of chaos to order—was in reality a teller of fortunes to women, doing so in a vaguely erotic manner (p. 21).

It might be expected that the legitimate younger son would appear in Comala to kill the older, legitimate one and then assault the Father's house in quest of the boon. But this is not to be, for at the time of his arrival the older son has already killed the Father and died himself. There is neither a brother with whom to struggle nor a boon to make it worthwhile. Nor does the act of patricide even partake of the heroic-tragic quality it has in the Oedipus myth; it is only the semi-conscious act of a drunken man. There is no conflict, then, at the meeting of the two brothers, for such a conflict can take place only to determine who is the one chosen to appropriate and apply the power of renewal, and there is none. Instead the dead brother has become a Charon-figure on behalf of the powers of nonbeing, in order to meet the other at a crossroads—which symbolizes the meeting of two worlds—and lead him to Hades. In a sense Abundio has managed to kill Juan, but there has never been any malice, any rivalry, involved.

What is needed in Comala is a hero who will come there from wherever Being is in exile and blast apart the order of death—if indeed there is Being anywhere. Then life can be reestablished. The problem, perhaps, is that the people, even before their death, had ceased to believe in the reality of Being, as in the case of the supreme feminine figure Susana San Juan, who believes in hell but not in heaven.

V

Julio Cortazar
Rayuela (Hopscotch)

In ordinary times the center always wins.
—Squalidozzi in *Gravity's Rainbow*

Rayuela, like *Los siete locos,* is an Argentine book consisting largely of a series of dialogues. The difference is that the dialogues take place in Paris, the participants are an international crowd, and rather than madmen they are, if anything, too coldly rational, at least where their discussions are concerned. Their goal is the same, however: finding some sort of coherence within the chaos they are living. In addition, the central character does go at least a bit mad.

The heroes of Argentine novels tend to be a strange lot; they drink a great deal of *maté,* talk incessantly about the meaninglessness of life, or simply decide to *quit* talking for a few years. Horacio Oliveira drinks *maté,* and its bitterness is as much a symbol as is the coffee that García Márquez' Buendía family drinks unsweetened for a hundred years. But there is little danger that he will ever stop talking, and one is reminded of the Dogon people. for whom speech itself is a reproduction of the original words of creation.[1] Perhaps in their view only their incessant chatter will assure the continued existence of their world. For that matter, Lezama Lima presents a character who seems to fear that he will disappear if he ceases to talk.

This hero is definitely not a man of action, but in the final analysis some of the most venerated heroes are not, Gautama Buddha being the best example. In the thought of India, the hero is "sometimes a fool, sometimes a sage, sometimes possessed of regal splendor; sometimes wandering, sometimes as motionless

82

as a python, sometimes wearing a benignant expression; sometimes honored, sometimes insulted."[2] If in addition to all this that hero sometimes has very little idea of what he is about, we may include Cortázar's Oliveira. Even then, however, it is a bit difficult to find a valid precedent for his initial over-intellectuality. Otto Rank's feeling is that "the hero should always be interpreted merely as a collective ego,"[3] and while the words "always" and "merely" smack of the overconfidence of many psychologists of a bygone era, there is something to the statement. This description of the hero seems inconsistent with so much introspection, even if Oliveira is the collective ego of an introspective generation. Dorothy Norman says, "Mythological heroes typify goals to be approached, rather than readily definable human figures" (*The Hero*, p. 3), and Kerényi would seem to be in agreement: "Gods and primitive beings have no inner dimension, and neither have heroes, who inhabit the same sphere."[4] Oliveira has quite a complex inner dimension, and is recognizable as a "readily definable human figure."

The question that then arises is, why call him a hero at all? The answer is twofold: because he himself is very conscious of being set over against the traditional hero, and because he is typical of several characters appearing in recent Latin American novels who are struggling to adapt the hero role to the twentieth century because the age of the Apocalypse *needs* a hero. Moreover, the epigraph to the first of the novel's three main divisions, "The Other Side," reads, "Rien ne vous tue un homme comme d'étre obligé de representer un pays."[5] Horacio Oliveira, in fact, is conscious at least of the need to serve as collective ego to his country. He says, "Reality . . . is always a conventional reality, incomplete and fragmented. . . . The problem of reality has to be planted in collective terms, not in the mere salvation of some elect persons. Fulfilled men, men who have taken the leap outside of time and have integrated themselves into a whole. . . . I feel that my salvation, assuming that I can attain it, has to be the salvation of others as well" (p. 507). So both author and protagonist have identified the latter as a representative figure, and Oliveira, in his solitude, also meets that paradoxical requirement that the hero's definitive victory must be achieved alone. His problem is that his shipwrecks of the spirit constitute a greater threat to his well-being than Odysseus' literal ones.

Like Odysseus, he is the hero as wanderer, but in a very different form: "Searching was my sign, emblem of those who go out at night with no set purpose, *modus vivendi* of the compass-slayers" (p. 20). In spite of this, he has considered attempting to be something of a conventional Western hero, although the heroic life and death he proposes would involve writing a book on defending with his life the ideas that redeem nations. In the end, however, he is the uninvolved observer, trying to make sense of the phenomena that assault his senses. He is a victim of "thingishness" (p. 84), of what Alvin Toffler calls overstimulation and overchoice. He is too sensitive to his surroundings to simulate the quest of anyone "lacking an inner dimension." At this point he is not far from Carpentier's hero, but instead of a retreat to the past in the form of his race's physical origins, he chooses that inner voyage which is neither traditionally Western nor truly Eastern in character. He can never let go of his consciousness enough for the latter, although he makes some bizarre attempts at it. His friend Wong summarizes a passage written by Morelli, the book's version of the Wise Old Man archetype, as follows: "The novel that interests us is not the one that goes about placing its characters in the situation, but the one that installs the situation in the characters" (p. 543).

Horacio Oliveira's name links him with the ancient Greek civilization, as is duly noted by the comic character Berthe Trépat. Horace was a poet who filled his works with great deeds, sound and fury, and the olive tree is the very symbol of Athenian civilization, re-arising as it did the day after the city's defeat by the forces of chaos. It is the tree of Athena, protectress of heroes, for she and they are charged with shoring up civilized order whenever it is threatened. The olive tree forms one post of the bed of Odysseus and Penelope, the Center of their cosmos. Nevertheless, in the opening scene of *Rayuela* there are only olive branches floating in the Seine, for this Oliveira whom they stand for is alienated from Odysseus' heroic mode. His is more the way of an uncertain Socrates.

There is the possibility that the olive branch in the river is the one brought to Noah by a dove to signify the emergence of a renewed earth from the flood waters. The problem is that the dove is associated with the White Goddess (Ishtar being the cause of the flood in the Babylonian version), and she is the one for whom Oliveira searches. The flood waters themselves are the bearer of the branches, for La Maga has apparently disappeared into the river, and those remnants of an olive tree now constitute the only remaining link between her and the hero. As for the dove, it appears near the end of the novel, turned gray from so much stroking by a mental patient, and symbolizing what has happened to even La Maga's image in Oliveira's mind.

His friend Ronald tells him, "Action might serve to lend some sense to life" (p. 198), but Oliveira wants to be certain it is well-directed action before he commits himself. La Maga too tells him he thinks too much before he acts, that he studies a picture but is not in it. For one thing he fears that "in every act there was an admission of a lack, of something yet undone which it was possible to do. It was better to renounce" (p. 31). What he has in mind may be analogous to a point made by Dorothy Norman: "Not only does every battle of the hero necessarily lead to a further one, but each victory can all too readily be but the prelude to a subsequent disaster" (*The Hero*, p. 143). For him the problem is to apprehend the sum total of acts that define a life without actually being a hero in any traditional sense.

Oliveira is committed to passively waiting, particularly in his Paris experience, but in Paris it is too easy to reproduce the archetypal deeds of those heroes of Beckett's, the tramps who perpetually wait for Godot. "He seemed born to be a first-row spectator," although, self-conscious about the fact, he says, "I also intend to be an active spectator" (pp. 475-76), whatever that may be. If he does decide to perform one of Odysseus' deeds, he says, it will be to leave La Maga with her child as Odysseus left Penelope with Telemachus. " 'Yes,' said La Maga smiling homerically." "I'm far from being a hero" (p. 103), concludes Oliveira. He tells her that his perils are not those of Odysseus, but metaphysical ones. She, who has considered drowning herself in the Seine, remarks that there are metaphysical rivers too.

At one point Oliveira feels as if someone were living him. This is very much the experience of Carlos Fuentes' triple hero in *Terra nostra*, but in the latter case this involves some unnamed force's having purposefully moved to express the archetypical solar hero in them; they truly do lack any inner dimension. In *Rayuela* no such pattern is apparent. Normally, according to the principles described by Eliade and others, there must be a determined effort on the part of a person to follow the guidelines laid down *in illo tempore*, in the age of origins, in order to appropriate the identity of the hero who established them. It involves living someone else rather than being lived. The fact is that Oliveira has become so passive in his mere contemplation of life that it is living him. One factor in this may be that he lacks the vitality of youth, in that he is well over forty, while the hero is supposed to be the *puer aeternus*, or eternal child. Ironically, however, he remarks to La Maga, "We aren't adults, Lucía" (p. 111). Lacking both the dynamic qualities of the child and the maturity of the adult, he is in a precarious position.

The act of creation is viewed by primitive societies as the divine revelation par excellence, so that the hero's successful completion of his task in repeating that act constitutes another encounter with the transcendental. The emphasis in *Rayuela*, however, is not on any possible manifestation of the divine, or hierophany, but rather on what Morelli calls "that anthropophany that we go on believing to be possible" (p. 452). Oliveira, for his part, feels sufficiently dehumanized to need it: "I'm a sack full of food" (p. 459). The significance of the inner quest is that this time there is no question of the hero's being transformed so that he may shed power on his society, the whole process being one more repetition of a rigidly prescribed, changeless procedure. This time there will have to be a return to the actual roots of the creation in order to make humanity human again. Thus, the emphasis will be on anthropophany rather than hierophany, and the transformation of the remainder of the cosmos can come later, if at all.

Yet the anthropophany will not necessarily be a revelation of the human being at a higher stage of consciousness, able to reason more incisively, for it appears that too much rationality is not good for the hero. Morelli comments, "The external forms of the novel have changed, but its heroes go on being avatars of Tristan, Jane Eyre, Lafcadio, Leopold Bloom" (p. 497). Oliveira, in fact, "seemed to specialize in lost causes" (p. 214), and this is the case whether he follows an overly intellectual route or not. The so-called Serpent Club in Paris leads him far down such a path, and their interminable discussions, he finally realizes, have led him no nearer the center of his labyrinth, no nearer to coherence, than he was before. When they actually meet Morelli in the hospital and are allowed into his room, which is a kind of shrine to them, Oliveira walks out and leaves the group. A shrine should be a Center, but there is no power for him there. Even earlier, however, Gregorovius has accused him of having become a brute for the simple reason that he no longer discusses literature the way he used to. Looking for a key to his existential experience, "he is beginning to realize that things of that sort aren't in the library" (p. 161).

Oliveira is unable even to explain what he is searching for in Paris; Berthe Trépat thinks it might be the Golden Bough. The significant point is that when she says it, he is already into another stage of his quest. In this one he finally appears to realize that the essence of any hero's quest, whether traditional or not, is in the experience through which that hero passes, not in any intellectual evaluation of the phenomena of existence. This is analogous to what Carpentier's narrator should have learned: cosmic harmony is sufficient in and of itself, and man's rearrangement of it is superfluous.

Oliveira and La Maga decide to run an experiment to learn whether there is any meaningful structure behind the events of their daily lives. What they pursue recalls Jung's synchronicity. According to Jung, his patients often experienced coincidences that were meaningful to them in some way. He felt that the existence of the phenomenon could not be denied, but that no cause and effect system could be discerned in the process. Oliveira feels nauseated at the thought that the sun comes up every day like clockwork, for what he really desires is a universe based on chance. That is, he appears to nurture the hope that in some fortuitous encounter of purely random events something meaningful to him may occur.

He believes that "a casual encounter was the least casual thing in our lives" (p. 15). He and La Maga refuse to make dates because that is the kind of thing done by people whose lives are characterized by too much order of the wrong sort. Once again we are in the empire of Holdfast, who may have things organized but not in any life-giving way. Therein lies the importance of the issue; the modern concept of order, our entire *Weltanschauung,* if not built directly on Newton's cosmology, at least shares its philosophical foundations.

The opening line of the novel sets the quest as one for the meeting with the Goddess: "Would I find La Maga?" It is significant that on previous occasions he has most often met her on a bridge, which, as noted in our discussion of *Pedro Páramo,* Jung considers a symbol of the passage to a new stage of existence. So we have the overly intellectual Oliveira, who as hero is a representative of the masculine principle of rational order, depending upon an acausal process to lead him to a definitive meeting with the non-rational figure who is an expression of Eros—meaning not just love but all the meaningful relationships of life. Probably without their realizing it, what Oliveira and La Maga are testing is the same structure that decrees that Odysseus and Penelope should be reunited after twenty years, no matter how many obstacles Poseidon and his allies might place in the hero's path. The significant difference is that Odysseus has the formidable Athena and her allies personifying the process and thereby guaranteeing his success.

The chance encounter principle works well for a while, but ultimately those encounters cease, and "Oliveira once more planted the problem of probabilities," while "for her it became simply a matter of fate" (p. 47). Nevertheless, the experiment has contributed to one aspect of Oliveira's quest to solve the riddle of the labyrinth; the Center which he suspects is found not by rational means but by chance. The effect of his time spent with La Maga is to draw him away from his exaggerated Logos-orientation and towards a more traditionally feminine construction of the world. When he loses her, however, and chance fails to restore her to him, he comes very near the insanity which can be entered from either extreme, that of Logos or that of Eros.

Although Oliveira's first meeting with La Maga is in a location proper to the quest of the solar hero, the Rue du Cherche-Midi, her bird, according to a palmist she has consulted, is the blackbird, and her time the night. Normally this situation would seem to constitute a repetition of Odysseus' time spent with Calypso, whose very name means darkness. It would then, according to the common interpretation, symbolize the sun's power being weakened by the winter only to burst forth reborn in the spring. This is hardly the case here, considering Oliveira's rejection of the regularity of natural cosmic rhythms, and his desperate need to find her again—as stated in the first line of the novel—rather than the necessity of leaving her to meet another woman. It is as if Odysseus were to spurn his appointment with Penelope and wander over the Mediterranean in a futile search for Calypso. For that matter, Gekrepten, a woman left back in Buenos Aires, serves as a weak Penelope-figure, and at the close of the narrative Oliveira is indeed living with her.

On the other hand, what if the force—if there be one—behind those previous chance encounters really is as strong as ever, but is determined that Oliveira should no more remain with La Maga than Carpentier's hero should stay with Rosario? What if that force really is impelling him away from his Calypso, his dark Yin-figure, whose purpose has now been served along the way of his "search for noonday"? Then even if Gekrepten is only good for a joking reference to Penelope, there must be some final, decisive encounter with the feminine, whether with an actual woman or with the anima within him, still to be sought. For him the prime candidate is Talita, who is married to his double, Traveler, and onto whom he insists on projecting the image of La Maga.

La Maga's real name is Lucía, a source of light, but not that of the severe rationalism of the Enlightenment. Her light is that of the moon, for as Eliade points out, "The complex symbolism of periodic regeneration . . . has its foundation in lunar mysticism."[6] Oliveira sees her as a mythic being; she is like the moon as she lies against him, which immediately raises the image of the *hieros gamos,* conceived as the reunion of sun and moon. However, one must keep in mind that Odysseus' sexual affair with Calypso is not the sacred wedding, for even though she is lunar in character (as is proven by her weaving), she is the dark side of the moon, not the side relating to fertility. La Maga says, "The moon always made me feel kind of cold" (p. 78). This is probably because the light of the moon *is* cold, and she, Lucia, identifies with it.

Her mythic character is further underscored in a zany *planctus* composed by the Club after her disappearance. For them, the exponents of the reason associated with the sun, she was a mirror: "From her we learned of the effects created by the rest of us," says Ronald. Later he describes her as "so vegetal . . ., so bound up with the most mysterious things" (p. 606), from which she seems to be emerging as the Earth Mother herself, with an innate knowledge of the reality of things; she was there all along. As a creature of the night she has cats as her companions; in fact, she is called a cat, a lioness, whose nickname is "The Sorceress." As such she attempts to kill Pola, her rival for Oliveira's affections, who actually does become ill and drop from the scene.

The Logos-oriented males of the Club make her feel inferior for her inability to reason and her lack of knowledge concerning literature and general culture. This is not to be mistaken, however, for a lack of the instinctive appreciation of culture, for she and Oliveira listen with pleasure to Haydn. As Carpentier's hero finally realizes, new worlds must be lived before being described, much less controlled, and to this group in Paris, Haydn, with his version of the harmony of the spheres, is a new world. The men serve as a personification of modern man in search of a soul, *homo sapiens* at the interface with what William Barrett calls irrational man. They gradually realize that, in spite of their knowledge and cultivated tastes, they have gotten precisely nowhere in terms of making sense of the multiple stimuli to which their lives are subjected.

Somehow La Maga always seems to provide an answer: "La Maga was right, as usual she was right, the only one who was right" (p. 171). The statement is more striking in the Spanish, where it reads, literally, "She had reason." This is not the reason of Diderot's Encyclopedia or Montaigne's essays, but a deeper reason rooted in the primordial essence of things. As Etienne puts it, "The poor girl understood so well many things of which we were ignorant by virtue of knowing them" (p. 606). It would be difficult to find a better statement of the despair of Logos standing naked before Eros. Logos, having unearthed the fact that spacetime is curved, or that time is affected by gravity, cannot understand those facts, but the Earth Mother-Eros *lives* the curvature of space. A man knows, moreover, that there is no center on the surface of a globe, but for Woman "the salt and the center of the world have to be there, on that part of the tablecloth" (p. 606). In an item on the Trickster-figure, David Leeming writes of a certain Turkish woman, "Always she confronted her friends and neighbors with a logic all her own which left them looking on in amazement at an absurdity that was somehow true."[7]

The entire phenomenon of the Eros way to truth represents an absurdity from the Western point of view, and yet it is increasingly recognized that the truly great advances in civilization have often come about in a manner quite foreign to our usual image of a person's "thinking it through," with no nonsense allowed. Psychiatrist Albert Rothenberg, partly on the basis of Albert Einstein's detailed description of the processes leading to the formulation of his theories of relativity, has developed the concept of "Janusian thinking," an apparent absurdity that "consists of actively conceiving two or more opposite or antithetical concepts, ideas or images simultaneously, both as existing side by side and/or as equally operative or equally true." Rothenberg explains, "In apparent defiance of logic or matters of physical impossibility, the creative person formulates two or more opposites or antitheses coexisting and simultaneously operating, a formulation that leads to integrated concepts, images and creations."[8] What Einstein calls "the happiest thought of my life," the one leading directly to his revolutionary General Theory of Relativity, was simply that "just as in the case where an electric field is produced by electromagnetic induction, the gravitational field similarly has only a relative existence. *Thus for an observer in a free fall from the roof of a house there exists, during his fall, no gravitational field*—at least not in the immediate vicinity. . . . The observer is therefore justified in considering his state as one of 'rest' " (Greenberg, "Einstein," p. 217). Out of such seeming irrationality the physical universe is constructed.

A man falling from a roof is at rest and the Center for which Oliveira is searching is there on the tablecloth with the

91

salt shaker. If this does indeed represent the "feminine" way to truth, the one despised since the time that Plato attempted to shove myths aside as tales told by old women (even while he made good use of them in his writings), something worthy of note is at hand. The American Indian Contrary, when not engaged in the traditionally masculine practice of warfare, would often dress in women's clothes to engage in absurd behavior, the purpose of which was to break old stereotypes and open the eyes of the people to truths beyond their usual tribal Logos-structures. Odysseus travels to Hades specifically in search of the boon of wisdom from Teiresias, who is considered particularly wise because he has spent some years as a woman and thus has experienced reality from both sides.

One of La Maga's characteristics is the avoidance of order *per se*, and she is always in some sort of trouble "on account of the failure of laws in her life. She was one of those who break bridges merely by crossing them" (p. 20). These, to be sure, are different bridges than the one on which she meets Oliveira; these are the bridges between the problem and its ordinary solution. Oliveira says of her, "She doesn't need to know as I do, she can live in disorder without any consciousness of order holding her back. That disorder is her mysterious order, that Bohemia of body and soul that opens wide the real doors for her" (p. 116). He also realizes that the apparent disorderliness is only such relative to his concept of order. She may be falling from one point of view, but at rest from another.

Pedro Páramo understands and applies the power that makes him master over a region, but even the madwoman Susana San Juan stands in silent judgment on him and his little empire, for only she and her moistness can make it live. By the same token, Oliveira, living in the dynamic city of Paris, feels "with so much knowledge a pointless anxiousness to take pity on something, to have it rain here inside, to have it finally begin to rain, to smell of earth, of living things" (p. 117). This is a plaintive call to the Earth Mother, the oldest goddess of all, who in the form known as La Maga "smells like algae. . . . Like the wave itself" (p. 612). She is the one whose body is eternal; she is capable of putting man into contact with the absolute, for Oliveira tells her, "You were always a terrifying mirror, a frightful machine of repetitions" (p. 17).

Still, true union with her proves to be as unattainable for Oliveira as union with Susana San Juan is for Pedro Páramo, and she leaves upon the death of her child Rocamadour. Her water-nature has continued to be stressed alongside her changeable lunar character: "I feel you trembling against me like a moon in the water" (p. 48). The water appears to attract her. She has long considered suicide; at one point she tells Oliveira, "An hour ago it occurred to me that the best thing would be to go and jump in the river" (p. 109). She senses that the sexual games engaged in by the two of them are leading to an inevitable sacrifice, whether of her or, as it turns out, of both herself and Rocamadour. In any case she states that she hopes Oliveira will kill her so that she can be reborn as a part of the Serpent Club. All she really desires at this juncture, then, is death as a ceremony of transformation, for neither she nor the members of the Club realize yet that her lack of ordinary intellectual prowess gives her property rights over the Center, where phenomena ultimately make some sense.

The sacrifice called for by the games they play is only the alternative to the achievement of their own sacred marriage, the fusion of Eros and logos in a profound love relationship. Oliveira continually stresses the lack of love between them, but it appears that she does love him after all. The ambivalence here is due, at least in part, to the fact that Oliveira, who consistently fails to understand the relationships inherent in Eros, feels that love must strike like lightning, in a strange image in which Aphrodite is replaced by Zeus. A significant combination of the *hieros gamos* with the harmony of the spheres seems to be in the making when Oliveira says, "We made love like two musicians who get together to play sonatas." Yet he is still moved to remark, "You see, we didn't meet in any deep sense" (p. 109). The fine duet does not imply any love between the performers.

Oliveira does realize the necessity of love: "Love, an ontologizing ceremony, giver of being," and yet "otherness lasts us as long as a woman, and furthermore only in what has to do with that woman." The problem is that "without possessing oneself there was no possession of otherness" (p. 120). After she has left he speaks of knowing himself to be in love with her, but even then it might be something attributable to other

93

forces. Instead of having achieved any meaningful union he asks, "Where will you be, where will we be from today on, two points in an inexplicable universe?" (p. 232), because "little by little, Maga, we are beginning to comprise an absurd figure . . ., an interminable meaningless figure" (p. 233).

La Maga's disappearance being triggered by the death of Rocamadour may be simply a novelist's trick to precipitate the act, or the child may represent something newly born in her or in Oliveira. Most likely, though, it is related to the fact that the baby, whose name is not far from "roca más dura" (hardest rock), is the fruit of his mother's experiences with life, love, and the violation of the latter, for he was born of rape. As he grew, her own Self (often symbolized by a stone, according to Jung) grew, especially in the potentiality of her relationship to Oliveira. When it becomes clear that Oliveira is incapable of incorporating Eros into his being, Rocamadour dies and La Maga's hope of fulfillment is gone. The reader is assaulted by the grotesqueness of the scene in her room, in which the members of the Club airily discuss their abstract ideas while Oliveira is the only one aware of the highly concrete presence of death there. On Cortázar's part the scene is a brilliant way of pointing up the irrelevance of their prattle to the existential situation.

Something is amiss from the outset in Oliveira's relationship with Pola. She is the opposite of La Maga in the sense that she has everything in order. He calls her "Pola Paris" (p. 481), and she seems to stand for something like the soul, the essence, of the city in which he is to search for the Center. She is "Pola microcosm, Pola summary of the universal night . . ., center of a chemistry endlessly rich and mysterious and remote and nearby" (p. 521). Whereas La Maga is something like his own feminine side, a woman from the River Plate region encountered at the Center that Paris is supposed to be, Pola is the personification of that Center itself; her name is indicative of that. She is the mysterious feminine figure which is Paris, but the Paris noted for its mania for categorizing everything. While Oliveira, as an Argentine "obligé de représenter un pays," is captivated by her as Buenos Aires has long been held in thrall by Paris, it is no lasting thing, and eventually she fades from the scene.

Talita is another matter. The novel is balanced between "The Other Side" and "This Side," and the pair consisting of Oliveira and La Maga in Paris is balanced by Traveler and Talita in Buenos Aires. When the balance is upset by Oliveira's loss of La Maga he eventually returns from Paris in search of her and meets her double, who, unfortunately for him, is married to *his* double. The resemblance between the two women is underscored at the outset when the couple meets him at the dock. La Maga has always been associated with cats, and Talita's arrival with a cat in a basket is not lost on Oliveira. Her name, although far from reflecting her character as revealed in the novel, serves as a warning to Oliveira of the negative anima potential within any woman. She is Atalia, and Athaliah was a queen of Judah, daughter of the infamous Ahab and Jezebel and notorious in her own right for crimes against decency.

Talita strikes Oliveira as being a positive anima-figure: "She gives the impression of going around carrying a lighted candle in her hand, showing the way" (p. 449), which is quite important for the hero who perceives himself as living in something of a labyrinth and therefore playing the role of Theseus. She takes on another face of the goddess, or a parody of it, when Oliveira engages in his comic descent into the realm of the dead, the morgue of the insane asylum where the three friends work. There "he was in his small, comfortable refrigerated Hades, but there was no Euridice to search for" (p. 372), since La Maga is not likely to appear there. When Talita does appear, he construes the scene in terms of a meeting with the Goddess, although he realizes that the kiss he gives her is intended not for her but for the one whose form he has projected upon her: "Somehow they had entered another thing, that something where one could be in gray and be in pink, where one might have died of drowning in a river . . . and have appeared on a Buenos Aires night to repeat on the hopscotch the very same image that they had just achieved, the last square, the center of the mandala, the vertiginous Ygdrassil by way of which one went out onto an open beach, a limitless extension, the world beneath one's eyelids which the eyes turned inward recognized and venerated" (p. 374). Just how ironically this statement is to be viewed depends upon one's opinion of the relative proportions of madness and sanity in Oliveira's unstable mind at this moment, for immediately after this scene he barricades himself in his room and apparently leaps out the window onto the hopscotch diagram.

What was overwhelmed him with a sense of the identity of the two women is the image of Talita whimsically trying her skill on that hopscotch figure in the semi-darkness. The fact that she is in a gray uniform is stressed, and probably not just because in such a color she fades more easily into the darkness, as is appropriate for one who has become essentially a psychic image. One of the patients whose form of madness seems deeply troubling to Oliveira is the man who constantly carries and caresses a dove, which has consequently become gray. The dove is one of the most ancient symbols of the White Goddess, and it would appear that just as the bird belonging to the patient has become gray in his monomaniacal obsession with it, the image of La Maga has also turned gray in his obsession with possessing her, even if only in the form of Talita.

This is the point at which the theme of the two brothers enters the work, for, Oliveira must dispute possession of Talita, even if only as a psychic image, with Traveler. It may be worth noting in passing, as we consider *why* Cortázar chose to provide a double for Traveler, that in the mythology of the Hopis, Spider-Woman creates twins who are responsible for keeping the world in order (Maclagan, p. 25). Perhaps the mythic impulse in Cortázar is similar, even though in his case it has to be ironic. His "twins" are hard-pressed to maintain any semblance of order in their own lives, particularly after the arrival of Oliveira back in Buenos Aires, feeling "that his uncertain quest was a failure and that precisely in that fact lay his victory" (p. 240), for "he realized that his return was really his departure in more than one sense" (p. 268). It would be futile to venture a guess as to his reasons for such an opinion, but in returning to Buenos Aires he is clearly still in search of the Center, obsessed with meeting the Goddess, and bound to end up in a terminal dispute with the other potential founding brother. Once again, as in *Los pasos perdidos,* there is a good deal of confusion on the part of the hero with regard to which way is home and who is the feminine figure with whom he is destined to remain.

96

In this case, despite Oliveira's paranoid delusions, the murder of one of the brothers does not take place, nor is there any sort of founding act. Oliveira calls Traveler his *Doppelgánger* and says, "It wouldn't surprise me a bit if you and I were the same person" (p. 400). The truth is that their characters and destinies are confounded in a rare manner. The one who thinks of himself as a man of action is, appropriately in view of that fact, named Traveler, but the man of words travels, much to the chagrin of the other. Oliveira tells him, "You . . . are in tune with the territory. You are my form that remains here watching me with pity" (p. 400). He is the 5,000-year-old child, basically satisfied to adapt himself to a civilization with its roots that far in the past, working in the circus which is a microcosm of the world of Buenos Aires as well as a Sumerian city of 3000 B.C. "At bottom Traveler was what [Oliveira] should have been with a little less damned imagination, he was the man of the territory, the incurable mistake of the misguided species" (p. 402).

Oliveira, says Traveler, is "a will in the form of a weathervane": "For you realities and memories get mixed up in a highly non-Euclidean manner" (p. 394). So Oliveira points whichever way the wind blows him at a given moment, but the rest of Traveler's comment is interesting because orderly systems such as that of Euclid simply are no longer valid at the extremes. Oliveira lives at the extreme, and Traveler's answers are insufficient for him.

There are at least two scenes in which the trickster mode is entered in Buenos Aires, one by the two of them and the other by Oliveira alone. This is significant because Oliveira, as one who rejects the conventional world, must set himself to abolish its boundaries. Therefore the justly famous scene in which Talita finds herself suspended on a shaky bridge over the street between the two apartments is significant not only in terms of the vision of the woman in a dangerous position halfway between them, literally riding for a fall, but in the medium itself, which is an outrageous trickster item calculated to avoid at all costs the mundane procedure of simply asking Talita to dress and carry the items in question—*maté* and nails—across the space between the buildings. That would have lacked all ceremonial value, and Talita herself recognizes the act as a sort of ceremony. This is exactly what the trickster is supposed to accomplish: the abolition of the boundaries of thought and behavior so that new perspectives may be gained. Even the "highly sexed" quality of Trickster is in view. Each man sits on the end of his own phallic piece of board while Talita straddles the one to pass to the other, which is tied to it—from Oliveira's genuine cedar to "that crummy piece of pine," as he calls it, belonging to Traveler (p. 290). Her eventual fearful retreat to her own apartment without ever getting to that of Oliveira foreshadows the events in the morgue, for even though Oliveira manages to kiss her, the kiss is not really for her. She is not La Maga and she is not his; she is only the fleeting vision of the dove turned gray by too much caressing.

The other trickster event in the Buenos Aires context involves Oliveira's locking himself in his room in the insane asylum and setting up an intricate system of defenses to prevent Traveler from getting to him. He perceives that, since he as one of the brothers has made a move in the very depths of Hades to steal the woman belonging to the other, the traditional murder could now take place. Here he acts as if he *were* a true son of the Hopi Spider Woman, as he weaves a web calculated to capture Traveler. Even though, as Daniel Reedy has pointed out, the spider's web is a kind of mandala too,[9] the narrator notes that "it was always going to be painful to Oliveira not to be able to construct for himself even a notion of that unity which at other times he called the center. There wasn't the remotest hope of unity" (p. 384). So Trickster—and in the Oglala tradition he is Iktomi, or Spider—in playing his pranks on others entraps only himself, as always the wounded wounder, the perpetual loser. Yet Jung points out that "the wounded wounder is the agent of healing" (Radin, p. 196). Trickster might often lament his uselessness, but he is among the highest gods of creation in the mind of the North American Indian.

Having wounded his brother, although not seriously, Oliveira becomes the wounded, a victim of his own tricks. To all appearances he leaps from the window in an attempt to land on the "Heaven" end of the hopscotch traced in chalk below. The author, however, seems less certain. Evelyn Picón Garfield says, "When I told Cortázar that Oliveira could not possibly commit suicide by jumping out the window and that *Rayuela* is an essentially optimistic book—two conclusions which are not shared by all critics—Cortázar smiled and said: 'No, no, he doesn't jump. One doesn't know for sure; but he doesn't jump, no, no, I'm sure he doesn't jump. But there are critics, of course, who when they reviewed the book stated that at the end the protagonist commits suicide. Oliveira doesn't commit suicide. But I couldn't say that. It would have destroyed the book. The idea is that you, or any other reader, have to decide. So, for example, you decide, as I do, that Oliveira doesn't kill himself. But there are readers who decide that he does. Well, I feel sorry for them. It's too bad for them. The reader-accomplice has to decide. Of course it's an optimistic book.' "[10] If Oliveira does not jump, however, the reader must account for his casts and bandages in some other way. It would appear that Cortázar is playing the time-honored Argentine authors' game of gently misleading the reader.

Assuming that he does jump, then, but without "committing suicide," one might note that the trickster Oliveira appears to be turning the fall of Icarus into another attempt at achieving what he fails at in the first instance. Having had to give up his search for the Center and cut off from his escape by any ordinary route, he chooses the only course open to him. He hurls himself, in place of the stone normally used in the game, onto the goal. Following that, we find him some time later with his lady of the "exacerbated penelopism" as she feeds her battered hero some fried delicacy. His attitude towards her indicates—somewhat tentatively—that he too is now in harmony with the territory. Perhaps the brother who remained has killed the wanderer after all.

Still, if the reader follows the order of chapters suggested by the author, the result is a continual circling back that never ends. This would seem to indicate that the soul of Oliveira, however bound it may now be to Gekrepten and the lifestyle represented by her, goes on making one assault after another on the Center, even though all that is achieved is a cycle of frustration. It also means that the book itself, now deprived of the hero it has defeated, is condemned to run madly in circles forever like the horse that killed Pedro Páramo's son Miguel.

One question that remains is what sort of quest for the Center this has been. Late in the novel Oliveira wonders "what kind of temples he was going around in need of, what intercessors, what psychic or moral hormones that would project him outside or inside himself" (p. 368). This recalls the statement in *Los siete locos* to the effect that *someone* would have to appear on the scene to save humanity. Here, in contrast, it is more clearly a matter of Oliveira's straightening out his own construction of the phenomena of life: "An analysis of the uneasiness, in the measure of what was possible, always alluded to a dislocation, to a removal from the center with respect to a type of order which Oliveira was incapable of specifying" (p. 476). He does feel—although he wavers—that there is some sort of Center to be found, but he is bothered by the fact that, even before Traveler has called him "a will in the form of a weathervane," he has perceived himself in the same manner, knowing he should be a compass instead.

For Prince Gautama or any other hero of his sort the quest is an internal one, particularly where the hero has a tendency to suspect that reality is no more than a projection of his own mind. If it is, to resolve the problem of the alienation of the mind from the Source is to come into harmony with all other things that proceed from that mind, and ultimately from the Source. Oliveira's feeling is "Really, I have nothing to do with myself" (p. 140) and "I would need . . . to approach myself better, to drop all that stuff that separates me from the center" (p. 28). Like Erdosain he fully realizes that the meaninglessness he experiences does not lie in the things themselves: "What is absurd is not things, the absurdity is that things are there and we sense them as absurd" (p. 194). Yet while Etienne argues that reality is within oneself, Oliveira expounds the view that reason itself may be a phanton concept: "The *cogito* . . . is situated today in a rather vague region, between electromagnetics and chemistry." It is not essentially different from the aurora borealis, but "maybe it's the other way around, and it will turn out that the aurora borealis is a *spiritual* phenomenon" (p. 511).

Madness is always a possibility. Even though Oliveira, as

he leaves Paris, feels that his uncertain search is a failure and that this is a victory in itself, his loss of La Maga and finally of all hope of coherence leads him ever more deeply into erratic behavior. He himself views the insane asylum as a microcosm and says, "I don't believe that we've come here solely because the Boss brought us" (p. 355). There is, in fact, a good deal of interest in madness as a solution when all else has failed, particularly in the work of R. D. Laing. Paradoxically, this is only a logical extension of the common conclusion that the way of reason is invalid, especially in view of the sort of world often produced by rational principles. Oliveira's position proves precarious, then, when the doctor says he suspects that all madness signifies the fixation of a dream, for this is what causes Oliveira to jump—the monomaniacal dream that *somehow* he must get to the Center, even if it be by jumping to his death.

The events in the institution are set against the backdrop of a mad plan for the reorganization of the world which appears in a letter from a lawyer named Ceferino Piriz. His cosmos is not one brilliantly born of chaos by the power and guidance of the realm of Being, but one thoroughly tainted by the chaotic nature of the mind that conceived it. The various divisions of labor within the military, for example, would be staffed by men born under the appropriate signs of the zodiac. It is as if Arlt's Astrologer were back, this time talking about his profession. Chapter 139 of the novel is even more striking, for it consists of the text appearing on the back of a record jacket and proposes an exotic mysticism dependent upon correspondences between musical notes, letters, and numbers. Again, in what has become a literary cliché, the craziest people may not be the ones inside the gates. Nor are they necessarily the patients as opposed to their keepers, as Oliveira demonstrates by his leap.

One gains the impression that Oliveira might bring himself into meaningful contact with the archetype were it not for the fact that the detritus of modern life stands in his way. He tells La Maga, "You're handing me an apple and I've left my teeth on the lamp table" (p. 484). This is a joke, to be sure, but nevertheless it represents an attempt to come to grips with whatever is preventing him from laying hold of what she offers him, the

101

Fall which at least leads to an understanding of good and evil. She remarks, "The fault belongs to that Morelli, who has you obsessed; his insane experiment is giving you a glimpse of a return to the lost paradise, you poor snackbar preadamite of the golden age wrapped in cellophane" (p. 485). She is wrong, though; Morelli has already abandoned the search for lost paradises, and Oliveira's idea is that one must "reinstall oneself in the present" (p. 113). His problem is the widely discussed one that Alvin Toffler and others have called sensory overload, which would effectively block the way from plastic wrapping to archetype. It appears that the greatest obstacle faced by today's hero is not the dragon guarding the gate to Paradise, but the very existence of false teeth and a lamp table to leave them on. To put it another way, he is likely to walk by the entrance without seeing it, because the boxes of consumer goods are piled so high that it is blocked from his view. It is another form of the invasion of existence by nonbeing, a particularly insidious form in which the way to Being and renewal is obscured, as it is by the flood waters in *Los pasos perdidos*.

In this framework the sense of *being lived* begins to come into clearer focus. Oliveira feels as if someone were living him in Paris, and later feels that, in a switch of media and their manipulators, "there are other things that use us to play" (p. 394). Even Talita says, "It seems as if something is speaking, something is using us to speak" (p. 323). These are expressions of the fear that the modern soul may be controlled by forces too large to fight.

At this point too the importance of disorder to the quest begins to make sense, for Oliveira states, "The disorder in which we were living . . . seemed to me to be a necessary discipline" (p. 25). For him, "all disorder was justified if it tended to emerge of its own accord; through madness one could perhaps arrive at a kind of reason that wouldn't be that reason whose inadequacy is madness" (pp. 93-94). At bottom this is simply another form of assault on the realm of nonbeing presided over by the tyrant Holdfast, whose order itself is absurd: "Only by living absurdly would one ever be able to break this infinite absurdity" (p. 123). What he proposes is similar to the practice of giving stimulants to hyperactive children, who are tranquilized thereby: one drives a process to the extreme in order to produce the opposite phenomenon. In this regard Morelli holds that the reader of the modern novel should be able, without laying aside the obvious disorder of the characters' lives, to perceive their reasons for being, "even if the latter were disorder itself." In reading his book, "one had at times the impression that Morelli had expected the accumulation of fragments to crystalize abruptly into a total reality" (p. 533), presumably because each character's reason for being will ultimately serve as focal point for the fragments. Here Morelli uses the kaleidoscope as *imago mundi*; it not only focuses on random collections of fragments in such a way that they are viewed as orderly and beautiful, but they even emerge in mandala form. In the end, however, Morelli seems not to be so sure, as he says, "I no longer know how to write 'coherent' " (p. 488).

The hope expressed by Morelli is akin to Kierkegaard's famous dictum that truth—and therefore coherence—"exists only as the individual himself produces it in action" (Norman, p. 56). Oliveira is not a man of action, however; he is a man of words, and one of his fears is that he will, in fact, become too ingenious. He allows that "our possible truth has to be *invention*" (p. 439), and "it would have been simple to organize a coherent scheme, an order of thought and life, a harmony" (p. 339), but it would be an abstract, artificial one. He seems to enter the world of Kierkegaard's existentialism as he asks, "Of what use is it to know, or think one knows, that each way is false, if we don't walk it with a purpose which is no longer the way itself?" (p. 340). The point is that truth must be invented, not discovered, and this may be what plunges Oliveira into his trickster role in Buenos Aires, and into the absurdities that lead finally to his dangerous leap which is no Leap of Faith.

Before he gets to Buenos Aires he has tried his hand at an extreme sort of tricksterism in Paris, for he has learned along the way that Heraclitus once achieved a cure by burying himself up to the neck in dung. Apparently Oliveira reasons that if the Greek could obtain a physical cure by a burial in physical excrement, a modern man might be able to achieve a metaphysical cure. The first major assault on this profundity is in his attendance at a supposedly serious concert by the pianist

Berthe Trépat. Cortázar handles it masterfully in the farcical mood appropriate to the trickster tales, and Oliveira is suitably enmeshed in the grotesque details of the life of a Parisian loser.

Finding no solution there, he wanders half-consciously into the range of the famous *clochards* of the city, and passively, in the manner, one supposes, of one buried to the neck in excrement, allows one of the women to begin performing fellatio on him. The subsequent scene in the vice squad paddy wagon, with two homosexuals making the appropriate comments and the *clocharde* sobbing on the floor, singing, "Et tous nos amours" over and over, is one of the comic masterpieces of our generation. Oliveira will never be farther from Odysseus, and even though he has found nothing yet, this is when he states that the success of his quest in Paris lies in its very failure.

For him the controlling image is the Center, whether it be the center of a labyrinth or mandala, or even the eccentric heaven of a hopscotch game, for, as Eliade states, "the Center . . . is pre-eminently . . . the zone of absolute reality" (*Eternal Return*, p. 17). It might be thought that the search by the hero of the age of depth psychology would be an interior one. The great labyrinth of Crete seemingly began as a spiral (Norman, p. 66), and according to Jung the spiral is a symbol of the movement into unconsciousness. That would fit well with Oliveira's use of La Maga as his guide into a non-rational, perhaps even unconscious, way to truth, but he concludes that the Center is not in his head. In fact, La Maga complains that for *other* people the mandala is only symbolic, while Oliveira admits that for him it might be geographical. It might be Paris, for, as La Maga tells him, Paris is a mandala, a center (the term "mandala" means either "circle" or "center"): "Everything there was nameless and without a history" (p. 486).

Oliveira realizes that the traditional mandala may be approached from any side, and as people do so, occasionally someone sees the Center. This is reflected in the major divisions of the novel itself. He plays with the concept, but always underlying the games there is a desperate desire to hit on something meaningful by chance. He contemplates, for instance, the existence of an Indian form of chess with sixty pieces on each side, in which the one who conquers the center wins. "From there one dominates all possibilities. . . . But the center might be in a side square or off the board" (p. 625). In Buenos Aires one game played by Oliveira involves the circus tent, with the pole rising to the opening at the top. He has a good deal of fun with such phallic symbolism and is pleased at having found one sort of Center. As Joseph Campbell points out, for the North American Indian "the opening at the top of the lodge . . . is the hub or mid-point of the sky."[11]

Oliveira is fascinated with the fact that a patient at the mental institution, known only as Number 8, plays hopscotch perfectly and ends up in firm control of Heaven. This may influence Oliveira's decision to make an assault on it from above. But Hades is also a kind of Center, and upon finding its surrogate in the institution's morgue he experiences his unsatisfying—and finally disastrous—meeting with the Goddess there. His only boon, as it turns out, is a cold beer from the refrigerator, which is close enough to the lotus to cause him to reflect on the possibility of a classic refusal to return.

Ultimately, however, he again touches on the province of modern physics in the course of his philosophical pilgrimage as he says, "There is no center; there is a sort of continuous confluence, of undulation of material" (p. 284). An indispensable quality of the Center is changelessness, motionlessness, the cessation of time. On a materialistic earth, with its continual flux of matter and energy, there is no such place. The Cuban writer Severo Sarduy expounds a concept of "the empty Center," which he says is analogous to the expanding universe.[12]

Perhaps it is inevitable that in all his reading and discussion of any number of approaches to reality and the restoration of meaning, Oliveira should also play with the concept of the creative word. At one stage he feels that the world he desires exists within the scattered fragments of his life as a line of the poetry of Garcilaso de la Vega exists in a dictionary: "Let us say that the world is a form; it must be read. By reading it let us understand generating it" (p. 435). That is, the creative reading of even a dictionary, which Oliveira considers a "cemetery" as it stands, and therefore presumably a potential source of new life, may be able to *select* and *arrange* those elements which by themselves are meaningless but when so selected and arranged signify cosmos.

Morelli too has said, "There is first a confused situation, which can only be defined in the word. . . . If what I want to say (if what wants *to be said*) has sufficient power, immediately there is initiated the swing, a rhythmic oscillation. . . . That oscillation [is the] swing in which confused matter begins to take form. . . . Thus by writing I descend into the volcano, I approach the Mothers, I achieve contact with the Center—whatever it may be. To write is to draw my mandala and at the same time to move within it" (p. 458). Here is the theory that order can and must be imposed on the *massa confusa* of the chaotic existential situation by means of the word. Where it diverges from the traditional is in its concept of the imposition of the word not as the *result* of a descent to the Source but as *constituting* it.

What Oliveira fears is the danger of surrendering to a purely verbal unity, for we live in a world in which the charge "Those are just words" is a damning one. Oliveira calls words "black bitches" or "an ocean of tongues licking the world's ass" (p. 484), and says he has not been to bed with them for some time. He has his fling, though, with a search for order through words, and at this point even the minds of La Maga and the Club meet. Their Wise Old Man, Morelli, has said that "only in dreams, in poetry, in play . . . do we behold at times what we were before whatever in hell it is we are" (p. 523), and Etienne strikes an even more basic chord when he declares that "language means residence in a reality, a dwelling place in a reality" (p. 503). One problem is that even that possible reality is fragmented, for the group spouts any number of languages, and someone calls the situation Babel.

La Maga, associated in her name and deeds with magic, is also the inventor of a language which they call "glíglico." It is no wonder that she always seems to have the answer if she has links with the invention of the language. Oliveira finds himself in Paris, where everything, as far as he is concerned, is without a name, time has not yet begun, and his companion is a woman who is in touch with the origins. This is at the same time identical to and a reversal of the situation of Carpentier's hero, for whom all these phenomena are present, but in the farthest reaches of the jungle, since for him Paris is not the source of new life but the epitome of decadence. For both of them, on their arrival, time must be set in motion, names given, and a general order imposed on the *massa confusa*.

Oliveira finds himself, on searching in Paris for the lost paradises forbidden by Morelli, experiencing a modified, pagan version of the Garden of Eden, as by her invention of *glíglico* La Maga endows things and acts with the names they have lacked till now. Chapter 68 of the novel is written in that language, and it clearly describes a sexual scene, which would seem appropriate: sacred wedding, new language, new creation. Of course, it fails to work out that smoothly, primarily on account of Oliveira's inherent inability to seal a love relationship.

Even in Buenos Aires there remains a trace of Oliveira's linguistic quest. He, Traveler, and Talita are viewed as forming a "trismegistic triangle," and the adjective used in the phrase is the one applied to Hermes. The nearest this division of the novel can come to linguistic renovation, however, is in the mention of, and a chapter written in, something called "ispamerikano" (chapter 69), involving some ludicrous attempts to reform the Spanish language.

The literary work itself, as constructed by author and reader, is an experiment in linguistic creativity. This is apparent from the outset as the reader is informed that one must decide whether to read only the first fifty-six chapters, the entire work with the optional chapters interspersed according to the author's suggestion, both, or even some or all of the chapters at random. It becomes apparent that the novel itself is a mandala, and as such it may be approached from any of several directions. The next revelation is that the reader is therefore responsible for making sense of it as Oliveira attempts to make sense of the world at large. The Center, if any, must emerge from the collusion of author and reader, who then finds out experientially what Etienne means by language as residence in a reality, and may accompany Cortázar and Morelli in their descent into the volcano, in an act which is to result in the creation of a new order.

Chapter 34 serves as an illustration of the difference be-

tween Cortázar/Morelli's concept of the novel and that of the nineteenth century. It has Oliveira reading a novel belonging to La
Maga, in a mind-numbing interlinear text in which Cortázar has
placed the Spanish novel in apposition to Oliveira's stream of consciousness. In the former the protagonist establishes his life and
love within solid bourgeois norms, while Oliveira comments on the
impossibility of such (including the language in which they are expressed) and on his complicated relationship with La Maga. The
Spanish character lives within a given reality, Oliveira attempts
to create another as he goes, and the reader is forced to formulate
meaning in the act of progressing through the novel. Morelli says,
"The true and only character that interests me is the reader, in the
measure in which something of what I write should contribute to
changing him, breaking him loose, alienating him" (pp. 497-98). He
wants to make the reader his accomplice in helping to bring about
the "anthropophany" mentioned earlier, evidently so that the two
of them can serve as messengers, for "there is no message, there
are messengers, and that is the message" (p. 453). This is linked to
his desire to "install the situation in the characters" rather than
vice versa.

The essence of what Morelli—and seemingly Cortázar behind
him—is saying is that where no hierophany is possible the goal
must be to achieve an anthropophany, a revelation of the human,
whether through literature or otherwise. This is accomplished
through the co-creation of writer and reader, another form of the
rhythmic swing which results from a play of opposites. What is
produced is a new human individual, who, however confused, at
least exists and struggles against nonbeing, thereby approaching
Being itself.

Thus, *Rayuela, as it is read and interacted with,* is itself the
equivalent of a quest for the Center on the basis of the Word, and
Morelli's doctrine of the search for the power of renewal as *constituting* that power in action supercedes the failure of the fictional hero to find the Center, achieve the sacred marriage, or renew his life or that of the cosmos in any conventional manner. The
power sought by the hero seems to be generated by the act of seeking; existence not only precedes essence but creates it. In the final
analysis the hero is above all a power bearer, and if the power is in
the kinetic nature of the quest itself, Oliveira does not come off
looking too badly after all.

VI

Gabriel García Márquez
Cien años de soledad
(*One Hundred Years of Solitude*)

No evil lasts a hundred years, nor could a body stand it.
Coastal Colombian version
of a Spanish proverb

Cien años de soledad opens with an excursion by the founder of
Macondo and its major heroic character to view ice. It ends with
the denial of renewal to any family condemned to one hundred
years of the kind of solitude symbolized by the ice. José Arcadio
Buendía calls it the great invention of his time, and one of his illegitimate grandsons, the mulatto Aureliano Triste, establishes
an ice factory in the city. But Colonel Aureliano, before he faces
the firing squad, reflects upon the fact that he is possessed by
an inner coldness which will accompany him the rest of his life.
Fleeing from it, he only demonstrates its hold over him, as he
condemns his lifelong friend to death for the crime of daring to
tell him the truth.

A book that begins with ice and ends with a denial of
renewal hardly provides a fit setting for an essentially solar
hero. Certainly the typical hero must be alone—must experience
a haunting temporary solitude—at the crisis point of his
transformation. At the same time he represents his people, actually embodies them, and therefore the warmth of the new life
he brings is theirs as well. In *Cien años de soledad*, in contrast,
there is a sterile kind of solitude.

Paradoxically, multiple hero-figures appear in the work,
and some are moderately successful, although in the final

analysis their solitude prevents the final renewal from taking place. Even the gypsies serve as heroes as they go periodically to the source of new marvels and bring them back to Macondo, if not to enhance the life of the people, then at least to amuse them for a time. Melquíades is first seen among them, demonstrating a preposterously powerful magnet. In fact the citizens of Macondo are most amazed by the wonders of technology taken for granted by most of the Western world, while what that world terms the paranormal—ghosts wandering through the house, for example—is a matter of daily reality, as any present day rural Colombian *costeño* can verify.

Many of the Buendía males and some of the females, notably Ursula, exhibit heroic characteristics. In the case of the men this is explained in part by the fact that essentially they are all only extensions of the original José Arcadio. The Sanskrit manuscript that tells the story of the family states that one hundred years of daily incidents have been compressed into a single instant; or, read in reverse, what has taken place is that a single cause-and-effect sequence has been expanded to allow one hundred years of additional happenings between the basic cause and its effect—namely the vaguely incestuous marriage between José Arcadio and Ursula and its expected result, the birth of a child with the tail of a pig. That child is not born to them but to the last Aureliano and Amaranta Ursula. In the one hundred years between, all the males are named either José Arcadio or Aureliano, and they exhibit, in greater or lesser degree, two facets of the character of the patriarch, who emphatically is a heroic figure in the *pattern* he follows, but not in the results he achieves.

José Arcadio has all the qualities of the hero as founder, including a run-in with a "brother" who must be slain to precipitate the wedding union and act of founding. His name begins with an allusion to the head of the archetypal Christian family, that comprising Joseph, Mary, and Jesus, and as we shall see, one of his sons does take on the proportions of Christ, or, more accurately, an antichrist. "Arcadio" is an allusion to the spatial roots of Greek civilization, for Arcadia was the first area of Greece to be settled and long served the poets as a primordial Paradise to long for, seat of the lost Golden Age. In the patio of the family home is a large tree known as a "castaño," which, while generally considered to be native to the New World, actually originated in the north of Greece.[1] The tree, José Arcadio, and the community founded by him all have some sort of roots in Greek civilization. Robert Lewis Sims suggests that the combination of "Arcadio" with "Buendía" suggests the dawning of the world.[2]

José Arcadio is tied to the tree when his madness has become too acute for the family to handle, and in this he is related implicitly to many traditional heroes: to Gautama, who sat under the Tree of Enlightenment to become the Buddha, but more firmly to figures such as Attis and even Christ, who actually were bound to trees. The tree in all these cases is the sacred one at the Center of the cosmos, whose roots reach down into the underworld and whose branches extend into the heavens. The narrator states of José Arcadio that "a power superior to any visible binding kept him tied to the trunk of the *castaño*."[3] From here José Arcadio continues to play a role in family life even after his death, when, like the townspeople of Rulfo's Comala, he continues to interact with the living. Apparently only the crumbling Aureliano is unable to see him there, as he walks out and absent-mindedly urinates on the shoes of his father's ghost.

José Arcadio comes to the startling conclusion that the earth is round, although no one believes him. Still, his act of founding sets him apart. The process begins in a variety of solitude based on Ursula's fear of the aforementioned result of their marriage, if it is consummated. The round of artificial sterility is broken by the inevitable taunting remark concerning his seeming impotence. Several modern novelists, aware of the often absurd symbolic interpretations by Freudian critics, appear to be deliberately employing Freudian imagery for its comic effect, and a prime example is the scene in which José Arcadio reacts to the insult on the part of the inappropriately named Prudencio. The offended man returns to his home for a horse and a spear, buries the spear in the offending part of Prudencio's body, the throat, and returns home to thrust the spear into the ground, symbolic of the Earth Mother, and to force Ursula to go to bed with him. He has achieved a quick run-through of the traditional hero's deeds to slay the dragon who blocks the forces of renewal and consummate the sacred wedding.

The matter takes on the proportions of a founding based on the murder of a brother when Prudencio's ghost returns and harasses José Arcadio sufficiently to force him to move to a new location with several other families and found the town known as Macondo. The name, which is given to him in a dream, has an interesting parallel in the Bantu language, in which "Makondo" corresponds to the Spanish for "plátano," or a banana-like fruit with magico-religious significance. Specifically, it is the food of the devil.[4] It appears, then, that name is destiny, as the foreign "devils" later invade the community to cultivate the fruit in question. Mircea Eliade has stated that every founding is a new act of creation. As in Carpentier's Santa Mónica, some things in Macondo are so new that they lack names, but only because of an epidemic of amnesia. Still, the re-naming of all that is represents the completion of creation.

A curious variation on the theme of founding results when José Arcadio attempts to "set" his town in space by learning how far it is from established civilization. The expedition finds an old Spanish galleon, symbolic of the heroic Iberian roots of their world. When Aureliano later views it, it has deteriorated badly: the Hispanic element in the *costeño* culture has faded. José Arcadio and the other men then find the sea, source of life and means of communication with the world at large.

In another parallel to Santa Mónica, Macondo is timeless at first, as it emerges from mythic spacetime and has not yet settled into mundane rhythms. José Arcadio sets traps and brings in large numbers of songbirds, who provide a connection between the community and the primordial harmony of nature. Not long after, however, the birds are replaced by synchronized chiming clocks. The rhythms of nature have been replaced by those of technology. Still, there remains a theme of musical harmony in the town, linked to the relative harmoniousness of the lives of its inhabitants. Francisco el Hombre, a genuine character from the history of the coast, appears from time to time, transforming the news of the regions he travels into the pleasant orderliness of music, as the *vallenato* composers of the region continue to do today. A player piano is brought into the Buendía household by the ill-starred Pietro Crespi and serves as a barometer of the family's spiritual fortunes. José Arcadio, as founder always obsessed with novelties, tears it apart in a futile search for its magic secret. Significantly, it cannot be repaired by the shamanic figure Melquíades, but only by the European Crespi, with his grounding in technology. Later there are so many deaths in the family that the piano is covered in mourning, but as the household is renewed subsequent to Aureliano's "death" and "resurrection" it is uncovered and again produces harmony. Aureliano Segundo becomes proficient on the accordion, and later there is a clavichord, in stark contrast to that plebeian instrument so typical of what Fernanda del Carpio considers the hopeless vulgarity of the coast. Fernanda plays the harpsichord, and her daughter Meme becomes a virtuoso on it, although her heart is not in it. Thus is the harmony of the spheres reflected in the life of Macondo.

As is the case with many heroes, José Arcadio's contact with the world of hard reality becomes increasingly tenuous once his major work of founding a new cosmos has been completed. Forgetting—or perhaps never having realized—that the realm of Being is outside normal experience, he attempts to prove God's existence by photographing him. His failure convinces him of God's non-existence. Nevertheless, even after death he maintains such an interest in modern marvels that he is unable to stay away when they begin flooding into the community. At this time, the narrator notes, "No one could know for sure any longer where the limits of reality were" (p. 195), which is a perceptive comment concerning mankind's problems with progress, and especially for the costeños, many of whom still steadfastly refuse to believe that human beings have walked on the moon. They have seen Disney Studios perform similar miracles on the television screen; why should this be any different? The problem is that the hero is by definition the one who places his people in contact with reality (as José Arcadio does by pointing out that the earth is round and finding the sea), but in Macondo the founder himself early on loses track of the line between physics and metaphysics, to say nothing of the one between illusion and reality.

113

The hero is one who should possess a profound understanding of the nature of time, for he periodically renews it. But in Macondo the founder, even while alive, becomes so attracted to the world of the dead that he, who first brought time to the community, loses contact with it. He talks all night with the ghost of Prudencio, whose friendship he has come to value, and in the morning he comes to believe that "the time machine has broken down," so that from then on every day is Monday (p. 73).

As was mentioned in our study of *Pedro Páramo*, the dream of series of rooms has to do with the transition to death. Here the same image is employed to show how, according to the Spanish expression, "he belongs more to that side than this one," as José Arcadio moves through the rooms to meet Prudencio coming the other way and later returns. One day he simply goes on, henceforth to return only as a ghost. At his death there is a rain of small yellow flowers, which, according to Joseph Campbell, is one of the accompaniments of spectacular events in Buddhist India.[5] The patriarch and founder is gone, but in two senses he is not: he can still be communicated with in the patio (Ursula often goes there in times of crisis) and his sons are an extension of his person.

The herculean son who bears his name is called a "protomacho" (p. 85) and is oversize in both physique and behavior, the very incarnation of machismo. His call to adventure is issued in a sort of meeting with the Goddess as Earth Mother, for the gypsy girl who enlightens him, like the woman accompanying Juan Preciado in his death, seems to dissolve in perspiration and emit "a faint odor of mud" (p. 36), with the significant difference that this occurs in what the French call "la petite mort" and not in literal death. His quest, if such it be, involves his circling the earth (which does prove to be round) sixty-five times and having every inch of his body tattooed. When he returns it is as if he had been gone only since that morning, as far as he is concerned, which indicates that he, as hero, has been functioning outside normal time. He arrives at the end of "a voyage that had begun on the other side of the world" (p. 83), which compares with the experience of Juan Preciado as well, since it is said that he comes from the other side of the world to Comala. José Arcadio Junior bears many marks of the hero, but his successful completion of the process of renewal is blocked by contamination on several levels, notably the prevalence of solitude where the traditional hero's task ends in the relational.

The relational character of his quest is damaged at the outset when the call is issued by a prostitute, and whereas the end of a successful quest should involve the union with the designated incarnation of the Eros-principle, José Arcadio returns only to become a crude prostitute for women, even raffling off his services to them. Apparently he has also made a pact with the devil somewhere in the course of his travels, for he wears what his people call a "niños en la cruz" (children on the cross) bracelet. The pact, according to my source on *costeño* folklore, usually involves the gift of great strength, which would seem to be the case here. According to tradition, the bracelet is all that remains after a cat is boiled and made to prophesy, and it is often embedded in the skin of the wearer's wrist.[6] This is far removed from the sort of boon with which the conventional hero returns from his travels.

He lives with Pilar Ternera and regularly returns from a day's hunting with great loads of game. Virtually his only creative heroic act is saving his brother Aureliano from the firing squad, which frees the colonel for the acts that eventually bring about a renewal of sorts. The manner of his death also relates to a feature of *Pedro Páramo* in that he, like Miguel, seems to be killed by his own excessive masculinity. Whereas Miguel is killed by a horse that seems an integral part of him, in José Arcadio's case the fatal blow is even more direct, in that he dies of what sounds like a gunshot inside his head. No wound is visible, but the smell of gunpowder issues from the cemetery for years, which is simply a symbolic expression of the fact that the so-called supermale tends to die of causes related to his own uncontrolled masculinity. Ironically, he dies of the gunshot from which he has saved his brother, in what would appear to be a substitutionary atonement.

Many hero tales speak of an astonishing wildness in the subject's childhood and youth, but this energy is eventually brought under control and made to flow in creative channels.

Often the transformation is brought about by contact with a positive female figure. Enkidu, the double of Gilgamesh, is a wild man among the animals until he is civilized by a temple prostitute—which is vastly different in context from a fling with an ordinary prostitute, for Enkidu's companion would have been considered an incarnation of the goddess herself. Therefore the meaning is that even a hero is essentially only a powerful beast until he achieves the integration of his personality which can be brought about only by his acceptance of the feminine within him. Working counter to this in José Arcadio is another force; the anti-relational power of solitude. Untempered by the softening elements, the power within him destroys him in the same way that Pedro Páramo crumbles like a pile of rocks. This solitude, by whatever name, is the most firmly established constant in the works we have considered so far, and is a determinative factor in *Tres tristes tigres*. That solitude is avoided only in a tragicomic manner in *Pantaleón y las visitadoras* and in a serious, purposeful manner in *Terra nostra*.

The original José Arcadio's other son, Aureliano, is a man of inner strength and will more than of physical prowess, and is perhaps the most extreme example of a solitary being in the work. His anguish is evident even before his birth, in that he cries in his mother's womb. He is born with his eyes open, as if untrusting and ready for action. From the beginning he is possessed of a strange psychic power, which takes the form of psychokinesis; as a small boy he can knock chairs over by simply looking at them.

Aureliano has a rare vocation for the practice of alchemy, and this should be a relatively good sign, for the true goal of alchemy is the transformation of the person, the conversion of lead into gold being only a side issue. The process is vitiated, however, by the very fact that his inner solitude isolates him in his laboratory, where he "seemed to have taken refuge in another time" (p. 50). Despite his conversations with Melquíades, this novel's version of the Wise Old Man, he ends up by transforming neither himself nor the physical elements, but engages instead in a senseless round of manufacturing little gold fishes, even turning the gold coins he receives for them into more of the same. Aureliano's name suggests the Latin word for gold, aurum.

He appears to find love for a time, albeit in an extraordinary

116

form, as he becomes obsessed with marrying the mayor's nine-year-old daughter, Remedios. He is so smitten by the child that he wanders unconsciously to Pilar Ternera's room to use her as a substitute. The marriage is arranged, and Remedios later dies in childbirth. His subsequent bitterness might be explained by the early loss of the love of his youth, were it not for the fact that it becomes evident that he never loved Remedios. What was involved was his pride, perhaps in possessing, although never truly relating to, the embodiment of those qualities of innocence, gentleness, and trust which he is incapable of finding within himself.

He is capable, nevertheless, of both pity and courage on behalf of others. The former is revealed when he finds himself impotent in the presence of the exploited young prostitute who serves as prototype for Eréndira in a remarkable short story by García Márquez. In addition to his self-consciousness at not being as well endowed as his brother, he feels the need to protect the girl, and helps her rather than taking advantage of her. Later his outrage at the senseless murder of a woman by government soldiers converts him into a revolutionary. He engages in thirty-two armed uprisings against the Conservative government, known popularly as the "Goths," and loses them all. In this connection his name ironically links him to the Roman emperor Aurelian, a successful general who defeated the Goths.

Aureliano does manage his successes, mainly victories that serve to harass the Conservatives and provide him with a reputation for ubiquity. This is his time in hell, and he returns transformed, but only into the sort of person that a long and hopeless war tends to produce. He has lost his compassion, and his sense of outrage at the brutality of the military has been replaced by an even more extreme brutality of his own. If "the hero is he who is immovably centred," he is a parody of the hero, for wherever he stops, even in his own house, he has a circle traced around him that no one else may enter, the apotheosis of solitude. Forgetting that in the beginning his struggle was against bad government, not against the Conservatives as such, he condemns the good and just mayor Moncada to die. He thereby sets himself up for the crushing disappointment of learning that the leaders of his own Liberal party have betrayed him and those who have died for the cause by making a deal to share personal power with the Conservatives. Later he burns the widow's house for her refusal to permit him to enter, has a charismatic officer whose popularity is a threat to his power murdered, and orders the officer who suggested the murder shot. He has now lost contact not only with the meaning of the war, but with reality as a whole.

Aureliano finally redeems both himself and his world by working for peace. The narrator comments that he was never a better warrior than in that battle, which is provoked by his realization that all his war efforts are being used only to establish the scoundrels within the Liberal party leadership in positions of power in Bogotá. At this point he has a good deal of trouble with *golondrinos,* which are large tumors in the armpits. They are symbolic of what has incapacitated him spiritually, for the word is also used for a military deserter. Thus, he arranges for a simple ceremony in which a peace treaty is signed.

In his youth he has been told by Pilar Ternera, who reads the cards, but not very accurately (at one point she reads the *past*), that he will be a great warrior, and specifically an accurate shot with a gun. Accordingly, he asks a doctor to indicate the location of his heart with mercurochrome, and when the signing has been completed he retires to his tent and shoots himself, but misses his heart. The doctor has deliberately pointed out a harmless spot. The importance of the act lies in the fact that he is subsequently treated as if he had actually died, although Ursula receives ambiguous psychic signals. She finds her cooking pot full of worms, indicating his death, and has a vision of him being carried home, but she fails to understand why his eyes are open. Throughout the episode he is treated as a martyr who has risen from the dead. Though he has been thought a traitor, his reputation is restored in his "resurrection."

What happens at this point in the Buendía household, Macondo, and the text itself indicates that García Márquez conceives his hero as a sort of antichrist, not in the sense of one opposed to Christ, but in the more basic sense of the Greek preposition "anti," which is "in place of." This is, in fact, the sense in which Jesus uses the concept: many coming *in his name* and claiming to be Messiah (Luke 21:8). To a certain extent Aureliano is to this novel what Christ is to the Bible. The chapter dealing with the incidents referred to above ends at almost the exact center of the text with a mention of New Year's Day. The following chapter begins with a paraphrase of the book's opening lines:

Many years later,	Years later,
facing the firing squad,	on his deathbed,
Colonel Aureliano Buendía	Aureliano Segundo
was to remember that re-	was to remember that
mote afternoon	rainy June afternoon
when his father took him	when he entered the
	bedroom
to see ice.	to see his first son.

This construction in turn forms a parallel with what the author of the Fourth Gospel does to indicate that Jesus has begun a new creation, opening, as does Genesis 1:1, with "In the beginning."

Seemingly the "wheel of time" has made one full turn, and when the energy that first set it in motion has ended in entropy there has appeared a hero whose death and resurrection—which is to say, his descent into Hades as source of the power of creation—has provided the necessary impetus to set it in motion again. Soon Ursula says, "It is as if time were going in circles and we had gone back to the beginning" (p. 169).

Whereas the family house has been in a run-down condition and even Ursula has allowed herself to behave as if she were worn out, Aureliano's return and the peace associated with his act of redemption encourages her to initiate the work of reconstruction and even dress herself in more youthful clothes. Furthermore, the spiritual renovation extends to the community as prosperity returns.

There appears one more parallel to the story of Jesus, whose followers, after his death, were often slain as martyrs. Aureliano has seventeen illegitimate sons, all named Aureliano, born during the war years of seventeen different mothers. In them he feels "dispersed, repeated" (p. 146), as they all come to

Macondo in the course of less than twelve years. The boys hold a wild celebration at the house, one vaguely reminiscent, as it turns out, of those ancient practices in which the sacrificial victim was treated royally before being sacrificed. Their marking for that sacrifice is unwittingly carried out by the local priest, who places on the forehead of each of them the usual cross of ashes, a mark that proves indelible only for them. The course of events leading to the eventual slaughter is established by one of them, a mulatto known as Aureliano Triste, who on his arrival in Macondo "had already sought his fortune in half the world" (p. 188). He establishes an ice factory, and this eventually necessitates the building of a railroad into the city. The railroad, in turn, brings in the North Americans to establish banana plantations. Presumably to forestall Aureliano's arming his sons for an uprising, a campaign of extermination is initiated in which sixteen of them die initially and Aureliano Triste only later, when after years of fleeing his pursuers he is refused admittance into the house by family members who know nothing of him. Thus ends the promise of the dispersion of heroism by multiplication which will be fulfilled only in *Terra nostra*.

Although he is tempted to go to war again, Aureliano remains in the solitude of his workshop, with few excursions outside it until one day he watches a circus procession go by and goes to the patio, where he dies leaning against the *castaño* tree. Apparently he is no longer able to live in a world of political injustice masked by the unreality of a circus. Later it will be debated in the city whether there ever was such a man as Colonel Aureliano Buendía, but, ironically, one of the jaded bullies searching for another Buendía family rebel in order to kill him reveals his great admiration for the man. He requests as a souvenir one of the gold fishes, which of course stand, as does the fish that symbolizes Christ, for the self-sacrifice which aims to renew the world and put an end to just such tyranny as is embodied in the officer.

In *Terra nostra*, El Señor remarks that the birth of twins announces the end of a dynasty. In *Cien años de soledad* it does not happen so quickly; rather, the line ends with a direct descendant of the twin Aureliano Segundo. As children Aureliano Segundo and his brother José Arcadio Segundo constitute a "mirror trick" (p. 151) or a pair of "synchronized mechanisms" (p. 159). The two are thought to have switched the name bracelets which are the only means of telling them apart. Ursula suspects this because Aureliano Segundo seems to have the character associated with all the José Arcadios, and vice versa. The Aurelianos, she concludes, "were marked with a tragic sign" (p. 159), which is all too literally true in the case of the original Aureliano's seventeen sons. The twins do appear to live lives each associated with that typical of the men bearing the other name, but they die at the same moment and are buried in the wrong graves, which presumably straightens out their identities.

The officer mentioned above stumbles upon Aureliano's workshop in search of José Arcadio Segundo, who has been involved in the protest against the banana company's barbarities and has been shipped towards the coast with a trainload of victims of the massacre. This is his descent into hell, and, like the Aureliano that he probably is, he retires from the disillusionment of war into the enchanted room where he feels protected. This is Melquíades' room, which exists apart from ordinary spacetime, and when the soldiers search for José Arcadio Segundo, even though he is sitting in what should be plain view, they fail to see him. It should be noted in passing that the ability to become invisible to one's enemies is a fairly common characteristic of heroes. José Arcadio is "protected by the supernatural light, by the sound of the rain, by the sensation of being invisible" (p. 265). Light and sound are two of the elements most fundamental to creation, and the soldiers, bent on destruction, are diverted by it. When they are gone he begins working with Melquíades parchments, and he becomes "illuminated by a seraphic resplendence" (p. 266). Outside that Center, however, he is unsuccessful. Earlier he has made a long and difficult trip to bring a boat into Macondo, a task at which he is finally successful, but the cargo is a load of French prostitutes. Even after his enlightenment he is unable to locate the boon of the horde of gold coins hidden by Ursula, as he digs up virtually everything within the indicated radius. The gold is found later at the center of the circle, at that Center and Source which is Ursula's bed. It is found by the last José Arcadio, the

121

one designated by the women to become Pope and sent to Rome to study. He has returned, not with the boon of the Papacy, but as a dandy; upon discovering the gold he holds a non-stop orgy described by the narrator as a saturnalia (p. 315).

The female figures are presented in a somewhat more positive light, as has often been noted in the work of García Márquez. Ursula is his White Goddess in this work. Her name relates her to the she-bear, which Robert Graves says was sacred to Artemis Callisto in Arcadia,[7] a fact that serves as another link between her and her husband and that region associated with the roots of Western civilization. Artemis is a moon goddess, and Ursula reveals characteristics associated with her as well as the closely related Earth Mother. Even when very old, Ursula at one point goes out "with some shoes the color of old silver and a hat with tiny flowers" (p. 119), silver being the metal associated with the moon and the flowers proper to the Earth Mother. She is a powerful force in the family throughout its hundred-year history in Macondo, and even has her say in the governing of the community, as her grandson Arcadio becomes the worst of all governors and she actually takes over from him. She even overrules Aureliano's outrageous decision to have his lifelong friend shot, threatening to kill her son with her own hands if he persists.

Earlier she has succeeded where José Arcadio had failed, as she and a group of women discover the route to the civilized world that her husband and his men had searched for in vain. In doing so they traverse a route so wild that Aureliano and his soldiers are forced to abandon it in a later time. In an age when many persist in believing in progress, she has her roots firmly planted in the concept of cyclical time, as she notes at several junctures that it seems to be going in circles and that they appear to have returned to the beginning. The narrator shows every sign of agreement. In accordance with her concept of time, before her death she becomes almost fetal, having the appearance of "a newborn old woman" (p. 290). José Arcadio, in contrast, has mistakenly believed that the machine of time has broken down.

Pilar Ternera, whose life spans most of the work, is the White Goddess in her prostitute aspect. Ishtar, for example, is known as "She who looks out of the window," a euphemism for the prostitute in the society over which she reigned. Pilar's name, although it would appear to have been invented as a joking allusion to a phallic symbol and the calf which is sacred to the moon, is in fact that of an acquaintance of the author who, I am assured by his father, bears no resemblance to the fictional character. Pilar forms part of the original group that founds Macondo and is associated with the revelation of their destiny, since she serves as card reader. She is somewhat deficient in living up to the archetypal role of Woman as revealer of hidden truths—as much so as Carpentier's Mouche—since her readings are none too accurate, and her laughter becomes so coarse that it frightens away the doves which are so closely associated with the moon goddess.

With Pilar the massive José Arcadio achieves his first Meeting with the Goddess, his sexual enlightenment. She becomes so deeply involved with all the Buendía males that she is forced to call upon the mysterious Santa Sofía de la Piedad at one point in order to avoid an Oedipal situation. Pilar, like Ursula, conceives the family history as a wheel. Near the end of that history she is still active in a zoological brothel known as "The Golden Child," which probably has to do with the atmosphere of orgy associated with the Apocalypse, the extravagant behavior that Eliade says represents a desperate effort to maintain contact with being. The golden child would be an ironic allusion to the desperately needed birth of the hero who might renovate time, but a brothel is not the appropriate setting for such a hope. There is an atmosphere of the creation there, nevertheless; the air is "as if it had just been invented," and Pilar Ternera herself "felt that time was returning to its primordial springs" (p. 333). Once again she is half right. In pre-modern thought the end should also be the beginning, but the time lived by the Buendías and Macondo is an exception, and that specifically on account of the sterile solitude best exemplified by a brothel.

Rebeca too is closely identified with the earth, as she is unable to abandon entirely her obsession with returning to it for nutrition. One suspects that her character might be drawn, in this aspect, from a comment of Don Quixote's concerning "the illness that certain women tend to have, who experience a desire to eat dirt, lime. . . ." Rebeca is the one who brings into Macondo the plague of insomnia, the worst symptom of which is amnesia, and which is cured only by a liquid brought back from the land of the dead by Melquíades.

Of all the women associated with the family, Santa Sofía de la Piedad most closely resembles what Jung would call a pure anima projection, for "she possessed the rare virtue of not existing completely except at the opportune moment" (p. 101). She is called upon when Arcadio, not knowing that Pilar Ternera is his mother, becomes determined to possess her. A common feature of Jungian psychology is that the male child holds his mother as a positive anima-figure until this fixation is diverted and he is able to integrate his own feminine side into his total personality. The danger is that he may be unable to integrate it, and thus abandon the projection of his feminine aspect onto his mother only to project it on another female. In this case Arcadio is diverted from his mother without even knowing who she is, only to unite with the ideal target for an anima projection, a woman so ethereal that her existence depends on her being perceived by someone in need.

The most fascinating of the feminine characters is Remedios the Beauty, an autonomous lunar being who goes her own way whether her actions correspond to the dictates of a civilized society or not, as the moon in its movements and phases appears independent of the sun. Like Susana San Juan, she "was not a being of this world" (p. 172), and therefore not bound by its conventions, feeling it perfectly natural to wander about the house completely naked. Nevertheless, as in the case of Cortázar's Lucía, or La Maga, "it seemed as if a penetrating lucidity allowed her to see the reality of things beyond any formality" (p. 172). That is, she too appears to be in direct, rather than derivative, contact with Being.

One expression of *hybris* rarely permitted to a mortal man is to possess a goddess. Out of the danger inherent in the attempt there emerge several myths in which a man is destroyed for his daring. If Remedios the Beauty is not of this world, if she belongs to Being rather than existence, then she may be met by the hero who, as Master of the Two Worlds, moves freely in both those realms, but she never will be *possessed* by him. Only by the aid of the powerful god of masculinity, Hermes, is Odysseus able to enjoy the favors of Circe and avoid being changed into a pig by her—that is, bound to Hades as nonbeing which is associated with the pig, rather than released from it with the power of renewal. Remedios is soon perceived as a destroyer; it is supposed that she "possessed the powers of death" (p. 203). The bold young man who manages to touch her dies. A young commander of the guard dies at her window when spurned by her, like Anaxarete's lover, Iphis, whom she treated "with such haughtiness that he hanged himself at her door," the difference being that in the latter story Artemis punishes the young lady by transforming her into the stone she so resembles in her behavior.[8] This incident is all the more significant for appearing just at the end of the first half of the novel, preceding the paragraph indicating full renewal. The presence of such a representative being at this end-point which is also a new beginning should signify the renovation of the male-female relationships which is the *hieros gamos,* the primordial unity of the opposing forces of creation. Instead we have at this point the destroying female, and the solitude goes on.

Another young man is doomed to death by reproducing an archetypal act, that of Actaeon, who saw Artemis bathing and was changed into a stag by her and then devoured by his own hounds. In García Márquez' version of the story the man removes tiles from the roof over the bathroom to watch Remedios bathing, which bothers her not at all; she even warns him of a possible fall. Having seen her, however, he is doomed in any event, and he does fall to his death, his body forever saturated with her fatal scent.

The most telling point within the solitude theme of the novel is provided by the narrator in one of his rare moralistic comments, to the effect that the reason none of the men desirous of possessing her was successful is that none of them hit upon the simple strategy of approaching her with love. The implication is that for this reason, more than for any deficiency in her, the shell of her solitude has remained unbroken, and moreover, the natural time for renewal in love should have gone by without that renewal's having taken place, but only the death of a suitor. Therefore she remains unattainable, even unreal, and according to a comment in José Lezama Lima's *Paradiso,* "The unreal . . . has a tendency to levitate."[9] This is true of Remedios the Beauty, who is unreal to the world because she has never been made a part of it by the love of a man. So she ascends to heaven, bothering Fernanda del Carpio a great deal by not only doing what Fernanda in her religious presumption would like to do, but taking along some serviceable bedsheets in the process. García Márquez has admitted, "Remedios did exist, but she was not beautiful; she was an Indian girl who did the housecleaning. . . . We don't know what became of Remedios; one day she left the house and we never saw her again."[10] Thus is memory converted into myth by the creative imagination of an author. Margaret Lester comments that Remedios "waits in life long enough to know that she will always be desired but never loved."[11]

Fernanda, for her part, is a representative of the cultural domination of the coast by the interior. Her entire orientation is towards death, as she supports herself and her father in Bogotá by fabricating funeral wreaths. She imposes a Holdfast order reeking of nonbeing upon the Buendía household once Ursula has become weak and her penchant for cyclical renewal is gone. Curiously, Fernanda's concept of time is linear, but on a line leading only to death. Her importance to the hero theme lies in her attempt to impose some order upon the family's eating habits. But rather than the communion indicative of the deep roots of civilization that characterizes *The Odyssey,* all that she achieves is a harsh, deadening formality that stifles all communion. Characteristically, she manages to achieve in death the incorruptibility expected by her father, apparently by means of the correct application of the formula that failed to work for Melquíades. Far from immortality, however, the best she has been able to attain is the preservation of the nonbeing that characterized her in life.

On the opposite end of the scale in terms of the meal as civilized act of communion is the competition of gluttony between José Arcadio Segundo and a huge woman known as The Elephant, which nearly kills him. Never is a balance achieved between the two extremes of lifeless formality and boorish gluttony, for solitude reigns over the dinner table as well.

Amaranta comes nearer than any other woman in the novel

to being a true Eros-figure or avatar of Penelope. The narrator informs his reader that she is the only member of the family capable of loving deeply, but that fear has prevented her from achieving love. In fact, fear is the basis of the hatred that she pours out on Rebeca, ultimately destroying both of them. Refusing each opportunity to marry, she becomes a twisted anti-Penelope, awaiting the return of no one, weaving not the shroud of a king but her own, seemingly undoing each day's work at night. She awaits only death, not her Odysseus. "She came to be, more than a specialist, a virtuoso in the rites of death" (p. 237), and eventually she begins to notice that an incarnation of Death is sewing alongside her. She receives the revelation that she will die when she finishes the shroud, and she recalls the vicious cycle of Aureliano's gold fishes: "It pained her not to have had that revelation many years earlier, when it still would have been possible to purify her memories and reconstruct the universe under a new light . . ., neither out of hate nor out of love, but out of the measureless compassion growing out of solitude" (p. 238). She is the complete Eros-figure by nature, a purveyor of both love and hate, capable of reconstructing the universe, but, chained by solitude, able to conceive the idea of doing so only out of the alienation from others to which she is condemned with the rest of the family.

Although it seems at times that a couple has grown into love, the relationship always proves to be faulted in some manner, whether by the overwhelming of love by lust, the superficiality of the love itself, or the incest taboo. The best relationships in the work are described in terms of "shared solitude." The incest theme is particularly significant in that the result of the act is invariably described in imagery proper to chaos and nonbeing. Even disobedience to parents can result in one's metamorphosis into a snake, symbol of cosmic disorder; how much more destructive must incest be? José Arcadio and Ursula are inhibited by a guilty conscience and the fear of "engendering iguanas" (p. 25), a New World variation on the Leviathan theme. The basic fear, however, involves bringing into the world children with the tail of a pig, a fear whose roots may reach far into the collective unconscious, to the point at which, if Graves is correct, the Spanish word for pig, "cerdo," comes from the name of the Celtic goddess Cerridwen or Caerdmon (*White Goddess*, p. 68). In many cultures, ranging from Europe to Polynesia, the pig is associated with the moon and with Hades. It is just possible, then, that some echo of these ancient associations between the pig and nonbeing (the Hades connection) may be productive of such a fear. The implied link between incest and such chaos then intensifies the solitude which generates the very nonbeing that the people are attempting to avoid. According to Julio Ortega, "García Márquez explains that *Cien años de soledad* is the story of a family that tries to avoid the child with a pig's tail; he affirms that this is the unifying theme of the novel."[12]

Closely involved with the lack of sound male-female relationships is the predominance of prostitution and illicit affairs in the novel. As noted previously, the only result of José Arcadio Segundo's minor hero quest is the entrance of a group of French prostitutes into Macondo, and one of the negative aspects of the arrival of the banana company is that even more of them invade the community. They are known as "Babylonian females" (p. 197) in an allusion to the Great Whore of the Apocalypse, and probably represent the fact that Macondo is prostituting itself to foreign interests with apocalyptic results, for the end of the affair is the chaos of mass murder and years of rain without sight of the sun. Pilar Ternera's "Golden Child" enterprise ends with her death, but only after she has sent the last Aureliano into a furious sexual bout with Amaranta Ursula that is not only incestuous but adulterous as well. Thus, the impulse for the final sterile act of incest is provided by a representative of the equally sterile profession of prostitution.

Petra Cotes is another Earth Mother or lunar figure. When she and Aureliano Segundo engage in sexual relations, and only then, the animals owned by him reproduce wildly. There is a "supernatural proliferation, for her "love had the virtue of exasperating [*sic*] nature" (p. 166). This is an example of the old pre-modern myth that led young couples up to recent times in Europe to copulate ceremonially in the newly planted fields. It is the *hieros gamos*: the masculine, fertilizing sky uniting with the moist, receptive, feminine earth. The problem, as it turns out, is that the process is vitiated by the lack of love between

them, as well as by the fact that Aureliano Segundo has married
Fernanda del Carpio for her beauty. He finds that he must continue frequenting Petra Cotes' house so that the animals will
continue to multiply, and eventually he leaves Fernanda altogether and moves in with Petra.

As Fernanda grows older, Petra is rejuvenated, like the
Nature that she symbolizes, and Aureliano Segundo along with
her. In Aureliano Segundo's case it means that he is a man in
contact with both the positive and negative aspects of the
White Goddess: with Petra, whose contact means an abundance
of life, and with Fernanda, dedicated to the cultivation of death.
No real sacred marriage takes place, because the relationship
with Petra partakes of the nature of chaos rather than order. Its
orgiastic character is more typical of those acts that *precede*
the *hieros gamos,* as at the conclusion of *Terra nostra.* The rain
following the banana company massacre puts an end to
Aureliano Segundo's wealth, and his attempt to arouse Petra
once more elicits only a response recalling the opening pages of
Pedro Páramo: "The times aren't right for such things any
more," and he concludes that "they themselves . . . were no
longer any good for those things" (p. 273).

In the early portions of the novel a good deal of imagery is
drawn from Genesis, and near the end much of it is associated
with the Apocalypse, particularly where Babylon, "the Great
Whore," is concerned. There is no better image of solitude and
the resultant sterility in a city than Babylon as prostitute. Not
only are there the "Babylonian females" brought in by the
North Americans, but there is Mauricio Babilonia, who fathers
the Aureliano who in turn fathers the child with the tail of a pig.
In these generations there has been no marriage. When
Aureliano finds he must learn Sanskrit to decipher Melquíades'
manuscripts, he discovers that the primer he needs is on the
bookstore shelves between *Jerusalen libertada* and a volume of
Milton's poems. The former is a 1581 work by Tasso, dealing in
a rather free manner with the "liberation" of Jerusalem during
the First Crusade, as Macondo was freed from nothingness and
made the capital of the Buendía tribe and their associates.
Their Paradise is followed on the shelf by the key to their being,
which is followed in turn—and rather ominously—by what may

be *Paradise Lost; Paradise Regained* is forbidden by the last sentence of the novel.

To summarize this point: From its beginnings as Eden, Macondo has become a sort of Jerusalem for its inhabitants, but it has, in the course of time, been invaded (as Jerusalem was in 586 B.C.) by its antithesis, which is Babylon. To continue the biblical analogy, the *hieros gamos* whose failure has caused the problem in the first place should be realized so that the New Jerusalem, the Bride of the Lamb, may be established. Furthermore, it is important to note what sort of behavior on the part of Jerusalem led to its invasion by the empire later to be viewed as a symbol of prostitution. Probably it is described most graphically in the book of Hosea, which is the focal point of Ergueta's madness in *Los siete locos*. Hosea is ordered by Yahweh to marry a prostitute in order to shock his people into a realization of the monstrous anomaly of his "marriage" to them when they are "whoring" after pagan gods. This sterile behavior, the ultimately solitary union between the people and the gods who are not real, leads to the final destruction of the nation by the people who have always worshiped those gods of nonbeing. Macondo has lived in the solitude that leads to nonbeing through its entire existence, so that it too, at the end, must be invaded by "Babylon" and annihilated by "an apocalyptic wind." Its solitude has been so profound that there will be no New Jerusalem.

Even so, there is a feeble example of that "desperate attempt to maintain contact with being" that has been discussed in connection with the sexual activities of Mouche and Carpentier's narrator during the revolution, as well as that in Paz's *Piedra de Sol.* In the latter case the sacred marriage is achieved and the world regenerated at the end of the cycle of Venus. The poem, consisting of the same number of lines as there are days in that cycle, proves to be circular and unending, always leading back to its original lines and the creation. In the case of Carpentier's hero with Mouche, this is not the case. Neither does the principle function in the novel at hand, in the case of Aureliano and Amaranta Ursula, simply because, to continue with the biblical analogy presented by García Márquez, they relate totally to the Babylon side of the Apocalypse and therefore are destroyed with it; there is no New Jerusalem side, in which the Bride descends from the heavens. Perhaps the potential bride was Remedios the Beauty, and her time was during the period of renewal at the center of the text. But at that point there is only the death of one of those suitors who never thought of approaching her with love. This is a family *condemned* to one hundred years of solitude.

The last Aureliano has one curious mark of the hero, which is that he arrives in a basket at the Buendía house, enveloped in mysterious origins. His grandmother, Fernanda del Carpio, propagates the story that he was found floating in the basket, a common feature of the story of solar heroes. The fact is that he is brought by a nun from Bogotá, where his mother, Meme, has died a virtual prisoner in a convent. His father is Mauricio Babilonia, who is paralyzed by a bullet in the spine. This is an inauspicious beginning, and at age three Aureliano is said to resemble the encyclopedia description of a cannibal, which is to say the grossest violator of eating as communion, exemplified in *The Odyssey* by Polyphemus. As such he is hardly fit to generate the child who could renovate the Buendía line. As he and Amaranta Ursula settle into their feverish routine of incestuous adultery, the house becomes the paradox of a "paradise of disasters" (p. 341), for their Eden of lust can only be destructive, never creative.

The irony of the case becomes more intense with the statement that the two "were beginning to be converted into a unique being" (p. 345). When their child with a pig's tail is born and named Aureliano, "Amaranta Ursula saw that he was a Buendía, one of the big ones, massive, willful like the José Arcadios, with open, clairvoyant eyes like the Aurelianos, and predisposed to begin the lineage again from the beginning and purify it of its pernicious vices and its solitary calling, because he was the only one in a century who had been begotten in love" (p. 346). Begotten in love, perhaps, but in the forbidden love of Oedipus, which pollutes the land and must be purged, not by the offspring of the union, who are polluted themselves, but by the cutting off of the offending parties from the land. "Then the wind began, warm, tentative, full of voices from the past, murmurs of old geraniums, of sighs and disappointments previous to the most tenacious nostalgias" (p. 350). In essence this is virtually identical to the experience of Juan Preciado, who complains that the murmurs of the past, of the dead, have killed him, cutting off the breath of life, and then, in the grave, that there is no rest, but only the incessant recital of memories. In both cases the potential hero is destroyed by an accumulation of negative soul-stuff from the past history of his community.

The case is seemingly prejudiced from the outset, for that fateful final sentence states that the family line was *condemned* to live its one hundred years in solitude, and that by a manuscript containing the entire history of the family, written beforehand. Its place is in the Center, the room built for Melquíades when he has ceased the wandering life of a gypsy to become a member of the Buendía family. Melquíades leaves instructions that when he dies definitively (having come back from the dead the first time) a certain procedure should be followed by the original José Arcadio so that he will be made immortal. It fails to work, as in the case of most of José Arcadio's projects, and Melquíades must be buried, to return several times over the years only as a ghost. Nevertheless, the room itself appears to have been removed from time, as the Center of the cosmos should be, since Being is not subject to change and the threat of nonbeing, as is existence. Comically, this means that, as José Arcadio had thought it was in the world at large, in the room it is always Monday and always March. This probably indicates the ideal situation of having moved just beyond Easter Sunday, when the world is new. Time, we are told, has become confused (no doubt by the burning of mercury) and has left an "eternalized fragment" (p. 296) in the room. Only when Melquíades' ghost fades out completely does normal time return to the room.

In the meantime it has suffered its vicissitudes. When Aureliano Segundo enters it he learns that time has not passed there. For him this is an important part of the hero's quest, for he has penetrated to the timeless Center in search of the boon of knowledge from the Wise Old Man. Even after having been shut up for years, the room does not need to be cleaned, and the ashes of José Arcadio's fire are still warm. This phenomenon has failed to affect Melquíades and confer immortality on him because it has been overruled by some mysterious personal powers which have banished his clan forever for having surpassed the limits of human knowledge. Melquíades himself returns from Hades the first time because he is unable to tolerate the *solitude* of death.

Later the room becomes hopelessly cluttered, and at one stage of the family's existence it is relegated to an ignominous status as the "chamberpot room," since it is used for the storage of a vast number of such utensils, bought to accommodate the friends brought home from boarding school by Meme. This is the room, notes the narrator, "about which in another time there revolved the spiritual life of the household" (p. 224). The family has come to ignore its spiritual affairs, as symbolized by the place built for the person "repudiated by his tribe, deprived of all supernatural faculties as a punishment for his faithfulness to life" (p. 49), with all his heroic attempts to hold onto Being. The best example of such neglect is seen in the first Aureliano, who actually lives in the room for years, yet without ever allowing its spiritual qualities to touch him. He sees the room as trashy, while the rest of the family remains astonished at its immunity to dust and deterioration. The key heroic figure of the novel is able to live, work, and sleep at the Center, all with an utter inability to participate spiritually in it. One wonders what would have been Horacio Oliveira's reaction to it. Aureliano's solitude cuts him off from its power as it cuts him off from the ability to perceive his father's ghost.

Melquíades himself is an ambiguous hero, and heroes are not supposed to be ambiguous. Even though he has the air of a man deeply immersed in the great mysteries, he fails to understand technology. He even attributes the functioning of a magnet to the concept that "things have a life of their own . . .; it is all a question of awakening their soul" (p. 9). As mentioned previously, he is unable to repair a player piano, yet he is presented as Master of the Two Worlds, in that "he seemed to know the other side of things" (p. 13). Having aged rapidly and left Macondo, he returns with his youth restored, yet the rejuvenation turns out to be firmly based on a new set of false teeth.

Melquíades is a bit like Gilgamesh in that his basic quest is for immortality. When denied this, he too returns to his "kingdom," which is the room containing the manuscript denying immortality to the Buendía line. When he dies it is of a fever on a beach in Singapore, and his body is thrown into the Java Sea, Although he also drowns in a river in Macondo; clearly he is capable of the occult practice of bilocation. Ultimately he dies a second time, decays and is buried, in spite of having announced the attainment of immortality. Upon descending to Hades he points Macondo out on a map for the masters of the dead, and death enters the city. This hero, far from bringing back the power of life from Hades, sends back death. From time to time he reappears in order to hold a conversation with someone. Aureliano Segundo, for example, receives a great deal of information about the world from him, even though Ursula fails to see him when she enters the room.

The name Melquíades appears to be significant. It may be compounded from a Hebrew name and a Greek patronymic, which would be fitting for the writer of a story with several structural and thematic links to the Bible. Apparently the first part of the name is a corruption of "Malaquías," the Spanish form of "Malachi," which is derived from the Hebrew *mal'ak* "angel," "messenger," and the first person singular possessive ending "i," so that the name means "my messenger." Malachi's prophetic book stands last in the Old Testament and ends with the announcement of "that great and dreadful day of the Lord," with a call to repentance, "or else I will come and strike the land with a curse" (Malachi 4:6, *NIV*). Melquíades, who would then be "Son of My Messenger," ends his manuscript in much the same manner, except that Aureliano is able to decipher the threat only as the curse is being carried out.

When Melquíades returns from the dead, he brings with him from Hades the text, written in an unknown script, which turns out to be Sanskrit. He is the author, for the narrator states that he "concentrated a century of everyday incidents in such a way that they would all exist in a single instant" (p. 350), which undoubtedly means that, as in all novels and histories, the events contained therein exist simultaneously on the pages of the book, even though they are to be read—and in this case lived—in chronological order. The major point of importance

134

here is a literary one with ancient religious overtones, for both in the Indian religions and in this novel, the Word precedes the emergence of created entities, since existence proceeds from the Word of Being. This concept relates quite well to that of Cortázar, who holds that a book lives only potentially until a reader interacts with it; that is, both sender and receiver of the Word must be active for creation to take place.

The implication seems to be that Macondo is neither more nor less than a projection of the Sanskrit words written on Melquíades' parchments. (Those parchments are *not*, however, coextensive with the text of the novel, as claimed by some critics. Melquíades' manuscript includes all the everyday activities of the entire family for one hundred years, which the novel obviously does not.) Commenting on the attitude of the people of India toward the Sanskrit language, Joseph Campbell says, "The words of this holy tongue are the 'true' names of things; they are the words from which things sprang at the time of creation."[13] It follows that, as Melquíades warns, no one will be able to decipher the manuscript until it is one hundred years old; if anyone could, of course, certain events might be forestalled. As it turns out, Aureliano is relatively successful in a hero quest, going to the Center to obtain from the Wise Old Man the boon of wisdom concerning the fate of his family and community, overcoming the obstacle of the Sanskrit language in doing so. But he is too late to bring about the renewal of his cosmos by means of that boon, for contained in it is the fact that the family has been condemned to solitude—including the solitude of Aureliano in the room with his manuscript—which aborts the possibility of a second chance on earth. Therefore it remains only for entropy to prevail, a "progressive corrosion of time" (p. 211), for "the family history was a gearworks of irreparable repetitions, a revolving wheel that would have gone on spinning into eternity had it not been for the progressive and irremediable wearing-out of the axle" (p. 334). The axle wears out, according to the last sentence of the work, because solitude, not love, has dominated the history of the family.

The predestination implicit in the word "condemned" raises the question of why the quest has failed, for "those families condemned to one hundred years of solitude" is quite different from "those families that choose one hundred years of solitude." By rights, solitude should come only with the running-down of the power of Being at the end of a temporal cycle; it should not enter with the very power of creation at the beginning. Moreover, there is a clearly defined and easily accessible Center for the family's heroes, and the Center is the zone of absolute reality, the point at which Being meets existence, where the transcendent becomes immanent. The specific point of contact is the manuscript from which, apparently, the community and its history proceed. The deadly fact is that the realm of Being—and it must be the realm of Being, for it has brought Macondo to life—in the form of Melquíades and his manuscript has condemned the family to a course leading inevitably to non-renewal.

Being is inextricably involved with love, the longing for reunion of all that has been separated, as symbolized in the sacred marriage, for all new life emerges from the return to union of opposing entities. Why, then, should Being produce a community utterly lacking the resources for renewal, the capacity to come together in a creative manner? Rulfo's Comala is different, for in that Center there seems to have been a complete takeover by nonbeing of a place produced earlier, when Being was in control. Macondo represents the phenomenon of a community brought to life by Being, which in the very act denies that community the power to stave off the nonbeing that inevitably threatens it.

The key seems to lie in the fact that Melquíades is faulted in the task in having been ostracized by his tribe for his fanatical love of life. His punishment is the loss of all supernatural power, which for the occult sciences tends to be associated with death. This takes place in the course of the writing of the manuscript, for Macondo has come into being before his first death. Then he angers his people by desiring to return on account of the solitude of death, is stripped of his supernatural powers, and reappears in the community with the manuscript. It would appear to be the loss of those supernatural powers— but not the power to maintain a cosmos in existence by the Word—that forbids him the ability to include in Macondo the prerequisites for renewal. In this case nonbeing has grown

136

strong enough to weaken Being's representative seriously in mid-cycle, so that all that remains is for entropy to complete its work.

In a certain measure Gabriel García Márquez is Melquíades. Ultimately he is the one who denies his characters the right to a second chance upon earth, perhaps because the world reflected and recreated in his novel truly is the world of senseless cruelty, exploitation. and betrayal. This world drives his Colonel Aureliano Buendía into a spiritual state in which even in the presence of the very source and explanation of his existence, he is able to see nothing but trash, and able to engage in nothing more heroic than the endless cycle of making little gold fishes.

VII
Guillermo Cabrera Infante
Tres tristes tigres
(*Three Trapped Tigers*)

Words are only an eye-twitch away from the things they stand for.

Thomas Pynchon
Gravity's Rainbow

The word is not dead; it is merely changing its skin.
Dick Higgins
"Some Poetry Intermedia"

If *Cien años de soledad* is presented to the reader as a manuscript describing the way in which a community and its one-hundred-year history grow out of another manuscript, *Tres tristes tigres* is an attempt to accomplish what is denied to the Buendía family: the regeneration of the cosmos by the Word. This novel is a linguistic phenomenon throughout, and a humorous one as well. The two are related in that, for the premodern person, both language and humor are creative. Carlos Fuentes speaks of a novel in which the central character is "the myth of a world maintained by the word: life is because it is named and named again."[1] That is a very good description of the world of Cabrera Infante's first novel.

Martin Heidegger refers frequently to language as "the House of Being,"[2] and this would be a fair expression of what language means to the characters of *Tres tristes tigres*—or at least what they would like it to mean. Theirs is a scanning search, trying out all the languages they can handle, all the variations of all the words, especially their names, and all the

138

combinations of words in which there could possibly dwell some reality in which they might take refuge from the ominous, cataclysmic events taking place in Havana in 1958. This is kaleidoscopic language, language reproducing the archetypal deeds of Proteus, who is the alchemists' *massa confusa*, the Old One, the trickster-figure who continually changes form as the hero attempts to entrap him and force him to tell the truth about reality—in this case, to *give* a viable reality as a boon. Proteus is the chaotic formlessness out of which gold, the Philosopher's Stone, the cosmos, emerge. One must know how to handle him, the shapeless result of the disintegration of the old world, before a new one may be brought into being. Thus, the book in great measure represents the phenomenon of language examining itself in order to find the key to the renewal of the cosmos.

Some readers have been misled by their failure to take seriously the author's warning that his writing represents "nothing more than an attempt to capture the human voice on the wing."[3] The text therefore is basically an oral phenomenon, even though there are sections written, as opposed to spoken, by the characters, such as "Los visitantes" and Delia Doce's letter; the latter, however, is written in one of the humorous spoken dialects of Havana. This point is important, for it has a bearing on whether the character Bustrófedon actually attains immortality through (or *as*) the Word, the fear being that once an expression is written it has lost its vitality.

There are five major male voices in the work, of which only Bustrófedon does no direct narration (his parodies of Cuban authors having been reproduced by Códac from tape recordings). In a sense they appear to be construed as the traditional four corners of the world in the process of creation, plus the Center of their adherence, which is Bustrófedon. Silvestre summarizes their quest in speaking of the actor Arsenio Cué, who in his mania for speed in his convertible "didn't want to eat up the kilometers, as they say . . ., but was running over the word kilometer and my thought was that his goal was the same as my goal of remembering everything or Códac's temptation, wishing that all women had only a single vagina among them . . . or that of Eribó getting an erection on the sound that moves or the late

Bustrófedon who attempted to be language. We were total-itarians: we wanted total wisdom, happiness, to be immortal by uniting the end with the beginning" (pp. 317-18). This is a remarkable statement, if only because the quest for immortality is a rare theme in the novel of the twentieth century. For that matter, even the first true novel, *Don Quixote*, is rather reticent on the topic. Cervantes' narrator formally parrots Counter-Reformation doctrine, but never comes to grips with immortality as a problem. The theme has never functioned well in secular literature, including the *Epic of Gilgamesh* of over 4,000 years ago. For the most part, recent literature has tended to ignore the issue, with some notable exceptions, such as Unamuno's *San Miguel Bueno, Mártir.* Even Carlos Fuentes' *Terra nostra*, with its highly optimistic outlook on cosmic renewal, fails to broach the subject of individual immortality in any meaningful way.

Silvestre and his friends desire total wisdom leading to the immortality that results from passing directly from the end to a new beginning. What is involved here, apparently, is the achievement on a personal level of what is normally possible only for the human race as a whole: participation in the endless natural round of renewal. That is, the race as a whole goes on as the cosmos itself does, but the individual does not. As the photographer Códac states it, "The only thing for which I feel a mortal hatred is oblivion" (p. 287). The challenge for the hero within this scheme is to manipulate the rules in such a way as to allow the individual to enter the cycle of cosmic renewal, as Fuentes' version of the Medieval heretic Siger de Brabant does in the strange little novel *Cumpleaños.*

Batista's Havana in 1958 was a city full of sensational sights and sounds, and, only half-consciously, four of Cabrera In-fante's heroes are engaged in a progressive rejection of the sights in favor of the sounds, which are far more basic to creation. Fur-thermore, visual imagery is more susceptible to falsification than is sound. Bustrófedon is associated with the Word from the outset, but Silvestre, a writer who comes to be known as Bustrófedon's disciple, is in captivity to visual imagery when he first appears in the text, as narrator of a story in which he and his brother sell the family library in order to earn money to attend the movie theater, described as "the Road to Santa Fe."

It is significant that Silvestre says the reality of a bizarre and brutal murder observed by the youths on the way to the theater overwhelmed the fantasy presentation on the screen, because the story as it appears early in the text is in fact the result of a creative writer's having reworked the original experience. At the end of the work Silvestre remarks to the reader that someday he will write down the story he has just related to Cué, and the first version in the text is that writing. The significant fact is that the story told to Cué, presumably more or less as it actually occurred, has the boys finding that the artificial reality of the film is more real than the jarring reality of the murder. In this version, more faithful to the living experience, the boy Silvestre is so thoroughly steeped in the contrived reality of the cinema that he is unable to absorb the full impact of a man's violent death. In the version written later, the viewpoint is that of a man now won back from fantasy to the reality of the word. One should note, however, that while the polished written version is not accurate in its portrayal of the events as they occurred, it is more "real" than the literal account in that it represents a creation by the Word. In the course of the novel, Silvestre is portrayed as progressively losing his attachment to the cinema and growing in his faith in language.

Códac is a photographer "converted" to sound and the Word to the extent that he is the narrator of the "Ella cantaba boleros" segments, dealing with primordial sound in the form of La Estrella, and the key "Rompecabezas" section on Bustrófedon. Finally, he says, he sits down to concentrate on nothing but sound, and as for Bustrófedon, Códac decides that one of his words is worth a thousand pictures. Eribó is won back from the visual arts to the world of the auditory as he leaves his job as a bongo drummer for one as an illustrator and then returns to drumming.

Arsenio Cué begins as a man believing himself to be a writer, undergoes a traumatic experience in which he becomes a television actor almost in spite of himself, and at the end is another man on his way back from sight to sound, as he is increasingly attracted to word play. This is difficult for him because he has undergone a powerful transformation ritual in his youth, one made more vivid by the fact that he is hungry and frightened when it takes place. He arrives at the home of a powerful man in the entertainment industry with a letter from his mother, who used to know the man. The scene is set by his perception of a number of phenomena in apocalyptic terms. He first sees what he thinks is another person and finally realizes is his own image in a mirror. There is a convention of German Romanticism in which a person may meet the double, the *Doppelgänger,* as an indication that he or she is about to die. The meaning would seem to be that one is at the terminal point of life and is seeing one's image on the other side of the mirror which is death. In this novel, in fact, being on the other side of the mirror is a metaphor for death, and Cué plays a good deal with the idea that he is not himself but his *Doppelgänger*: "I am my mirror image. Eucoinesra. Arsenio Cué in the language of the mirror" (p. 400).

Cué meets a butler whose name turns out to be Gabriel, linking him to the statue of an angel standing on land and sea and holding an open scroll, which Cué feels like eating. This is an allusion to the scene in Revelation 10 in which John is handed a scroll and told, "Take it and eat it. It will turn your stomach sour, but in your mouth it will be as sweet as honey." He also sees a girl named Magalena, who appears to represent the Great Whore of the Apocalypse. In the course of his conversation, the entrepreneur, who has been taking target practice, apparently shoots Cué in the stomach, and Cué believes he is dying. The portion of the story near the beginning of the text ends at this point, and the reader learns near the end that Cué was not actually shot, but that the entrepreneur was so impressed with his supposed acting ability that he launched him on his career in radio and television. Thus, the bitter shot in the stomach has become sweet in his mouth.

The importance of all this is that it constitutes the only fully achieved hero quest in the novel: the separation in Cué's abandonment of his small town, his penetration to the Source of power, his ritual death and rebirth, and finally his return to the world (although not to his home town) with great power. He points out to Silvestre that time stopped for him that day of his "metaphysical resurrection" (pp. 426, 431). Eliade's comment on the subject is pertinent: "What is of chief importance in . . .

archaic systems is the abolition of concrete time, and hence their antihistorical intent. In the last analysis, what we discover in all these rites and all these attitudes is the will to devaluate time."[4] For Cué this means that he has managed to abolish past time with his poverty and non-identity and to establish himself in a comfortable present. For him it is important to freeze time at that point, and this becomes a playful, comic obsession with him. Silvestre says, "Cué had that obsession with time. I mean that he was looking for time in space, and our continual, interminable voyages were nothing but a quest, a single infinite voyage along the Malecón" (p. 296). Time is getting away from him; and bordering the sea which stands for death, he must now make a desperate, heroic attempt to recover it. Ironically, in speeding along the Malecón at one hundred k.p.h. he actually does age less than he would at rest, but only a few billionths of a second, which hardly constitutes the effort a successful quest. In the final analysis, however, he is racing over the *word* "kilometer," according to Silvestre, and this is quite a different process than searching for the fourth dimension in the other three. It involves, instead, the search within a word for the power that burst forth from it on the day of creation.

Cué becomes very nervous in the midst of the veritable explosion of imagery from the book of Revelation in the last third of the novel. That is understandable since it was to the accompaniment of such imagery that he descended into Hades the first time; any repetition of the event can only correspond to that second death about which Circe warns Odysseus. He becomes highly curious when he and Silvestre pick up two women, one of whom turns out to be the Magalena whom he saw briefly at his first encounter with death, although he does not recognize her initially. He questions her as to whether they have met before, and she too fails to remember. Later, as he and Silvestre have left the women and are entering a night club, he becomes intrigued by a statue of a nude woman which is kept wet by a fountain. At this point he does not understand the fascination it holds for him, but later, when he has Silvestre repeat the girl's name as "Maga Lena" (magic spirit), he exclaims, "I knew it!" (p. 413), but fails to explain anything. What has occurred is that the wet statue has reminded him that the

Magalena in the car was the same one who had appeared, dripping wet, at the time of his transformation. The recognition is triggered, apparently, by his having perceived her at that earlier time as some sort of goddess associated with the waters of rebirth.

Cué is the novel's chief enigma, and the reader is forced to wade through quantities of extremely complex imagery in order to learn what is actually taking place in his life. Not without reason does Delia Doce misspell his name as "Harsenio Qué" (p. 30). There are hints throughout the work that he may be homosexual, seemingly based on a typical Cuban suspicion of male actors. When his friend Livia teases him with nudity she says she is doing it for the purpose of learning whether he is a man or just a gentleman, and he informs the reader that he is indeed a man. This is reinforced by the fact that he is genuinely disappointed at finding only nude photos rather than the genuine article on the bed. He contributes to the mystery, however, by loudly insisting that he would *never* become engaged to anyone, even though Sibila seems to be his fiancee. Her name does not indicate that she is a prophetess; it is only "alibis" spelled backward. What sort of alibi she is is revealed later, but her brother Tony implies publicly that Cué is a homosexual, as he calls to him from a swimming pool, "Arsenio Quackquackquack" (p. 103). A duck is a homosexual in Cuban usage, and the term tends to be applied especially to actors.

There is a good deal of stress in the novel on the fact that Cué has a secret that no one knows. The reader is tempted to conclude that Cué's extreme discomfort indicates the truth of Tony's allusion, but something must be done with the incident involving the nude women. It may be pure coincidence, but the word "cue" in Nahuatl means "skirt" (as in "Coatlicue," the goddess with a skirt of serpents), and several times the saying that in every actor there is hidden an actress is applied to Cué.[5] The last time this happens Silvestre indicates both that it does *not* mean he is effeminate and that Cué does know how Silvestre means it. Later, under a good deal of pressure, Cué reveals to Silvestre that he is the one who went to bed with Vivian, but little more.

This revelation of his secret is placed in the midst of a passage that constitutes the conclusion of an earlier unit, which is extremely confusing if taken by itself, the "Seseribó" section, narrated by Ribot, otherwise known as Eribó. It opens with a short item in italics, a tale from Afro-Cuban folklore in which a girl named Sikán hears the river deity Ekué singing, captures him, and takes him to her village to show the people. The god dies of shame and the girl is put to death for her extreme imprudence, following which the skins of the two of them are made into the ceremonial drums known as Seseribó. The drum covered with Sikán's skin is never to be played; it is decorated and intended for display only.

What does seem to be clear is that Cabrera Infante is having two of his characters (or three, as will be explained) reproduce the archetypal deeds of the heroes of their society's mythology; the names Eribó/Seseribó and Cué/Ekué are an indication of that. Nevertheless, the story that follows does little more than raise questions concerning how Cué, Eribó, and presumably Vivian Smith Corona Alvarez del Real may have lived through a modern version of the Afro-Cuban tale. As it turns out, the reader must attempt to solve the mystery by assembling several fragments: the story told by Eribó (for he is the bewildered narrator of the section), earlier narrations by both Eribó and Cué, and statements made later in the text, including the aforementioned confession by Cué to Silvestre. Then this material must be assembled on the framework of the Afro-Cuban origin story, which, as it happens, suffers a key modification as applied to the modern characters. That is, one must realize the significance of the fact that, whereas the living god Ekué is half the drum called Seseribó when he is dead, Cabrera Infante's Cué and Eribó are two separate characters whose identities become intertwined in a special manner.

They are, in fact, a twisted version of the two brothers, one of whom must "die" so that the other may go his way. The first faint indication of their destinies is in their twin experiences as narrated by them near the beginning, one following the other. Eribó tells the story of his ascent of a staircase to see his employer and request a raise in his pitifully low salary, a quest in which he fails and is mocked and humiliated into the bargain. Later the reader learns that Eribó has then returned to the lowly position of bóngo drummer. In Cué's story, in total contrast, he ascends a set of stairs to see the man who can provide employment for him, and, as we have seen, he is eminently successful, becoming a celebrity on the basis of that experience. The two incidents are indicative of the contrast between two types of Classical hero: Icarus, who ascends only to fall on account of the inadequacy of his power, and the one so favored of the gods that he is placed in the heavens among the stars.

From then on Eribó has his problems ascending. In *Tres tristes tigres* there is a good deal of play on the metaphor of altitude, symbolizing either success or the revelation of some powerful truth. In Eribó's case it always involves the former, or the lack of it. He believes himself to be the one who discovered Gloria Pérez and made her into Cuba Venegas, the star singer, even though Silvestre actually saw and heard her earlier. In "Seseribó" he meets her in the nightclub known as La Sierra (the mountain range), and she refuses to go with him to the one called Las Vegas (the fields). Furthermore, when he goes out with Vivian he must wait for her on the street as she descends from her elegant apartment; she tells him the doorman would not have allowed him to go up anyway. He is a mulatto bongo player, and the social weight of that fact is a burden allowing him to ascend only on pure primordial sound.

Eribó first meets Vivian in the Capri, when Cué enters with Sibila, whom he later describes, not as his "novia" (fiancée), but as his "no-vía" (no way), and Vivian motions to Eribó through a window separating the upper crust guests from the mere employees. (Later Cuba Venegas is to speak to him only through her mirror.) Cué, a bit intoxicated, suggests that the two of them marry, and when he dances with Vivian he does so with a king-size cigar in his mouth, which, as it turns out, is the Freudian equivalent of the mast to which Odysseus has himself tied—a prop for the hero's masculinity in the presence of the devouring female. Another day he goes to visit her at the swimming pool, and arrives there on a hot day in sunglasses and a raincoat, bringing Eribó with him.

On another day, Eribó manages to go out with Vivian and she informs him that she is dreadfully sorry she has gone to bed with someone, who she says is Tony, Sibila's brother. She swears Eribó to silence, and he ends the "Seseribó" section with the words, "Seré una tumba" (either "I'll be [as silent as] a tomb" or "I'll be a drum"). So this is a clue; Eribó has become the Seseribó, it seems, or half of it. Earlier Cué has told him that Vivian Smith Corona is a display typewriter, one made to look attractive but not be touched, which would be a nice modern equivalent of the decorated and untouchable half of the Seseribó drum. Her name, which with the addition of an accent can be read as "they lived" in Spanish, supports the idea that she and Eribó have in some sense died and been made into the dual drum. The question that remains is what act of hers constitutes her pulling of Cué/Ekué out of the river, and how someone other than Cué becomes the drum. The key to that is revealed only near the end of the text, when Cué is quite drunk, for his involvement with Vivian always entails a good deal of inebriation.

Vivian is the name of the sorceress who enchanted the powerful Merlin. This is perhaps the only reason for the inclusion of the otherwise puzzling and out-of-character passage in which Cué is seen dabbling in Afro-Cuban magic rites, for then he too appears as a sort of shamanic figure enchanted by a sorceress named Vivian. As he reveals to Silvestre, it was he and not Tony who went to bed with her, when both of them were drunk. She is the actress hidden in him, and he feels fatally attracted to this fifteen-year-old even while he fears her. She is an actress in that she has been feigning an interest in Eribó in order to make Cué jealous. Cué in turn has used Eribó to shield him from her at the pool, as he has also used Sibila/alibis. The raincoat is a symbolic form of protection against the wet girl, since he "died" the first time he met one, and the sunglasses keep her or anyone else from seeing in his eyes what he feels for her. He puts them on even in a dark nightclub when Silvestre questions him about her.

Cué is a man with a mortal fear of surrendering to the power that women may exercise over him. He speaks against them and makes known in no uncertain terms his opposition to marriage. Vivian/Sikán has drawn Cué/Ekué from his sanctuary, but he is only in *danger* of dying from the ignominy of the situation. Perhaps he realizes that he may be near repeating the

147

mythic tale, so he eludes that fate by appearing before Vivian with a woman who represents no danger to him, while actually supporting the ill-starred relationship between Vivian and Eribó. The latter, finally convinced that he has no chance with her, becomes a *tumba* in a substitutionary atonement on behalf of Cué, while Vivian pays for her own sin of presumption by becoming the silent display drum or typewriter. In fact, Cué at one point specifically denies being a "ñañigo drum," while Eribó, doing a bad job of acting in Vivian's presence, describes himself as "another Arsenio Cué." He is also jokingly referred to as "Sese Eribó," while late in the text Cué is Ekué.

One mystery never fully unveiled in this novel full of revelations is why Cué fears the destructive aspect of woman so much, although some hints are given. As has been mentioned, he bears a firm imprint from the experience of seeing a dripping-wet Magalena just before his apparent death by shooting. This may aid in explaining why he is fascinated by the wet statue and the thought of Vivian in the pool, as well as the reason for the raincoat routine. He was attracted by the beauty of Magalena, but her appearance on the scene was followed by his violent "death," and her return may result in a death with less pleasant consequences. Another clue is in his otherwise puzzling remark that he likes Hemingway's *Across the River and Into the Trees;* he calls it "one of the few novels truly about love in this century" (p. 147). The curious fact is that the love of Colonel Cantwell for a noblewoman (and it must not be forgotten to what class Vivian belongs) is followed by his death, which he knows is immiment from the beginning of their relationship. Somehow Cué has come to be preoccupied with the notion that becoming too closely involved with a woman sets time in motion and therefore leads inevitably to death. His fear of Vivian may be heightened by the fact that the influential Bustrófedon seems to call her "arsenic for the Cués" (p. 219). After Cué has told Silvestre that he places all his faith in numbers, so that when two and two no longer equal four it is time to run, he recounts a dream in which everything around him, including the woman at his side, bursts into flame. At that point he runs; seemingly, when a woman such as Vivian becomes passionate, his cosmos has become chaos. Then he runs, mainly in his Mercury convertible, searching in the word "kilometer" for an escape from nonbeing, the fate of the god Ekué.

It never occurs to him that Mercury, although the messenger of the gods, is also the one charged with delivering the souls of the dead to Charon to be ferried across the Styx to Hades. The hero must go to Hades, but only as Cué has done earlier, in order to return with the boon of a new life. When he is in the cold hands of Mercury, no return will be possible, even though the conversation may be what Silvestre calls "the Greatest Show in Hearse" (p. 375).

Silvestre's fate is closely tied to that of Cué, not only in his awareness of riding in the "death seat" of the speeding Mercury, but in some rather remarkable ways as well. It becomes evident that he and Cué, once referred to as "Silvestre Ycué" (p. 222), are Cabrera Infante's dual representation of Lewis Carroll, whom he considers "the true originator of modern literature,"[6] in the two aspects of his love of play, the verbal and the mathematical. At only one point is Silvestre's full name used; it is Silvestre Isla (p. 141), alluding to the forested isle which is Cuba. If he is indeed a representative of the nation as a whole, the reader should be able to see in him something of Cabrera Infante's vision of Cuba's trajectory in the recent past and its ideal course in the future. As has been indicated, Silvestre has long been addicted to the cinema, and some of the more comical imagery in the novel arises from his descriptions of events he has lived in terms borrowed from the films he has seen and cinematic techniques with which he is familiar. In what should be a love scene with a girl known as Ingrid Bérgamo (a nickname based on her pronunciation of the name of her favorite actress), she becomes his "co-star," as he seduces her "a la Cary Grant"; he sees her forbidding hand "in big close-up," and "at the moment when old Hitch would cut to insert an inter-cut of fireworks, I'll be frank with you, I didn't get beyond that" (pp. 165-66). The fact is that, even near the end of the work, he simply feels more comfortable with illusion than with reality. Even when he is at a table with Vivian, whom he later admits to himself that he likes very much, he becomes totally involved with the show on stage, which even Eribó realizes is "a desert of sex" (p. 95), a play of mirages.

149

Both Cué and Silvestre have had disillusioning experiences with artificiality as it applies to women, but only Cué has been deeply affected by one. He has been invited to go and see Livia Roz and Mirtila Secades in their new apartment. Cué arrives at the opportune moment to watch them as they dress and apply makeup, realizing in the process that there is far more illusion than reality to them, and understanding why they now go out only at night. The scene serves as a perfect backdrop for a refrain applied to Cué in various forms throughout the text: "You never change" (pp. 145-56). This, of course, is his goal. Within this portion of the novel, entitled "La casa de los espejos" (house of mirrors), Silvestre undergoes an ordeal which is the mirror image of that experienced by Cué, in that he sees his "co-star," Ingrid Bérgamo, *lose* her artificial beauty. He is thoroughly puzzled as to why she allows him to sleep with her, but without the consummation of their sexual involvement. Apparently it is because she is totally bald and fears that her wig may fall off in the act of making love. In the end it does so in spite of her precautions, and as he awakens Silvestre sees it as "an abyss of falsehood" next to him (pp. 165-68).

At this stage of the game, however, Silvestre evidently does not yet grasp the importance of avoiding artificiality, as Cué does. One problem is that Cué now knows all he needs to know concerning the reality underlying the apparent beauty of Mirtila, Livia, and the latter's former roommate, Laura Díaz, who has been converted into an "Avon swan" (p. 149). Silvestre, in contrast, announces at the end of the text that he is thinking of marrying Laura. Cué's reaction is to pretend he does not know her, but still to protest firmly that Silvestre is making a serious mistake, which Silvestre seemingly takes as nothing more than another expression of Cué's general dislike for marriage. It seems safe to assume, nevertheless, that the marriage does not take place—that is, that Silvestre does not ultimately bind himself to artificiality—for the book itself clearly stands as his editorial work, constituting a concrete attempt to build reality out of the spoken word; the movement is away from the delusions of visual imagery and towards the primordial creative power of sound and the Word.

Silvestre's increasing problem with his vision would itself

150

tend to force him away from a strong attachment to the theater. Throughout the work he is increasingly drawn to the Word as represented by Bustrófedon, so that he is described a number of times as the latter's disciple. He has other metaphysical concerns, although the major one is presented in the "Rompecabeza" section devoted to Bustrófedon's last week. His theory is that a hexagon is nothing but a cube that has lost its third dimension, which he demonstrates by drawing in the lines that give the figure the illusion of being a cube. When that third dimension is found we may also find the fourth dimension, the loss of which—running out of time—signifies death, and presumably attain immortality. Other dimensions beyond that may be discovered, and humankind may learn to pass freely among them. Cué, on the other hand, believes speed may transform time into space, or vice versa. His quest for the fourth dimension involves endless movement, the conversion of the street into a Moebius strip, which has only one surface—that is to say, no "other side."

The game has to do with memory, for Silvestre is the one of the group whose aim is to remember everything. For him as a writer this it is undoubtedly related to the fact that Mnemosyne, or memory, is the mother of the Muses. If literature has value, that value is in its creative transformation of past experience. Yet Cué prefers not to remember whence he came; his is the goal described by Eliade as the will to devaluate time.

This point has been raised in order to begin laying to rest the simplistic equation of humor and play in literature with frivolity. *Don Quixote* too is a humorous book, and no less a serious work of literature for it. *Tres tristes tigres* is an apocalyptic work before it is a humorous one, and one simply does not behave in a frivolous manner in the Apocalypse, at least not if one's stated aims are total wisdom and immortality. Both this novel and the next one to be considered, *Pantaleón y las visitadoras,* have been treated nervously by some critics because they are humorous, but if Joseph Campbell is correct, as I believe he is, humor is the very touchstone of the mythic mode, which has as its goal nothing less serious than the re-creation of the cosmos. Paradoxically, Guillermo Cabrera Infante himself has been taken seriously in stating that *Tres tristes tigres* is, after all, nothing but a joke that got out of hand. Like the captain of the enchanted vessel beheld by Count Arnaldos, our author teaches his song, his hymn to the night, only to those who travel with him.

Thus, Lewis Carroll, the erudite Victorian mathematician who made literature out of his humor-filled encounters, dominates this novel in many respects.[7] He is present throughout the section entitled "Bachata" in numerous allusions and even in one fascinating incident from his life, re-lived by his dual alter ego, "Silvestre Ycué," the "duet" or the "jimaguas" (twins) (pp. 107, 114). The episode is all the more strange for the fact that the two seem to be bewildered by their own behavior, as if, like some of the heroes of the other novels here considered, they were "being lived." In this case they are the heroes reproducing the archetypal deeds of the model character Lewis Carroll, who once found himself in a delightful setting with one of his favorite nymphets, the fifteen-year-old actress Irene Barnes, who describes the events as follows: "His great delight was to teach me his game of logic [which was a method of solving syllogisms by placing black and red counters on a diagram of Carroll's own invention]. Dare I say this made the evening rather long, when the band was playing outside on the parade, and the moon shining on the sea?"[8]

Silvestre and Cué discover two young women walking down the sidewalk; they are Beba Longoria and Magalena Cruz (who narrate sections on pp. 34-35 and 43-45). There is a Carrollian play of mirrors as Silvestre watches Cué approach them and bring them to the car, and even Silvestre wonders why he is so attracted to young girls such as Beba. He tells himself, "You're going to end up where Humbert Humbert started" (pp. 369-70)—that is, with a twelve-year-old Lolita. The scene is set for one of those torrid amorous adventures that are supposed to take place in the Havana night, but it never happens, even though Silvestre realizes that the women expect to be seduced in a normal manner. Rather, the men engage in a dizzying display of verbal pyrotechnics that would cost James Joyce (whom Cué calls "Shame Choice") a good deal of effort to follow, and which instantly baffles the fundamentally illiterate women.

152

Silvestre realizes this, but he says, "No one could stop us now" (p. 384)—no one except the author, who is so fascinated by the incident in Lewis Carroll's life that he feels compelled to manipulate his characters into repeating it. The women are increasingly cold to the jokes, and Silvestre remarks, "Nevertheless, we kept on making up rib-ticklers for them, stringing together Fallopian jokes, hilariating [sic] one gag-after-another. Why? Maybe because Arsenio and I were enjoying ourselves. Possibly there was still some stylistic alcohol in our jocular veins. Or we were pleased with the facility of it all . . ." (pp. 386-87). Later he asks, "Wouldn't it have been easier just to seduce them?" (p. 391). Undoubtedly it would, unless one is unknowingly playing the role of a Victorian clergyman whose interest in females was not basically a sexual one, and for whom in any case mathematical and word games were of even greater import.

There are further allusions throughout the work to Carroll and his fifteen-year-old friend Irene, to whom he was attracted even while avoiding all romantic involvement. Cué's partial reproduction of his character may even help to explain his mysterious ambivalence towards Vivian, who happens to be fifteen when they go to bed, as is Magalena when he first meets her. Furthermore, the name Irene appears with Irena, who is the size of a young girl and clearly represents a salute to the Cheshire Cat, as she fades into the darkness with only her smile remaining (p. 62) and continually appears from and disappears back into the darkness throughout the work.

The importance of their strange action—which is consistent with the theme of the book in its abandonment of normal relationships to search for renewal in language—is that it recovers for Cuba in its hour of crisis the character of Lewis Carroll as a Contrary. The sociological data on that remarkable group of tricksters within the warrior caste is discussed at some length by Silvestre and Cué and applied to literature. The Contraries could "permit themselves to break the laws of the tribe at will" (p. 408), always doing the opposite of what was expected of them, and therefore presumably maintaining the options of the society open so that Holdfast could gain no foothold by stagnating tribal traditions. When one is living in the Apocalypse as Silvestre and Cué are, one must not be caught

153

clinging to a column the foundations of which have been blasted away. Having concluded that all great literary characters are Contraries, they ask whether they themselves are; the answer should be obvious from their behavior scant hours before.

At this point they return to the theory that they are just one person. Both Magalena and Irena have said that they are "just alike" (pp. 395, 412); Silvestre comments, "We are identical," to which Cué replies, "The same person? A binity. Two persons and just one true contradiction" (p. 419). The term "binity," along with the theme of the Contrary, may be significant, in that the trickster in North American Indian mythology, as well as the fool in many other traditions, is unquestionably a divine creator-figure. This would seem to be related to the fact that creation can only take place when the boundaries have been broken down and new possibilities opened up, and the pre-modern mind is astute enough to perceive that this is often the role of humor. Cué bears a name recalling that of a major god of the Afro-Cuban religion, and interacts closely in his humorous, language-related quest for immortality with the one whose name constitutes him a representative of the land itself.

It would occur only to a Contrary to combine the work of Johann Sebastian Bach with the sort of unbridled chaotic activity engaged in throughout the last third of *Tres tristes tigres*. That section is entitled "Bachata," which in Cuba means a game or joke, but its connection with Bach is underscored at both the beginning and the end. Significantly, though, Silvestre and Cué are mistaken concerning whether a piece of music on the radio is by Bach or not. If Bach's composition is the epitome of music as an expression of the belief in an orderly, Newtonian cosmos, these heroes' failure to recognize it may indicate some deficiency in the state of their spirit. In any event the title is a stroke of genius, for it summarizes the contents perfectly: the quest, by way of a typically Cuban outburst of play, for a viable cosmic order such as is reflected in the music of Bach. The two concepts are united in the title as creative Word.

As he makes quite clear, Cué's approach to the problem of recovering cosmic order involves a belief in virtually nothing but numbers. There is an evocation of Pythagoras, who was convinced that numbers—geometric structure—underlay the harmony of the spheres. Cué, says Silvestre, is either a late Euclidean or an early Pythagorean, depending on one's viewpoint (p. 330), which is to say that he takes his stand somewhere between the first significant development of geometry and its quasi-religious usage. He feels that he is safe as long as two and two equal four, for there should be nothing more fundamental and changeless within reality. This is a crucial point, for both he and Silvestre are aware of some of the unnerving pronouncements of modern physics to the effect that on both the micro- and macrophysical levels the laws do not hold, so that ordinary language is often inadequate to express the concepts of physical reality. Cué has then gone beyond that inadequacy to the language in which physicists still do converse, that of mathematics (although it must be admitted that his semi-mystical treatment of numbers, when it goes so far as to find significance in the fact that the sign for "number" [#] is above the 3 on a typewriter, or that 8 on its side means infinity, is hardly the philosophical equivalent of a Unified Field Theory). His trust is basically in the concept that mathematical relationships represent an absolute within the structure of reality, that they are what we might term the expression of Being.

His personal move from the inevitably abstract realm of numbers into geometric structure is seen in his numerical square, which is represented as follows:

4 9 2
3 5 7
8 1 6   (p. 329)

This Chinese magic square, according to Marie-Louise von Franz, "is a number mandala, the so-called Lo-shu (pattern of the river Lo), which was considered *the* basic numerical pattern of the universe . . ., according to which architecture, music and even menus were arranged."[9] Not only does it add up to fifteen in any direction, but it is made up of sets of three numbers, nine of them in all. For Cué three is the greatest number, for reasons that Carlos Fuentes develops far more fully in *Terra nostra*, and nine is the square of three: "9 added to itself is 18 and multiplied by itself is 81. Backward and forward, the number in the mirror. . . . When its two digits are added we find ourselves

155

with the 9 again" (pp. 328-29). Fifteen, although he fails to mention it, is the product of the Great Number multiplied by the traditional number of man, or five, which is to say that his magic square could represent an attempt to bring the number of the heavens into union with the number of man, which would be the proper result of a Pythagorean hero quest, and might speak to Morelli's "anthropophany" in the process. Significantly, Cue says his square is worth as much as a circle, which is probably an allusion to Bustrófedon's linguistic mandala on p. 214, rejected by Cué.

Words are too changeable for Cué, and even as he engages in a dazzling display of word play, going so far as to use nine languages in one brief discourse (pp. 376-78), he will never entrust his destiny to language as Bustrófedon and his disciple are so eager to do. He eventually expresses his reason for not believing in Bustrófedon, which is that the latter always treated words as if they were written, an ironic statement in view of Cué's tendency to treat *numbers* as if they were written. He says, "I deal with sounds" (p. 359). Presumably he means by this that the living word, once committed to paper, loses its vitality. Bustrófedon likes palindromes as words in the mirror— that is, as a visual phenomenon—while Cué's version is a remarkable display of skill in taking a sentence he has heard and pronouncing it backwards, as a tape recorder can do. The ominous point, viewing the scene long after January 1, 1959, is that he declares that the result sounds like Russian: "Spanish in reverse is Russian" (pp. 359-60); Bustrófedon, with his prejudice toward the written word, has already declared the Cyrillic alphabet to be the Latin alphabet in reverse, all of which appears to represent the judgment of Cabrera Infante that Fidel Castro and his Soviet backers have reversed Cuban reality, based as it is on the Word. Russian can be read in the mirror, the reader is told, and one must keep in mind that in this work the reverse side of the mirror signifies death.

Cué also finds it significant that Bustrófedon, for all his obsession with discovering new palindromes, never hit upon the best of them: "Yo soy" (I am) (p. 358). Clearly, if there is to be any sense to such a quest, it will be in an application to the problem of existence and its continuation beyond the Apocalypse, and this palindrome is the most basic expression of an individual's being. In *Tres tristes tigres* the palindrome is related to the mirror and has to do with the heroic status of the Master of the Two Worlds, who can pass freely between the world above and that of Hades—that is, return from death, as Juan Preciado cannot and Melquíades can, although even he is able to accomplish the feat only once. "Yo soy," more than coincidentally, is also the powerful name revealed by Yahweh, the Ground of Being, to Moses to enable him to deliver his people from their state of nonbeing in Egypt and found a new nation, which is to say, to perform a new act of creation: "I AM has sent me to you" (Exodus 3:14, *NIV*). "I am" is also the declaration of Jesus which, according to the Fourth Gospel, precipitates his crucifixion (*ego eimi*, reflecting the Hebrew *ani hu* of the Exodus passage; John 18:5,6). These allusions would not likely have escaped the attention of Cabrera Infante, familiar as he is with the Johannine literature.

Cué, for all the attention he devotes to numbers and their implications for stability in his life, remains quite uncertain of anyone's ability to impose order on the chaos he observes: "There are those who consider life to be logical and orderly, others of us know it to be absurd and confused. Art (like religion or like science or like philosophy) is another attempt to impose the light of order upon the darkness of chaos. Blessed are you, Silvestre, who can or think you can do it by the word" (p. 334). Lucidity, for Cué, is actually a vice, because reality itself is disorderly, leading to his pessimistic declaration that life itself leads ultimately to the worst (p. 401).

Thus, neither side of the dual hero has a great deal of confidence in his own ability to find or create coherence. The excursion of Ekué and the Forested Isle around the Havana night, declared at the outset to be a quest for immortality, ends with Cué's "Please end well your trip around the underworld" (in English, p. 443) and silence, this in a world whose existence is patently dependent upon words.

The character known to his friends as Códac conceives his quest as a modified version of the sacred marriage, for his aim is to discover and unite with Woman, which, as expressed by Silvestre, seems to mean all individual women at once. Even an amateur nightclub rumba dancer is viewed by him as inventing movement, the dance, the rumba, now before my eyes: all movement, all Africa, all females, all the dance, all of life" (p. 67). His version of the mandala, corresponding to Bustrófedon's word wheel and Cué's numerical square, is presented by him as follows: "Is life a concentric chaos? I don't know, all I know is that my life was a nocturnal chaos with a single center which was [the nightclub known as] Las Vegas and in the center of the center a glass of rum. . . ." (p. 272). Shortly thereafter he tells Cuba Venegas, "Cuba, you are the center of my chaos" (p. 273), the equivalent, one suspects, of the glass of rum. While the concept of a mandala as nothing more than chaos with a center, rather than the existence of order within a surrounding disorder, appears to be a new one, it is particularly appropriate for Códac. He is prone to become so intoxicated that he sits down at a table to eat a steak and looks up to discover that, even though the steak is the same, he is in a different nightclub. A rum drink is at the outside limit of his ability to focus on a center.

The male characters in the novel have such negative experiences with the females that Silvestre concludes at one juncture that the latter are no longer worth the trouble (although, as mentioned, he later admits he is thinking of being married anyway). Only the sea is worthy of attention, as the ultimate source of life and rebirth, and therefore a primary symbol of woman and the only thing that is truly eternal. Códac, for his part, feels the sea is another vagina, perhaps the universal one in which he may unite with all women simultaneously in what would be a rather sensational expression of the *hieros gamos.*

In the meantime Códac is subjected to some unnerving experiences with individual women. It becomes evident as the reader assembles the jigsaw puzzle pieces which are the novel's "voices" that he has had an ongoing relationship with Cuba Venegas from the beginning of her career. Delia Doce, in her letter to Cuba's mother, describes her as coming to the house with a photographer whose description matches that of Códac. On a symbolic level he should naturally be attracted to her, given his preoccupations, for even in her stage name she becomes an image of what the nation has come to be in its attachment to the superficially visual. She received the new name because "no one known as Gloria Pérez is ever going to sing very well" (p. 91). Eribó calls her "All Cuba" (p. 116), but even Silvestre, with his tolerance for the artificial, says she is "the National Whore" (p. 368). The primary point is that at one period she becomes the entertainer whose beauty causes the public to accept her as a singer, and this lasts until the advent of the apocalyptic bolero singer who calls herself La Estrella (the star). The text actually loses sight of Cuba Venegas as Códac admits his ignorance of where she is. Later his version of the hero's descent into Hades takes place when, in accordance with the novel's predilection for metaphors of altitude, she has descended from the Sierra to the Mil Novecientos, which is in a basement. At the end of one of his all-night binges Códac arrives above it and, hearing music emerging from among the trash cans, thinks it is coming from hell. Realizing that it is rising through a grating with the hot air from the nightclub, he descends the red stairs. There he hears Cuba singing "The night of love has ended" and realizes that no one who hears her and actually listens can love her (pp. 277-78). She who in her first appearance in the novel has announced, "Look at how I've come up" (p. 30) has hit the bottom.

The fact is that Códac has come into contact with pure, primordial sound as embodied in La Estrella. In India, according to Joseph Campbell, "all this universe is but the result of sound."[10] Indeed, La Estrella herself appears to be, at least for the obsessive, image-oriented Códac, a microcosm, the sound which is already something of a world in itself. She is often described by him in absolute terms, as "a power of nature or more than that, a cosmic phenomenon" (p. 84), even an "infinite body" (p. 68); in her "great cetacean mouth . . . there was room for an ocean of life" (p. 75), and when Códac is unfortunate enough to have her as an uninvited guest in his bed, she is "that universe piled on top of me" (p. 161). She is something of an ironic fulfillment of Códac's wishes, a woman who is Woman, Earth (when first seen she is in a brown dress the color of her skin), and Sea. In the dream preceding her rolling over on him, which is a hilarious parody of Hemingway's *The Old Man and the Sea*, the fish on his line "was long and looked like Cuba and then shrank and it was Irenita and became dark, negrescent,

159

black and it was Magalena"; then it grows to enormous size in the boat and he awakens to realize it is La Estrella (pp. 160-61).

Such is the nature of Códac's experience with her from the outset. He first sees her when he has spent the end of the night in a love clinch with Irenita, who is described as a tiny version of Marilyn Monroe. After the darkening effect produced by his mention of Cuba Venegas singing "in the vague semi-darkness" (she herself being moderately dark), he suddenly sees La Estrella on stage in the early morning, as if a huge black star had suddenly appeared in the sky. For this photographer, whose stock in trade is the play of light and shadows, the jolt of the sudden transformation from the visual and tactual phenomenon of the tiny blonde Irenita in the darkness to the huge black auditory apparition of La Estrella in the spotlight is nearly too much to handle, and he quickly becomes preoccupied with her. He is warned that she is Moby Dick's black cousin— that is, that such an obsession could destroy him as it does Captain Ahab—and indeed she proves to be too much for him. This is his Meeting with the Goddess as Earth Mother, and its importance lies in the fact that this encounter of some months duration with pure sound draws him away from visual imagery to the extent that he becomes the narrator of the section on Bustrófedon, remarking as he does, "If I talk like Bustrófedon from now on, I don't regret it; I do it consciously." He wants only "to forget about light and shadows and chiaroscuros" (p. 219).

There is one more meeting with La Estrella that illustrates the effect she has on his transformation. He is, metaphorically, underwater with Cuba Venegas, thinking he is "the Captain Cousteau of the nocturnal waters" (p. 273), in the element that he sexualizes, when La Estrella appears and "sinks his table to the surface." She and Cuba never speak to each other, for the singer who depends on her appearance and instrumental accompaniment is like antimatter to the singer who "is her voice" (p. 115) and holds out as long as she is able against using any accompaniment at all. The contrast is somewhat analogous to that between the primitive music discovered by Carpentier's narrator and the composition he intends to build on it. When La Estrella leaves, Códac finds himself dancing with Irenita, as if

Cuba Venegas had been shrunk and bleached by La Estrella's presence.

Códac remarks that at the time of Bustrófedon's death La Estrella was the "eternal theme" of the group, which is similar in some ways to Oliveira's Club (p. 213). Eribó considers her a monstrous new goddess, a siren whose song is irresistible to everyone: "We were Ulysses tied to the mast of the bar" (p. 115). But this "metaphysical monster" star is destined to reach her apogee only to be extinguished. The first indication of things to come is her inadvertently signing a contract requiring her to use makeup and musical accompaniment, which represents the supreme irony after she has blasted Cuba Venegas from her position and replaced her. In one more example of the altitude metaphor, she becomes another Icarus-figure as she rises to the heights of Mexico City to perform. The combination of a weak heart and a gluttonous meal at that altitude causes her death, and she is buried there.[11] Thus the black star apparently portending a revolution so radical that it would return to the very foundations of creation in sound is dead, although not without having had her effect on the fivefold hero.

Códac, of course, never does achieve his desired union with Woman. His descent into the Hades of the Mil Novecientos involves a meeting only with a fallen goddess, and the night of love is over. There is no boon to be had but the revelation that he must lend his ears to sound. There is, in fact, no positive union between any male and female within the present time of the text. Cué's night with Vivian not only seriously frightened him but took place earlier. His vision of Livia and Mirtila nearly nude and without their makeup serves only to disillusion him. His and Silvestre's experience with Magalena and Beba is a Carrollian disaster. Silvestre spends the night in bed with Ingrid, but the result is nothing but entropic disintegration. Significantly, just after La Estrella's death and immediately preceding "Bachata," Códac and Rine Leal pick up a pair of showgirls, one of whom is Irenita, and take them to a beach hotel. The dreariness and meaninglessness of the incident constitute the dominant impression and set the stage for the apocalyptic imagery of the words to follow in the next section. Once again, nothing vaguely resembling the *hieros gamos* is in evidence, and where there should be the creative unity of the androgyne there are only the monosexual pairings of "Laurilivia" and "Silvestre Ycué."

Marriage is out of the question for all of the characters except Silvestre, although, for reasons already noted, his wedding probably does not take place either. Bustrófedon is described as an enemy of marriage, and his adversary, Cué, fears it. What remains is either casual sex or nothing. Códac complains that "one ends up slaying love with every move until nothing but sex is left" (p. 273). Eribó too, as he enters his "Saint-Exupéry of sound" routine, reflects on the possibility of picking up a chorus girl, which would involve waking up in all the dreariness of the morning to hear her saying, "You love me, Sweetheart, asking me that, when what she should be doing is asking my name . . ., which she probably doesn't know and because I probably don't know hers either I would tell her, A lot Sweetheart" (p. 111).

The characters are troubled from the beginning by what appears to be an inexorable movement towards a homosexual orientation on the island, which is twice described as "the isle of Lesbos" (pp. 129, 368). The first "show" of the novel, immediately following the emcee's introduction, has two young girls engaging in lesbian acts as they watch a heterosexual couple in more conventional lovemaking. The significance of this Paradise Lost sketch lies in the fact that lesbianism causes the exposure and expulsion from their lovers' paradise of the heterosexual lovers. Stated in another way, homosexuality is viewed as *displacing* heterosexuality. Early in the work, even a young prostitute is named Lesbia, and near the conclusion Cué calls Beba "Lesbia" twice.

Códac is a bit unnerved by one creature of the Havana night which he knows as the centaur, in this case half woman and half horse. Earlier he has been a party to another of the Carrollian mirror experiences, in which he first picks up an attractive girl known as Manolito el Toro who introduces him to another girl whom she calls Pepe (Joe). Afterward he meets Alex Bayer, a homosexual actor who lives with a homosexual doctor and is known to local wags as Alex Aspirina. The transition between the two experiences for this photographer consists

162

of his meeting with a negative image consisting of his black friend Rolando in a white suit. The "mirror" in this case serves as a division between the sexes. Properly interpreted, the occasion of the second meeting, with Alex Bayer, is one of the most humorous incidents in the novel. Alex pleads with Códac to make La Estrella a star in order to induce her to move out of his and the doctor's house, which she has simply invaded and taken over. This is La Estrella, not as sound, but as one of those grotesque prehistoric Earth Mother figures exemplified by the Venus of Willendorf, assaulting the sensibilities of two men dedicated to effeminacy in the male and the avoidance of the female as such. Again a process has gone to an extreme and met its opposite at the juncture.

There seems to be an unconscious attempt at a linguistic compensation for the sterility inherent in both the homosexuality and the casual sex in the work, and it is found in the characters' favorite obscenities. Obscenity is associated with the classical comedy, which was Dionysian in character and therefore had to do with fertility and the renewal of life. Thus, it may be significant that certain words are used with a good deal of frequency in our text. Perhaps the best example is seen in Códac's reaction to the announcement of Bustrófedon's death: "*Carajo* everybody is dying . . ., everybody and people like Bustrófedon too . . ., *Coño*" (p. 221). The long sentence begins with "Carajo" and ends with "Coño," which is also capitalized. The former, according to Robert Graves, alludes to the donkey phallus of a cult that persisted in the European unconscious long after the cult itself was banned, while the latter is an obscene term for the female genitalia. Given the work of both Freud and Jung on linguistic slips based in the unconscious mind, it seems safe to assume that the frequency with which these words are used reflects the primordial desire for the restoration of a general fertility.

All of this is a part of the apocalyptic situation existing in Cuba in the summer of 1958 and reflected in numerous allusions to the book of Revelation, many of them highly complex and obscure. A consciousness of the political situation, although suppressed by the characters' dislike for politics (as well as the author's disgust with the direction taken by the Revolution),

163

cannot be avoided altogether, and when it does emerge it tends to be in apocalyptic terms. Perhaps the most striking example is the dream recounted by the psychiatric patient in her second session, in which, in a generally apocalyptic setting, a dog lies dead and burning in a large bonfire, and various other dogs burn their muzzles attempting to extract it. The dreamer inadvertently frees a large, dirty gray dog with red eyes which is able to retrieve the dead one and return to the house with it. Evidently the dead dog is the Cuban government under Batista, and the dogs with their muzzles burned are those who have attempted to displace him. The huge red-eyed dog, then, would be Fidel Castro, who is easily able to take control when set loose by the people. The menace of this situation causes a certain vague uneasiness in the characters, although it must be stressed that the Revolution represents only a small part of the overall disintegration of this cosmos as far as the novel is concerned.

The task of any astute individual in an Apocalypse is, as Silvestre states it, to join the end to the beginning—not to allow everything to end in cataclysm, but to locate and apply the power to restore order to the fragments. This is the ambience of "Bachata," and Cabrera Infante has very cleverly tied in the atmosphere of the book of Revelation with Silvestre's and Cué's quest, which is taking place within it. When there is some confusion concerning the name of a certain bar, Cué says, "It's called La Odisea" (The Odyssey), to which Silvestre replies, "And the owner is Homer." Cué answers, "You're not going to believe this, but the name of the bar is Laodicea and it's the last name of the owner, Juan, Juan Laodicea" (p. 319). The allusion is to the church at Laodicea, one of the seven churches of Asia Minor addressed by St. John (Revelation 3:14-22). Laodicea is not only the last of the churches, which are often taken to stand for historical periods of Church History, but the one criticized for being lukewarm and therefore about to be spewed out of the mouth of the Lord. To complete the effect, the bar is on a bridge, a transitional form. Later Cué rebukes Silvestre for viewing the Havana skyline as if the city were the New Jerusalem, telling him that he and the city are both lukewarm: "With pleasure would I vomit you up" (p. 354). Then he combines Sodom and Gomorra, which represent another terminal situation, into Havana as Somorrah or Godomah.

There are far too many allusions to the biblical Apocalypse to be mentioned here, but one of them in particular is not only important in itself but serves as an example of the way in which the men's perception of their environment is colored by that book. Immediately after they view a huge fish that they conclude is the Beast from the sea and must have the number 666 on the other side, Cué speaks to a child whose sex Silvestre, standing at a distance, is unable to determine at first. When he realizes it is a girl, he reflects Lewis Carroll's well-known statement "I am fond of children (except boys)" by saying "I don't like boys, but I find little girls charming." This is important, first because the child gives Cué a white stone, and it was with such that Lewis Carroll marked his pleasant days spent with little girls. The imagery is dual, however, for the girl is called by someone with the words "Angelita ven" (Come, Angelita), an evident allusion to Revelation 6, in which the Four Horsemen are called out with the command, "Come." Previously, the "little angel" has been skipping stones on the water, in a pale reflection of Revelation 18:21, in which a gigantic angel casts a stone representing Babylon into the sea. Cué points out that the white stone she gave him has something written on it, but Silvestre, whose eyesight is failing, is unable to see it. This is an allusion to the statement of Jesus in Revelation 2:17 concerning his faithful disciple: "I will ... give him a white stone with a new name written on it, known only to him who receives it" (*NIV*). Cué, having been reborn as a star, which is tantamount to receiving a new name, is the one who receives a token of that privileged status.

Cué is also equated with the rider of the white horse, the savior, but this is only a fleeting fancy of Silvestre's. His Mercury even becomes a time machine, a "Quatre Chevaux," which alludes to the horsepower of the Renault 4CV and to the four horsemen, the question being whether Silvestre and Cué are headed for Sardis (the dead church of Rev. 3:1) or the sea, which represents rebirth. The problem is that Cué, even though favored with the white stone, has little faith in the reality of anything to be retrieved from the realm of Being: "*Ah oscarwilder-*

ness: 'There is a land full of strange flowers and subtle perfumes . . . a land where all things are perfect and poisonous' " (p. 327). His belief is that "there is more nothingness than being. Being has to make itself manifest. Being comes out of nothingness, struggles to become manifest and then disappears again, into nothingness. . . . Being is nothingness by other means" (p. 323). Here, evidently, is a man who instinctively understands *Pedro Páramo*. He feels that life is only a parenthesis within the context of death, which is also a fair expression of the nature of Macondo's one hundred years, non-renewable because of a solitude not unlike that of this novel.

The nature of that solitude is evident in the apocalyptic implications of Silvestre's and Cué's experience with Magalena and Beba. Mary Magdalene is the prostitute redeemed by Christ. Beba, for her part, is a highly complex character. With good reason, Cué calls her Babel, which serves to raise her telephone conversation near the beginning of the text to an archetypal level, for she too is reproducing some deeds from the time of origins. She describes how she has risen in the world as she and her lover have been allowed into the exclusive Vedado Tennis Club. As a result, in addition to her usual mishandling of the Spanish language, she includes some ill-pronounced English terms: "Senkiu" and "Solón" (pp. 44-45). Once more, following the creation of the world by the Word (of the Tropicana's emcee) and the Fall from innocence and expulsion of the lovers, Babel has risen in this linguistic cosmos, and as in the first instance the result is the confusion of tongues.

Cabrera Infante has realized that the Babel of Genesis is the Babylon of Revelation (the Hebrew "babel" stands for both), and has Beba reappear near the end of the novel, where she and Magalena together seem to constitute the Great Whore who is Babylon. They, bombarded by the men's play with words and concepts, "were dead for being as well as for nothingness" (p. 390). Beba, at least, represents the disintegration of language, and the creative Word is what deprives the two of them of being. The name of the game is "Carpe diem irae" (p. 403), as opposed to Magalena's expression of the more conventional *carpe diem* in her first appearance (pp. 34-35).

To a great extent "Bachata" is a repetition of the namesake of one of the bars visited by the two men, Johnny's Dream. Near the end of the segment Silvestre is introduced to Irenita by Cué as "Silvestre Noche Desán," an allusion to St. Sylvestre's Eve, which is December 31. This is not only the end of the Western world's year, one of our cosmic cycles, but the date on which, in the year in which the novel's action takes place, Fulgencio Batista fled Cuba, permitting Fidel Castro to assume power as 1959 opened. The name of the novel's fictional editor is itself an apocalyptic one as given by Cué, especially since the book that begins with the sound and fury of a creation by the Word (and the name of the emcee at that time was Miguel Angel Blanco, easy enough to read as "Michael, White Angel") ends in multiple repetitions of the phrase "in silence."

Out of the linguistic *massa confusa* of this novel with its Protean word play there emerges an improbable biblical structure, as the mundane occurrences of the characters' lives are related to the exemplary deeds of that book. This is similar to the technique of Cabrera Infante's fellow Cuban author José Lezama Lima in *Paradiso*. What is striking in both novels is the phenomenon of an entire novel rising from the chaos of its own words to a meaningful, structured whole on the basis of the power of those same words. As Paul Tillich puts it, "The vitality that can stand the abyss of meaninglessness is aware of a hidden meaning within the destruction of meaning."[12]

Between the creation, Fall, and Babel episodes and the Apocalypse is what one might expect to find within such a framework, the story of a redeemer-figure. Bustrófedon, however, is highly unconventional in such a role, and thus serves as an antichrist, a mirror image of the New Testament's central figure. This is especially evident in the fact that, whereas Jesus Christ, according to the Fourth Gospel, is the Word who became a human being, Bustrófedon is the human being who made an attempt to become language, and there is every reason to believe that he has attained his goal. R. D. Laing states that "William Blake in his description of split states of being in his prophetic books describes a tendency to *become what one perceives*" (*Divided Self*, p. 198). Bustrófedon has perceived language as few others have. His is the central "Rompecabeza" section, the title of which bears a triple allusion: "Rompecabeza," literally "headcracker," means a riddle or puzzle, which Bustrófedon certainly is; his head is literally broken open in an autopsy; and the longest of his linguistic games consists of several imaginary literary viewpoints on the death of Leon Trotsky, who died of a pickaxe blow to the head. In any event, Trotsky is something of an alter ego for Bustrófedon, as the ideological deviant whose head is cracked for his pains and whose influence continues.

The very end of "Rompecabeza," I believe, indicates that Bustrófedon has in fact become language, for as his head is divided, the language divides and becomes random. Furthermore, the randomness resolves itself into the device known as boustrophedon, or writing first in one direction and then the other (p. 270). That is to say that in death his personality has passed into the language needed to describe that death. Códac, who is the narrator at this stage, leaves the reader another subtle hint that he too, like Silvestre, believes Bustrófedon may now be immortal. In questioning what Bustrófedon would prefer, he uses the form "prefi(ri)era" (p. 216), indicating that the past tense might not apply, for Bustrófedon might be able to prefer one option over another in the present.

Bustrófedon chose his own new name from a dictionary, presumably because it might allow him to become "the two-way man," as Cabrera Infante calls him in an interview,[13] the master of the two worlds of Being and existence. As stated previously, his preferred form of word play is the quest for the palindrome, which is heroic in that it should allow the possibility of a return from Hades for the one who is language and is able to make it move in both directions. Furthermore, he attempts to communicate his supposed power to his friends by combining his two-way name with theirs. Ribot's name seems to be drawn from the French word "ribote," as in the phrase "étre en ribote," which means to be drunk or on a binge. With a slight change Bustrófedon has assimilated him to Eribó, the supreme deity of the secret Afro-Cuban society called the ñañigos. Códac, whose original name does not appear in the work, but which turns out to be that of a certain photographer whom Cabrera Infante knew, called Korda, remarks, "His was my other baptism and the idea came, fully developed, from Kodak

168

and thus he masked my prosaic Havana name with a piece of universal graphic poetry" (pp. 220-21).

Paul Tillich has said, "The most vital being is the being which has the word and is by the word liberated from bondage to the given" (*Courage to Be,* p. 82). Thus, Bustrófedon, dissatisfied with the given—a disconcerting deterioration of his society in addition to his own mortality—"began to change the names of things" (p. 220). In fact, he engages in the destruction of the Spanish language, believing that, "in contrast to what happened in the Middle Ages, when from a single language, such as Latin or German or Slavic there emerged seven different languages in each case, in the future these twenty-one languages . . . will be converted into just one, imitating or stuck together or guided by English" (p. 221). This is another application of Plato's doctrine that at the end of time all processes will be reversed; the result of this reversal is to be "a stable Babel." Placing names on things is the work of Adam, and changing them implies the advent of a new Adam and a new creation. Bustrófedon wonders if Adam's name in Catalan might be Ada, a palindrome, presumably so that he who embodied mankind in Paradise might return from the death which results from the Fall. He is even tempted to become a Muslim because of the Spanish name of its supreme being, Alá.

Códac presents his "Rompecabeza" section in terms of Bustrófedon's Last Supper and Holy Week, at the end of which he dies. In the midst of the section Bustrófedon comes forward with his magic circle, which also has messianic connotations. Appropriately, considering Bustrófedon's opinion of three as a magic number, it is based on a phrase of three words: "Dádiva ávida: vida" (avid gift: life). According to Códac it is another representation of the serpent devouring its tail, which is to say the symbol of the Eternal Return. It is also a "wheel of misfortune," one supposes, because Bustrófedon dies in spite of having invented it. The wheel contains the word "David," whose son is Messiah, and is a star; therefore, according to Códac, it is related to La Estrella. Robert Graves mentions "the White Goddess's Starry Wheel . . . multiplied into the twelve signs of the Zodiac."[14] Just as Bustrófedon is the reverse image of Christ in this inverted world, its twelve-part wheel is associated

169

with a sort of *Black* Goddess. Shortly after its unveiling Cué becomes the anti-Judas of this anti-Messiah by leaving the supper (pp. 213-15).

Perhaps the most mysterious relationship in the book is that between Bustrófedon and La Estrella. She is represented by his linguistic wheel of perpetual renewal and is the group's "eternal theme" during that fateful week. It becomes clear that she is more than simply an impressive, innovative singer for this "club," which is missing its La Estrella as Oliveira's Paris club misses La Maga. Consciously or unconsciously, they seem to have laid hold of the fact that La Estrella represents pure primeval sound, and any search for immortality through language will have to take her into account.

Even though Alex Bayer vehemently denies it, La Estrella insists that she has a son, whom she calls "the fool" (p. 70). Later, after the death of Bustrófedon, she dissolves in tears and alcohol, mourning her dead son (p. 275). No other clues are offered, but at the party given by Códac in La Estrella's honor the latter sets in motion a chain of events that causes Bustrófedon to trip, and he avoids falling only by some skillful gymnastic moves. Two important phenomena follow this event: Silvestre says Bustrófedon was like never before in his word play, and he becomes very ill. Soon afterward he is dead. The most likely explanation is on the mythic plane to which these characters are elevated. Bustrófedon is language and La Estrella is sound, which in a sense is the mother of language. Furthermore, as the birth of Christ was announced by the appearance of a bright star, the death of this antichrist-figure is portended by the ascent of the black star. In this way the circle of interlocking words becomes a wheel of misfortune: it must perforce be based on sound, and when the cosmos is experiencing a return to origins so radical that the center of attention is primitive sound itself, even language must die, for the universe has returned to a position beyond it.

Bustrófedon becomes more proficient at word play immediately before his death because the growth on his spinal column both produces his linguistic creativity and causes him to die. The question that remains for his principal disciple, Silvestre, is whether or not he will return. Throughout

170

"Bachata" he expresses his wish that Bustrófedon could be with him and Cué "to make three" (p. 442). Eventually Silvestre becomes lost in a reverie in which "Superbustrófedon" returns, spouting his usual obscenities and generally continuing in his divine trickster role, seemingly anxious to shatter the old consciousness in order to stimulate the new.

Nevertheless, there is an infinitely more satisfying resurrection or Second Coming of Bustrófedon, which is nothing less than the book itself. P. L. Travers has remarked, "If I were a hero the maiden I would set out to rescue would be language,"[15] and in this consists Silvestre's ultimate hero quest. After his disconcerting experience with women, the "sojourn in hell" of his reflections on death, and his intention to surrender to artificiality in marrying Laura, he tells Cué, "I'm going home to sleep, wrapped up in a little ball: I'm returning to the womb, going back to the maternal breast" (p. 403). Until he does so he is still able to tell Cué he is thinking of marriage, but the production of the book itself as an act of creativity indicates that he has not surrendered to artificiality. Furthermore, his inclusion of Cué's comments on Laura's having become an "Avon swan" proves that he has finally heard the full story from him. The root meaning of "apocalypse" is "unveiling," and the Revelation is not complete until both the false and the true have been uncovered.

The point of all this is that the silence at the end of the novel, reflecting the fact that both La Estrella and Bustrófedon, as sound and language, are dead, is only the silence that traditionally precedes the new song of another creative act. Silvestre, who reveals in "Bachata" that he has not been writing, returns from the sleep of his initiation reborn to rescue language from the dead. The epigraph, from Lewis Carroll, has Alice imagining what a candle's flame would look like after it is put out, and this attempt to capture the spoken word of Havana 1958 on the wing is just that. Language opens this "show" and maintains its existence until it dies in silence. Now the operation of Mnemosyne, mother of the Muses, upon that language, plus the creative imagination of a writer, rebuilds the world and imposes order on its chaos. Language is the house of Being and makes Being known, says Heidegger, and the hero Bustrófedon has returned to his house.

VIII

Mario Vargas Llosa
Pantaleón y las visitadoras
(*Captain Pantoja and the Special Service*)

Great men are meteors that consume themselves to light the earth.

Napoleon

In reading *Pantaleón y las visitadoras* one is confronted once more with the question of which way is home and which way is the Source. As in other such novels, notably *Los pasos perdidos*, there is a reversal of many heroic values, including an attempt to maintain a union with a Calypso-figure. The difference in this case, however, lies in the attempt, not to transform chaos into order, but to organize the chaos itself. Yet Pantaleón's career is almost orthodox if one stays with the superficial and ignores the essential. All lists of the typical stages of the hero's career are matched more or less well by any given incarnation of the hero, even while none corresponds perfectly. What is striking in the case of Pantaleón Pantoja, however, is the close correspondence of his trajectory to the second half of the list presented by Lord Raglan. Raglan's first nine points have to do with the hero's childhood, which does not come into play here or to any significant degree in any of the novels we are considering except *Terra nostra*; the remainder is as follows, with Pantaleón's career appearing in the right-hand column:

10. On reaching manhood he returns or goes to his future kingdom.	On becoming a successful organization man, he is sent to the jungle.

11. After a victory over the king and/or a giant, dragon or wild beast,	After *swallowing* the dragon,
12. He marries a princess, often the daughter of his predecessor, and	He begins an affair with a devouring female, and
13. Becomes king.	Becomes "king of vice."
14. For a time he reigns uneventfully, and	For a time he reigns uneventfully, and
15. Prescribes laws, but	Is known for his organizational work, but
16. Later he loses favor with the gods and his subjects, and	Later he loses favor with his superior officers and the public, and
17. Is driven from the throne and city, after which	Is driven from his assignment, after which
18. He meets with a mysterious death,	He meets with a mysterious sacrificial "death,"
19. Often at the top of a hill.[1]	In the high Andes.

The call to adventure is issued by Pantaleón's superior officers in Lima. It must be understood that in most Latin American societies the army is the primary source of order and stability (it goes without saying that this tends to be the order of the Tyrant Holdfast). Thus it becomes a matter of concern when the troops in the Amazon region, isolated for long periods from any contact with women, go on a sexual rampage whenever they arrive in a populated area, raping every female in sight. The forces of order have then become promoters of one of the worst forms of disorder, and that precisely at the time when a lunatic religious leader known as Brother Francisco has appeared in the same area, announcing the impending end of the world. Pantaleón Pantoja, known as "an officer without vices," a discreet and reliable organizer, is ordered to assemble a system by which prostitutes may be taken to the troops. Since it will never do to have the forces of order *known* as purveyors of the disorderliness of prostitution, this must be a clandestine, ostensibly civilian operation. The times are apocalyptic, however, and, as was noted previously, the etymology of "apocalypse" has to do with unveiling. The unveiling of the true nature of the bizarre scheme is what topples Pantaleón from the throne he rejects at first and then comes to enjoy. For he has engaged in the traditional refusal of the call, which is equally futile whether the call is issued by a representative of the Argives to Odysseus or by a Peruvian general to a captain under his command.

He is called because he is an elect being, not one of the herd, as he continually insists: "I'm not like other people, that's my rotten luck."[2] He is marked from the beginning as a sun-hero among a people whose ancestors worshipped the sun, a bearer of enlightenment and order, as even his name appears to indicate in its allusion to the lion that so often stands for the sun. Pantaleón is a common enough name in Peru, but I believe Vargas Llosa chose it because it fits the character of the hero, for it can be read as a combination of *león,* "lion," and the Greek word of "all" in its neuter plural form: "all things." He is called in to receive his new commission because he has been a lion in all things, the organization man *par excellence.* His mother, Leonor, also bears the lion in her name, as does the madam with whom he works. The problem is that even a solar hero can fail miserably by abandoning his solar nature for a time, and this is particularly true when he falls under the sway of the destructive aspect of the Great Goddess. Samson (whose name is a play on *shemesh,* "sun"), in his loss of power to Delilah, would seem to serve as a perfect example of such a loss, but he is not. In the order of things the sun's power must inevitably be limited by the darkness of the night ("leilah" in Hebrew) for a time, and it must just as inevitably be released in the spring. Odysseus must remain for a while with darkness in the form of Calypso. Disaster would strike only if he decided never to leave, or if he did not have himself bound to a symbol of his masculine strength and did succumb to the power of the sirens, which is a destructive rather than a retaining power. In the case of Circe, too, Odysseus must, by the aid of Hermes (the masculine half of the *herm*aphrodite), dominate the devouring female aspect so that he may receive her aid, rather than being converted into the pig that would identify him with Hades. It is essential that the hero unite with the feminine, but equally important that he avoid being destroyed by it. Gilgamesh, too, is very aware of what dangers lie in store if he allows his solar character to fall under the dominance of the lunar Ishtar.

What Pantaleón does, on the contrary, is not in the order of following the normal seasonal entrapment of the solar power by the night. He is perhaps predestined by the very perverted nature of his quest to fall into the trap. He enters wholeheartedly into anything to which he is assigned, and if the assignment involves illicit sex he must give himself fully to that as well. Thus, in effect he succumbs to the temptation to remain with Calypso/darkness, as does Carpentier's hero, alienating his Penelope-figure in the process, and losing any chance for renewal, which has been forbidden by the nature of the assignment in any case. Herein lies the ambiguity of the direction of home, for he is called away from his true home situation to what is clearly a source of transformation for him, but for the purpose of renewing *it* for the powers that have called him out. Moreover, he is to accomplish this by what amounts to managing the prostitute-aspect of the goddess. The result is what is termed a "dismal odyssey" (p. 158), and only the negative features of Odysseus' quest seem to be his lot. Like that hero storing up trouble with Poseidon by revealing his name to Polyphemus, Pantaleón begins his downfall by being frank with the muckraking radio commentator Sinchi.

The most outstanding characteristic of the hero quest in the novel lies in the transformation process undergone by Pantaleón. In his youth the conventional hero tends to possess a tremendous amount of undirected, and therefore destructive, power. This is a reflection both of the fact that he is born into the very chaotic situation that he is eventually to remedy, and the fact that order does not replace chaos but is imposed on it; it is the *massa confusa* itself that comes to order, in the hero himself and in the cosmos he embodies. It may involve the slaying of a dragon, but the dragon's body is nevertheless likely to be used as the material out of which the world is constructed. The Inca prince Viracocha of whom Garcilaso writes is said to have been born of chaos; hence there is no surprise when he becomes so unruly that his father feels it necessary to exile him. The purpose of transformation is to bring the power with which the hero is born under control and direct it into creative channels. Adrian Thatcher, in his work on Tillich's ontology, speaks of "a blind power principle which is tamed by the structure-imposing *logos*."[3]

In the case of this officer destined to manage the chaos of prostitution, however, the process is reversed, for he never sowed his wild oats in his youth. When he realizes that he must not only carry out such an unsavory project, but do so in the guise of a civilian, he remarks, "It's going to be . . . like changing my personality" (p. 13). In one sense it is and in another it is not, for throughout the three-year project, however disorderly he becomes in his personal life, all is done in the name of giving himself properly and unreservedly to his assignment. His sense of the proper, orderly way of carrying out any charge is actually what forces him into unacceptable forms of behavior. This in turn is nothing more than a personal application of the army's aim, which is to restore order to the Amazon area by managing its chaos instead of forcing it into order.

What is demanded of him, essentially, is that he be transformed from Apollo into Dionysus, and do so in the name of Apollo, who represents reason, justice, and civilized order. On the other hand, the shrine of Apollo at Delphi was occupied for three months of each year by the priests of Dionysus, seemingly in recognition of the need for fertility to take precedence over reason occasionally. Coincidentally, such a metamorphosis of Pantaleón is demanded by "Tiger" Collazos; in the Prado Museum is a painting in which Dionysus is portrayed as riding in a chariot drawn by a tiger.

Whereas the ordinary hero sets out to slay the serpent of chaos, in whatever form, Pantaleón is asked to assume its character. Joseph Campbell points out that "the hero . . . discovers and assimilates his opposite (his own unsuspected self) either by swallowing it or by being swallowed,"[4] and this is Pantaleón's experience: "The potion called *viborachado*, a cheap brandy in which a poisonous snake, preferably a fat one, has been marinated, is . . . truly fiendish," Pantaleón reports to his superiors (p. 67). To make the imagery even clearer, he has drunk it in an Iquitos nightclub known as The Jungle, and its aphrodisiac effect on him, although probably based only on the power of suggestion, is powerful. The drink takes him back to his childhood, in that he has recourse to masturbation, which he thought he had abandoned many years before. The Garden of Eden imagery is clear as well, as he becomes involved with a serpent in The Jungle, being enlightened in the process and, in doing so, rendering his eventual expulsion a certainty.

Dionysus, as a god of fertility, is a lunar phenomenon; his mother is Semele, or the moon. As such, he never becomes associated very strongly with the symbols of masculinity. Kerényi says, "Dionysus . . . is never represented as a noticeably phallic deity: he is shown either clothed in a long robe, or in some other effeminate form."[5] That phallic character is associated with the solar being, while a lunar deity should by rights only be able to promote the exaltation of the phallic. This appears to be the case with Pantaleón, whose responsibility is to create a situation in which the phallus (but certainly not fertility) is central, and his own member is in a sense separated from him in its behavior: "This work is to blame for what's happening to my birdie," he says (p. 168). The occasion on which he points out that he is different from other people is when his paramour, the Brazilian, protests that no one becomes sexually aroused out of mere duty.

From this point on he is associated with the reptilian creatures that represent primordial chaos. Madam Leonor, whose nickname is that of the highly poisonous snake known as the "chuchupe," calls him "Crocodile" (p. 93). Not long afterward Sinchi arrives to attempt to blackmail him, and Pantaleón has him thrown into the river. Even as the order is being carried out, Pantaleón is reading of Yacuruma, who is "an angel or demon of the waters, who causes cyclones and floods. He rides on the back of crocodiles or on the skins of giant water snakes" (p. 106). Sinchi is the demonic figure, the hypocrite thought to be an angel by his listening public. He calls himself a cyclone. Significantly, Pantaleón is associated only with the chaotic aspect of the serpent and not its traditional symbolism of immortality. Immortality arises out of chaos when the snake changes its skin to initiate a new cosmic cycle, but paid prostitution is sterile, and even though Pantaleón eventually changes back to his uniform from civilian clothes, it is only for the purpose of being sacrificed.

The effeminacy of Dionysus is applied to Pantaleón. His dreams reveal a fear of it, and when he reveals to his wife, Pochita, that he has been unable to obtain a house for them on the base, she comments, "Once again, Panta, you're not enough of a man" (p. 14). She should know; she has just excised the "lion" portion of his name. The initiate must lose his name as when he loses his old identity, as Odysseus becomes Noman for a time, and true to form, Pantaleón announces, "I can't tell who I am" (p. 10)—this coming shortly after his announcement that he will virtually have to alter his personality. His name then changes a great deal in the mouths of his associates, becoming "Pan-Pan" (p. 89), which bears multiple allusions, to wit:

1. The god Pan "was believed to wander among the mountains and valleys of Arcadia . . . leading the dances of the nymphs," and "was one of the gods to whom Socrates prayed for beauty of soul. In works of art Pan is represented as a sensual being."[6]

2. In the course of his work, after the followers of Brother Francisco crucify an infant, there begin appearing rolls ("panes") in the bakeries, in the form of the child, thus foreshadowing Pantaleón's own sacrifice as he is identified with it.

3. In this part of Latin America "panes" also means the female genitals, and this seems to be in view as, in the cinematic interweaving of scenes of the novel, the announcement of the appearance of the rolls is immediately followed by Pantaleón's complaint about the presence of an excessive number of candidates for the Service: "I asked you for ten and you bring me twenty" (p. 108). The identification of the prostitutes with the rolls, particularly in view of the allusion to the indicated part of the body, marks them as sacrificial victims as well.

178

Pantaleón even descends into Hades in a dream, which is based on his memory of a painful case of hemorrhoids; in it he is "suddenly transported in flesh and spirit to hell" (p. 58). He has an operation to remove the hemorrhoids, and the enema given later, says his doctor, "will take away all the mortal and venial sins of your life." He continues, "Console yourself with the thought that after this experience, everything that happens to you in life will be better" (p. 61). Again we may perceive the "will to devaluate time," the desire to abolish history with its sins, as described by Eliade. At the end of the dream Pantaleón roars like a lion and grunts like a pig, for the latter symbolizes what Hades has left in the former. The pig is particularly appropriate here, since it is associated with both the underworld and the moon. When the transformation has been completed, Colonel López López is able to remark, "Now he's in his element" (p. 173), and Pochita comments, "It seems to me I've switched husbands" p. 47). In a later dream Pantaleón leaves his logistics center like a soul carried away by the devil, who, after all, looks a good deal like Pan in some of his representations—or, for that matter, like Dionysus.

So this "officer without vices," the "born organizer," establishes the requisite bureaucracy of chaos, and at all points the tension between his fundamental nature of a solar lion and the newly imbibed serpent-nature is evident. His has been a transformation in reverse, from the mature man with an established solar identity to the chaotic child, still in the grip of the Leviathan he is born to conquer. His fundamentally puritanical character emerges in strange ways; in search of books that might provide a certain insight into the world of prostitution, he naively enters the Augustinian bookstore. St. Augustine is the Church Father who went from a life of pagan licentiousness to that of a saint, and this cannot be completely lost on Pantaleón, who is being forced in the opposite direction. One of the churches in Iquitos also bears the name of St. Augustine; Pantaleón takes the prostitute known as Knockers there to have her baby baptized.

Pantaleón, who as a good public relations man is conscious of the need for morale building, creates an insignia for the Service, using green, which is the traditional Hispanic symbol of lust, and red, which has a long-standing association with prostitution. He has chosen these appropriate colors for the wrong reasons, however, selecting "(1) green for the lush and beautiful countryside of the Amazon Region, where the Service is going to forge its destiny, and (2) red for the virile ardor of our recruits and soldiers, which the Service will help to appease" (p. 42). At every juncture he engages in an attempt to raise the disreputable to the level of his own lofty ideals, but the ultimate effect is quite the contrary.

Soon the Service has become famous, which is exactly what its creators have attempted to avoid, and the logistics center becomes popularly known as Pantilandia. General Scavino's wish is that Pantaleón would have the good sense to organize it, if he had to do so at all, in a mediocre, defective manner, but this is out of the question for a solar hero. Handed his commission, he has created a highly efficient machine; given the nature of the commission, the result must be what General Scavino perceives as he complains, "We've set an infernal machine in motion" (p. 187). *La Machine Infernale* is the title given by Jean Cocteau to the structure of the cosmos by which Oedipus is led into a pair of horrible sins against his will and then exiled for them. Something very similar is happening to Pantaleón—there are even light Oedipal overtones in the fact that his mother and the madam have the same name—although by the will of a few officers, not that of an overall cosmic structure.

References are made to the two "jungle disasters," or the "jungle nightmares," which are the Special Service and the lunatic religious cult of Brother Francisco. The adjective "lunatic" is used deliberately, for Brother Francisco goes astray in attempting to lead Christianity from its fundamentally solar orientation back to a lunar state of affairs, which always tends to imply human sacrifice.

The Service is not brought down by any solar principles, as might be expected. Rather, it is destroyed by the most grotesque forms of hypocrisy. Sinchi, finally convinced that he cannot enrich himself by means of payoffs from Pantaleón—although the latter does give in for a time—states on the air, "The time has come to confront the monster and, just as St. George dealt with the dragon, to chop off its head in a single blow" (p.

180

145). Sinchi is far from an avatar of St. George in his motivations, based as they are on the failure of an attempt at blackmail, so that a more apt image might be that of one dragon battling another for dominance over the territory. Within the military establishment the opponents of the project are no more admirable. From the beginning great moral indignation has been expressed by both General Scavino and Chaplain Beltrán, yet at the end of the novel the former is heard to say, "This will be the peaceful country of the old days again" (p. 240). The person to whom he makes the remark is the prostitute Peludita, who, having lost her job with the Service, is back at work under the dismal conditions involved in serving such as the general. Later she is in bed with Beltrán, who is no longer a chaplain.

Sincerity on the part of Pantaleón, on the other hand, is what drives the final nail in the coffin. So grief-stricken is he at the violent death of his lover, the Brazilian, that he gives her burial with full military honors and appears in uniform to deliver a eulogy. Not only the sleazy business of a prostitution service, but his own adulterous affair, must be conducted with decency and in order. This concern with justice within a false framework ultimately brings the Service crashing down and sends him into exile. The revelation of the fact that in running the Service he has been acting on official orders from the military is called "apocalyptic," and again, as in *Tres tristes tigres*, that word takes on its etymological sense of the unveiling of a truth previously hidden, accompanying the dissolution of cosmic order.

In ancient mythology the hero, while it is essential that he meet the Goddess in her various forms and unite with her in a positive manner, must avoid falling under her spell. Like the moon she is changeable, and her devouring, castrating side is to be feared. Significantly in view of this fact, Pantaleón gives to the Service's transportation units, the historic boat and seaplane that are used to carry the personnel, the names Eve and Delilah. Such a use of the nation's monuments is rightly considered a literal prostitution of history, and there is great irony in their having been named for two of history's most notorious devouring females. Although her name means "life," Eve is paradoxically the figure who brings ruin to the primeval world,

181

enticing the man to sin with her and bringing about an expulsion from the Garden. The choice of a name for the boat, then, constitutes an unwitting prophecy by Pantaleón concerning the fate awaiting him as he takes Eve into "towns that live in biblical purity" (p. 107)—at least in the popular imagination.

Delilah is the foreigner who so fascinates the solar hero Samson that she gains complete control over him and destroys his effectiveness as a hero for a time. This choice of a name by Pantaleón is prophetic as well, for the "foreigner" known as the Brazilian (actually a Peruvian who has lived in Brazil) eventually causes Pantaleón's total downfall. Her nickname, too, like the names of Calypso and Delilah, speaks of darkness, for "brazil" is the name of a dark wood. Pantaleón's problem is that he focuses on the light side of her character, that indicated by her true last name, Rosaura, which conjures up visions of a pink aura such as that in Homer's oft-used "Dawn," with fingertips of rose." The reader steeped in the lore of the hero stories might conclude in the midst of this tale that Pantaleón's affair with her is only the hero's required dalliance with Night for the winter season—that even her concealed name promises that he will burst forth with solar power once more as Odysseus recovers his kingdom and Samson slays more Philistines. Pantaleón, though, experiences no such success before going into exile, simply because he becomes too attached to the goddess-figure with whom he should by rights spend only a short time, if any. In fact, in a sense she is an embodiment of the entire ill-fated adventure.

The Brazilian is presented as a *femme fatale* like Remedios the Beauty, although she most assuredly is a being of this world. Rumor has it that two men have already died on account of her, one a young Seventh-day Adventist missionary who, after a torrid affair with her, took his own life. She is also reputed to be half witch, and this would place her in the same category with the two "Magas" previously dealt with (in *Rayuela* and *Tres tristes tigres*), as well as Celestina, the Dama Loca and La Señora in *Terra nostra*. Ironically, she does nothing positive to destroy Pantaleón. On the contrary, she is the one who dies, in another of those plays on Freudian symbolism of which some authors have become so fond, when her body actually seems to attract bullets from the men attacking her boat.

Pantaleón's wife Pochita herself has a bit of the castrating female in her. In a letter to her sister she remarks that she is so angry about her new circumstances that "I swear I'd cut off General Scavino's you-know-what" (p. 46), and then, in the same letter, concerning Pantaleón, "I wanted to cut off *his* you-know-what too" (p. 48). All three of the women with whom he is closely involved, Pochita, his mother, and the Brazilian, treat him as if he were a child, which in a sense he is after undergoing his anti-initiation and transformation: the hero as *puer aeternus*.

There is something ominous in the fact that the madam with whom he works bears the name Leonor, the same as his mother's. Indeed, in two of his dreams the identities of the two are thoroughly mixed. Although there is no specific mention of the fact, there is probably a play here on the fact that in Spanish a madam is often called "madre," so that both of these women are "mothers" for him, one corresponding to his solar side and the other to the new lunar identity. That identity having been gained by his imbibing of a poisonous snake, Leonor fits into the scheme perfectly, for, as previously mentioned, her nickname, Chuchupe, is that of the most poisonous snake of the Amazon region.

It goes without saying that in this novel as well as in the six previously considered there is a violation of the principle of the sacred marriage, as prostitution for pay must always be. Paradoxically, temple prostitution in the ancient world was considered to be a ritual facilitating the *hieros gamos,* since by uniting with one of the consecrated priestesses a man was believed to achieve union with the goddess of life herself, thereby assuring that fertility would come to the land. Pantaleón's Special Service hardly belongs to that category, and within a general atmosphere described from the outset as apocalyptic, everything begins to disintegrate as the operation is set in motion. It may be symbolic of the blow to the doctrine of love inherent in the *hieros gamos,* and of the resultant lack of renewal in a new generation, when two items of news coincide, one concerning the tremendous success of the prostitution service and the other having to do with the crucifixion of a baby.

The twisted nature of reality in the situation in which

183

Pantaleón is involved is seen also in the fact that one of the prostitutes, Maclovia, elopes with a soldier she is serving, marries him, and is immediately fired for it by Pantaleón. In her naiveté she writes Pochita and reveals all, including Pantaleón's affair with the Brazilian. Later, being interviewed on Sinchi's radio program, she comments, "Maybe it's a sin to get married?" (p. 152). In the system of inverted values into which Pantaleón has been forced, and within which he now functions enthusiastically, in which prostitution is not sin but redemption, the reader is jarred into the realization that marriage is indeed a sin.

At first glance the two "disasters of the jungle," the careers of Pantaleón and Brother Francisco, are difficult to integrate. The fact is that together they comprise a special reading of the two brothers theme. They represent the military and the Church, the two most honorable professions of the Middle Ages. Both are enveloped in the apocalyptic atmosphere that pervades the jungle at this time, and which Brother Francisco transforms into an atmosphere of human sacrifice. Panteleón is "to represent the military in Paradise" (p. 3), which is a contradiction in terms in any event (one recalls Don Quixote's Golden Age discourse concerning the need of arms to *restore* Paradise), but the scene shifts quickly to one recalling Genesis 3, with a sex-related fall from the supposed "biblical purity" of the area, followed by the killing of brother by brother. The novel opens with the report that Brother Francisco, newly released from a mental institution, has crucified himself to announce the end of the world, so that his career coincides in its beginnings with Pantaleón's new one. An impending Apocalypse calls forth heroes, but these two hardly match the archetype.

Brother Francisco establishes an organization known as the Brothers of the Ark, but in this ark animals are not saved from destruction but crucified. By the same token, Pantaleón has his boat carrying prostitutes, who are often viewed as society's victims. He comes to view them as a necessary part of the military service and does in fact provide them with much better working conditions than they might have outside. He forgets the grotesque character of the profession until his liaison man with the military, Lieutenant Bacacorzo, jokingly

184

asks him what he will think if the son Pochita is expecting turns out to be a "little specialist" instead. The question shocks and infuriates Pantaleón as his professional and family lives, with their mutually exclusive sets of values, are unexpectedly brought together.

The high-ranking officers who thrust Pantaleón into the assignment do so in full awareness of what may be dire results for him, so that the operation is described in terms of a human sacrifice from the outset: "He's going to think we're sending him to the slaughterhouse" (p. 2); Pantaleón himself is told directly, "The only way to avoid any reflection on the army is by sacrificing you" (p. 14). Then Pochita, who has not been informed concerning what is taking place, dreams that she and Pantaleón are being crucified. Not long afterward, the Brothers of the Ark perform their first human sacrifice, that of the baby: "They thought that with the sacrifice God would postpone the end of the world" (p. 100). If we allow that there is a parallel with the prostitutes as sacrificial victims offered to male lust, Pantaleón's career clearly matches Brother Francisco's in this instance too, for his victims are brought in to put an end to the cataclysmic orgy of rape by the frustrated jungle troops.

The hero is always a representative of his people, and Pantaleón is no exception, for he is made to bear the guilt both of his countrymen in general and of the military leaders who are ultimately responsible for such an insane scheme. At this point the theme of hypocrisy ties into that of the hero as guiltless sacrificial victim, for every male in the work, with the exception of Pantaleón and Brother Francisco, appears to be guilty of the twisted sexuality that brings on the whole sordid situation. Incredibly, Pantaleón only succumbs to temptation out of professional dedication, yet he is the one who must bear the wrath, first of General Scavino and the Chaplain, and then of society at large, which was guilty when he was not. The principle is that of the choice of perfect lamb—in this case "an officer without vices"—for the sacrifice, so that it will be evident that the victim must die for the sins of others rather than for any defect of his own. In this regard Mary Davis, quoting Géza Róheim, points out that while the Hebrews used a perfect animal, the Greeks preferred "a monstrous, idiotic or misshaped person for

185

their sacrifices,"[7] which may be significant in view of Brother Francisco's ultimate fate.

The situation involving human sacrifice becomes increasingly intense as the novel progresses. After the Brazilian is shot, her body is hung on a cross, precipitating Pantaleón's fateful funeral oration. Eventually Brother Francisco, who has often had himself hung on a cross without dying, finds that he can no longer elude the army, and he crucifies himself deep in the jungle and dies. His body, already badly decayed when found, is thrown into the river. The pimp known as Chameleon, having witnessed the bizarre scene and gotten into the spirit of things, says, "I'm a sacrifice" (p. 232).

The twin careers of Brother Francisco and Pantaleón have lasted the three years of Christ's ministry. For his part, Pantaleón, having "committed professional suicide," is called before a board of superior officers who are nearly as uncomfortable as he is, and, refusing to resign his commission, is sent from the steamy jungle lowlands to a place of virtual exile in the rarefied atmosphere of Lake Titicaca. His sole consolation is that he is still in his beloved army, the only context in which he knows how to function, and is reunited with his wife and daughter. The verdict has included the words, "It is imperative that the people forget about the existence of the famous Captain Pantoja" (p. 243), for he bears away the sins they wish to forget.

The instructions given in the Law of Moses for the highly important Israelite Day of Atonement read, in part:

From the Israelite community [Aaron, the High Priest] is to take two male goats for a sin offering . . . and present them before the Lord at the entrance to the Tent of Meeting. He is to cast lots for the two goats—one lot for the Lord and the other for the scapegoat. Aaron shall bring the goat whose lot falls to the Lord and sacrifice it for a sin offering. But the goat chosen by lot as the scapegoat shall be presented alive before the Lord to be used for making atonement by sending it into the desert as a scapegoat. . . . He is to lay both hands on the head of the live goat and confess over it all the wickedness and rebellion of the Israelites—all their sins—and put them on the goat's head. He shall send the goat away into the desert in the care of a man appointed for the task. The goat will carry on itself all their sins to a solitary place; and the man shall release it . . . (Leviticus 16, *NIV*).

186

Thus, these two brothers, who never meet, reenact a ritual renewal, one of them dying, but the other, instead of founding a new society, going out into a desert place bearing the sins of a nation.

Human sacrifice tends to be inseparable from lunar religion, so that the Hebrew people were torn away from both by the priests only with great difficulty and more or less simultaneously, to be established in a more solar type of faith in which animals substituted for sinners. Only with the resurgence of a lunar viewpoint does human sacrifice reappear, as it does in this novel. The fact was discussed earlier that Pantaleón's transformation experience, rather than fortifying him in his position as bearer of the enlightenment and civilization associated with the sun and its symbol, the lion, has him imbibing the obscure, chaotic, relational lunar serpent. This is remarkable, for when the hero is metamorphosed from Logos to Eros there is an attendant reversal of the values inherent in the monomyth, especially when a mutilating form of Eros is involved. Even though the Greek dramas of both types were dedicated to Dionysus, their hero was plainly a Logos-figure, destined to unite with Eros at the conclusion in the comedy and be sacrificed according to her principles in the tragedy. In *Pantaleón y las visitadoras*, however, while we have the licentious atmosphere pervading the comedy, and the sacrifice of the tragedy, in the end the requirements of neither are complied with, for no renewal of the world results from the process, nor does the dual sacrifice result in any modification of the guilt that called it forth. It is clear at the conclusion that we have returned to the status quo. The fact is that, even though Pantaleón has quite faithfully reproduced the pattern presented by Lord Raglan, the values inherent in those events have been violated.

In this case the problem would seem to be that the call to adventure is not issued by any representative of the realm of Being, which under normal circumstances calls forth the aggressive Logos to go in search of power, apply it, and then unite with the more passive, relational Eros. Rather, the call is issued by a group of misguided souls who have been infected by the idea that if the troops behave like lunatics in the jungle, the

187

only way of dealing with them is by a program of controlled lunacy, recalling the "Bureau of Entropy Management" in Thomas Pynchon's *Gravity's Rainbow*. It is as if Rio de Janeiro's *Carnaval* were to be perpetuated and simply brought under bureaucratic control, passing through Lent, Good Friday, and Easter without taking note of them. Entropy must be confronted aggressively, for it is the tendency for the energy *in a closed system* to run down. The hero's task is to leave that system and then return to open it up temporarily to receive a new influx of the power with which he has returned from the Source. Mardi Gras and Easter celebrations, though vastly different in character, are parts of the same religious cycle. What the generals fail to realize is that the chaos of the former must be done away with by the cosmos contained in the latter. One cannot control *Carnaval* and live by its kinetic power; it must be superceded.

The question may be posed once again with regard to this novel, as with all the others: how does the hero achieve cosmic renewal without the fruitful union of heaven and earth symbolized by the sacred wedding? How is the principle of enlightenment and order to unite with that of life and fertility when something prevents their making contact in any meaningful way? Arlt's madmen engage in something like the ultimate anti-heroic task in attempting to renew society on the basis of a chain of brothels. Pedro Páramo is so dominated by his adherence to nonbeing that he is alone even with Susana San Juan. No one can reach Remedios the Beauty, the perfect woman, because of an incurable solitude which is only perpetuated by failure, and so on. Here Brother Francisco, while preaching in the name of Christ, forgets that the latter's sacrifice is described as a once-for-all bout with nonbeing to establish forever the availability of Being to all, and the preacher spreads a cult of nonbeing affecting everyone, including himself. Eros means Being only when in a *hieros gamos* it achieves full union with Logos. The prevalence of prostitution in these novels is symptomatic of the failure of the process, for in it a woman is not even truly Eros, much less able to relate fully to the male principle. It will remain for Carlos Fuentes in *Terra nostra* to attempt to crack the vicious cycle and inject some new metaphysical power into what has become all too closed a system.

IX

Carlos Fuentes
Terra nostra

Man humanizes the cosmos . . . .: he turns it into language.
Octavio Paz

I don't see why a man of our time can't get excited over an achieved archetype.
Jose Cemí in *Paradiso*

In the last two chapters we have witnessed the case of the novel that presents language as the hero and itself as proof that he has returned from the dead with power, and the case of the hero successful at what no hero should undertake in the first place and then sacrificed for the sins of those who forced him into it. *Terra nostra* has something of both, but on an immeasurably more ambitious scale. The sacrifice is the final one and the hero, not language himself but nevertheless patently fabricated of words and human will, finally achieves the full *hieros gamos* and enters the third millennium A.D. as the beginning of a totally new creation. The reader is implicitly invited by this author to hope that the earthly reality of the new millennium might spring from a metaphysics such as the book contains.

The novel revolves around the Mediterranean world, particularly the Spain of the Black Legend as land of nonbeing; America as land of the struggle of Being and nonbeing as expressed in human sacrifice; and Paris as "Capital of the Third Age of Mankind" and "Fount of all Wisdom." The novel is a rewriting of the history of the two thouand years since the death of Christ on the basis of certain processes set in motion by that death and other events in the reign of Tiberius Caesar. To borrow the term used by Guillermo Cabrera Infante of Lewis Carroll's work, this is a case of "oneirolalia," dream-speaking, in the hope that the words emerging from the dream may prove to be those capable of constructing on earth the world of that dream. Eliade has said that "ritual abolishes profane, chronological time and recovers the sacred time of myth,"[1] and for Fuentes fiction is a ritual, so that his novel constitutes a return to the origins of Western civilization in order to renew it—the novel as cosmogenesis.

The author deliberately engages in a severe fragmentation of time and space in order to make it clear that the events portrayed in the work belong strictly to a mythic spacetime. The scene in Paris with which the novel opens and closes may be viewed as a product of events that precede it in time, as is normally the case. It may also be viewed as creating that past time, the events having been projected from the mind of Polo Febo as he reads books and contemplates certain artifacts in his room between July 14 and December 31, 1999. The reader is free to conclude that Polo Febo has never left his room between those dates, never left Paris or traveled in spacetime to take part in all the hero-events of the work. But between the July 14 of the beginning and the December 31 of the conclusion he has undergone a transformation experience, for his identity has changed from that of a sandwich board carrier to that of a heroic guerrilla from Mexico. That is, the hero quest in this novel may involve the journey in imagination of a man literally enveloped in his generation's materialism, back into the events of the past two thousand years to transform them and be transformed himself, in order to return to his present time and bring about the sacred marriage and renovate the world.

On Bastille Day, 1999, Polo Febo is working for a Paris restaurant to attract customers. As he leaves his apartment he witnesses the birth of a ninety-year-old woman named Madame Zaharia of a son with twelve toes and a red cross on his back. A note to Polo Febo from "Ludovico and Celestina" informs him that the child is his, but in another time, and is to be known as Johannes Agrippa. The complexities woven into this event are comparable to what Cabrera Infante does with "Seseribó," and are based on the principle reiterated throughout the work, that "many lives are necessary to integrate a personality." The personality in question is that of the solar hero, who bears the identities of (1) Jesus of Nazareth, (2) the pretender to the imperial throne of Rome, known as Agrippa, and (3) a slave called Clemens. The name Johannes is the Greek form of the Hebrew phrase, "Grace is from Yahweh," and is the one given to John the Baptist.

John the Baptist was born to an aged couple named Zacharias and Elizabeth; his function was to announce the advent of what Fuentes calls the Second Age, following that of Moses. This Johannes Agrippa is born of a woman bearing the name of the *father* of John the Baptist, recalling Eduviges Dyada in *Pedro Páramo,* who considers herself both father and mother of her children. The earlier Juan Agrippa of the novel is born to Elizabeth, wife of the second El Señor, the father being the first El Señor. The point seems to be that in "integrating the personality" of this hero, who will both announce and bring into being the Third Age, the author has had him born in different times and places, but of mothers bearing the names of both parents of the Johannes who announced the Second Age. The author probably means us to understand that the father of the baby in Paris is Polo Febo in his incarnation as the Johannes Agrippa born of Elizabeth, who has taken on the identity of Don Juan Tenorio and slept with his own mother. A complexity of this magnitude serves as an alienation device to prevent the reader from handling the work as something like a historical novel overwhelmed by what used to be called magic realism.

On the other hand, those who insist on treating it as a mystery challenging the reader to assemble all the pieces will fail even where Polo Febo is concerned, for, the nature of his travels aside, his identity in Paris is totally obfuscated. As has been mentioned, when he appears at the end of the novel the date is December 31, 1999, and he is no longer the sandwich board carrier, but seemingly a Mexican nationalist insurgent in exile, the one seen earlier in a final desperate stand against a series of bombing raids and then assassinating his brother for selling the nation out. One looks in vain for Johannes Agrippa, who should be five and one-half months old and playing some role in this apocalyptic scene, according to his elect character.

Evidently he perishes along with the rest of the human race—Polo Febo and Celestina excluded—as the millennium comes to an end. The previous Johannes Agrippa, having taken on the identity of Don Juan, has escaped the clutches of El Señor and gone to Mexico to father many children. One may surmise that it is one of these, born in another time with reference to both Don Juan and Polo Febo, who has become the guerrilla leader and then escaped to Paris, taking the identity of Polo Febo as the sandwich man who has disappeared into the Seine on July 14. Still, it is always possible that Polo Febo imagines the entire experience, including the fall into the river.

The most important point to bear in mind is that the author wishes to stress the identity of Polo Febo *as archetype.* The basic outline of his hero quest has him viewing the birth of an avatar of himself, traveling to many other locations in time and space, and finally returning by way of Mexico on a date a few months later. He can also say with sincerity that he never left Paris—that it was only a literary experience for him, as we know it has been for us. Fuentes seems to want to underscore the *reality* of the events, the fact that they are viewed *as happening,* on whatever level, for therein lies the creativity of myth. He also clearly feels that whenever in the history of the past two millennia a person has been found doing the creative work of Apollo, Christ, or Quetzalcóatl, that person has in fact taken on the identity of that solar hero with one of his thousand faces. Therefore this novel consists of a series of key events within that period, viewed as if someone actually stamped with the marks of that archetypal hero had been active in them, rather than Hieronymus Bosch, an anonymous heretic, or a Latin American guerrilla.

Paris is the center of enlightenment from which the solar hero departs to undertake a two-millennium quest, overcoming ever more formidable obstacles, and to which he returns with power to effect a new creation. The choice and handling of dates is significant. Fuentes wants to unite the date of the Revolution that broke the power of a false "Roi Soleil" (in the person of his grandson) with the solar hero's victory on the final day of the millennium, for he casts Polo Febo's major victory in terms of a confrontation with Felipe (not to be too closely identified with

Philip II, for he is a composite Spanish king). The situation is clearly apocalyptic, as Polo Febo continually wonders whether the world is growing older or younger. Both are true at this juncture in time when the end is united with the beginning. He is aware of the sights and sounds of multiple births and multiple sacrificial deaths, the Armageddon of this struggle between the forces of Being and nonbeing. At the point where the latter have seemingly gained the upper hand and slaughtered the entire human race, the two who remain, Polo Febo and Celestina, unite to form the seed of a new humanity.

The author skillfully avoids portraying the struggle as a battle between the solar forces and the dragon of chaos, for the latter would lead merely to the "manichaeism" that he abhors. Rather, the villian Felipe is depicted as a potential solar hero himself, largely a victim of his own corrupt lineage, and the three youths into whom Polo Febo's character is divided quite openly take on a devil's role at times in order to break down the all too orderly reign of nonbeing. One of the major discoveries of the so-called Pilgrim in the New World is that in the character of Quetzalcóatl he must accept the fact that he is also his own demonic brother, for life and death nourish one another in the prevailing system. This sort of rhythmic duality must be done away with, for Fuentes appears to be impatient with the thought that accepts the rightness of gods trampling human beings into the dust in order to create new ones. The only struggle of opposites he wishes to allow is that of the *hieros gamos,* which allows both partners to live and yet produce a third living being. To achieve this the enmity inherent in the duality of the founding brothers theme we have met in all the previous novels must be superceded by the harmony of resolution found in the number three. When the *three* founding brothers have returned to primordial unity in Polo Febo without having slain one another, there can be a *hieros gamos* productive of a different sort of human race.

The two brothers theme does enter the picture, but in the form of the struggle between El Señor on the one hand and the three youths on the other, all of whom he is convinced are sons of his father and therefore pretenders to his throne. He has desired to be the last of his line, probably because he realizes how degenerate it has become with him, and for this reason, as well as their ideology, which is diametrically opposed to his, he must eliminate them by any means possible. His father has a strong heroic cast, modeled as he is on Charles V, who is "blond as the sun,"[2] but his warfare is against the forces of life and renewal, and his union with women takes the form of an extreme promiscuity. The son, instead of supplanting the father in the normal order of myth, reestablishing the kingdom under the banner of new life against the stagnation into which it has fallen under the father's rule, supports his father's reign from the beginning, even leading crowds of celebrants to their death in the palace on the pretext of opening up a new era of love, justice, and the exaltation of life. The heretical university student Ludovico recognizes the potential Felipe has denied in himself, telling him, "Behind us is the illusory past, living, latent, everything that had no opportunity to be because it awaited your birth to be given that opportunity" (p. 614). Felipe is the hero who has definitively refused the call to adventure issued by Ludovico before the palace massacre and again by the same person after Felipe's victory over the Adamites in Flanders. To refuse the call is to condemn oneself to an existence characterized by the insistent encroachment of nonbeing; as El Señor remarks, "My age is measured by the increasing extension of its shadows" (p. 706).

Instead of associating themselves with the sun, symbol of rational creativity and order, the monarchs of Spain ally themselves with the wolf, consecrated to Mars, and through it with the decrepit Roman Empire under Tiberius, whose curse strikes terror into Felipe's heart when he sees its fulfillment begin with the arrival of the youths in the palace. Even apart from the curse, however, it might be recalled that in the realm of mythology Mars is conquered on various occasions by both Diomedes and the solar hero Heracles, the former employing the aid of Athena. The message, seemingly, is that warfare is ultimately dominated by enlightenment.

The Spanish royal family's motto is "Nondum," "not yet," and is taken throughout the novel to mean that the tyrant dedicated to death will not yet relinquish his hold on power to the forces of renewal. The line has deteriorated so severely, however, that Felipe is a hemophiliac and subject to bleeding to death if he receives the slightest wound. Symbolically speaking, this is a serious matter in a king, who is viewed as the embodiment of his people, in that blood represents life, which then must have only a tenuous hold in Spain. The dog Bocanegra is kept near El Señor during the hunt to protect him from attack by a wild boar. Solar heroes are often attacked by boars and usually die as a result. Odysseus is recognized in his own house by the scar left by such an attack. The boar is an animal associated with the underworld and the moon's death-dealing aspect. Its frequent attack on these heroes would seem to signify an attempt by the realm of nonbeing to capture the hero permanently before he can penetrate to Hades alive and return with the power of renewal. Thus, El Señor's vulnerability takes on added meaning.

He is associated with the falcon, which seems to stand for his repressed potential for life and freedom. La Señora caresses a falcon with great sensuality as a substitute for her husband, whose genitals have rotted away on account of venereal disease passed on to him from his own father by way of Celestina. One of the symbolic motifs of the work involves the necessity of keeping the royal falcons from total darkness, for, believing it to be limitless, they will attempt to fly and dash themselves against the walls. Clearly this is the case with Felipe, who believes, who wills, his self-imposed darkness to be endless, and eventually destroys himself against its unperceived limits. His aide Guzmán also associates himself with the falcon as he takes on the role of the cruel Conquistador establishing in the New World a kingdom identical to that of El Señor in Spain, having admired the bird's merciless way of falling upon its prey. Guzmán's plan is to "duplicate and congeal" Felipe's empire of death in America: "The New World will fit within your tombs," he tells him (p. 504).

El Señor believes the world to be orderly, and furthermore, well ordered. His refrain is, "Short life, eternal glory, immovable world," to which end he could even desire that the sun stand still. To encapsulate his ideology he builds the Escorial, the name of which means "dung heap," although Fuentes avoids what must have been a temptation to underscore this

195

point. The palace is built on the site of an ancient fountain that had never run dry, and is in the shape of the grid on which St. Lawrence was tortured to death. In its location and shape, then, it speaks of the suppression of life and an agonizing death. Felipe himself wonders if it might not be only "a gigantic stone reptile" (p. 258)—that is, for all its orderliness, another image of the dragon of chaos to be slain by the representative of life. As such it is a significant image used by the author in equating the order of Holdfast with chaos itself, for the dragon *is* Holdfast in many stories.

Felipe's desire is that his palace be an *imago mundi*, the "double of the universe" (p. 293). He brings into it the corpses of all his royal ancestors that can be located, with all their stories of cruelty, madness, lechery, physical deformity, and perversion, to impose their deathly rule on his anti-cosmos. Furthermore, although it fails to work out as he intends, he desires that the corpses all arrive on his birthday so that "the celebrations of life and death would be blended into one" (p. 186). This may be recognized as a mirror image of what takes place in the Apocalypse, for there the threat of death at its peak is overwhelmed by an influx of life. In spite of Felipe's best efforts, this is what takes place at the conclusion of the novel.

The nun known as Inés confronts him directly with his reversal of values, telling him that his race has confused hell with heaven. If heaven may be described as the experience of Being in its fullest manifestation, then hell must consist of its negation, the total experience of nonbeing, as in Juan Rulfo's Comala. In the Cathedral of Flanders following his victory over the heretics, El Señor is told by Ludovico, "You represent the principle of death, and we the principle of procreation," and "If you defeat us you defeat yourself" (pp. 54-55). El Señor has just seen his glorious victory turned to excrement before his eyes as the mercenary troops he has used against the heretics have defiled the very altar of the cathedral. As he himself realizes, he has been associated with excrement all his life, having been born in a Flanders latrine during a campaign of his father's. Now he too has been victorious there, only to return to his unsavory origins and be reminded of them. Years later, when a chest of gold—described as "the excrement of the gods"—

arrives from the New World, he sees it converted into the more ordinary variety. Later he dies as he was born, surrounded by the substance that vital beings cast off during the normal rhythmic cycles of life.

He is generally supported by his mother, called the Mad Lady, in his establishment of death. She, who believes that her husband was the sun, travels about Spain, generally at night, in a black funeral carriage which is totally dark inside, with his corpse. She says, "I bequeath to Spain what Spain cannot offer me: the image of death as an inexhaustible and consuming luxury" (p. 74). So ascetic is she in her madness that she exposes herself to the elements for many days in the palace courtyard, eventually being nearly devoured by the royal hunting dogs and losing all her limbs in the process. Her plan for the continuation of the family dynasty is to revive the thirty corpses in reverse order until the kingdom reverts to the first of the line.

She is installed in a niche above the funerary vault of the palace and continues to give advice to her son long after she is believed dead. Even when, in the midst of great confusion in the palace, she falls and is trampled, she lives on. Later in the text she takes on the identities of other mad queens, including Carlotta, for she too represents an archetype. Even after her death she speaks to the situation of the New World: "We shall impose the kingdom of nothingness upon the land toward which they gaze with hope" (p. 503). For her the palace is the abyss, which is to say the very Center of the cosmos (p. 277), which relates closely to Inés' comment, for the Center is where the hero enters in search of the Source. In Tillichian thought, too, the abyss is inseparably connected with Being. This one, however, is the source only of the power of nonbeing; it is the pit of perdition, the royal Spanish equivalent of Rulfo's Comala. Guzmán is the corresponding kind of hero, taking the power of nonbeing from the Escorial to found the kingdom of nothingness in America.

For her part, La Señora, who has originally wanted rose gardens in the palace, ends up by employing witchcraft to construct a composite ruler from bits and pieces of the corpses in the chapel. She is unable to bring it to life except in a bizarre scene in which the homunculus that has grown up from her mandrake serves as ventriloquist for the grotesque mummy. El Señor finds it and comments that it is ruling in his place, which in a sense is true, for, as he himself admits, he is a prisoner of the progressive corruption of his own dynasty.

When the final assault on the palace takes place, Felipe senses that it has closed the circle of his life. In his youth he provoked and put down such a revolt, and in a grotesque mockery of the marriage to the princess with which the conquering hero is rewarded, he was given the hand of Elizabeth for his treachery. In the heat of the later revolt, a peasant named Jerónimo finds him and is about to kill him in revenge for his acts of villainy, but upon learning that death is what the king desires most, he leaves him to suffer and finally die a horrible death, overwhelmed by his own filth and surrounded by piles of relics which are only another reminder of his necrophilia. Fuentes depicts the death skillfully, carefully avoiding the portrayal of any decisive break with life, for this man has already lived his death for many years. Having done so, and in accordance with the principle that many lives are needed to integrate a destiny, he must continue to live the nonbeing he has chosen, and do so through several centuries.

The rebels of all sorts within this context realize that new life is always born "of the rupture of an earlier state of equilibrium" (p. 692). El Señor learns too late that his palace dedicated to nonbeing, far from the *imago mundi* that he would like it to be, is nothing more than a refuge within a world in which Being is clamoring for an opportunity to manifest itself. He himself toys with the heresy which threatens to undermine the Aristotelian, Thomistic foundations of his ideology (which foundations he has admittedly perverted in the best of cases). This heresy he has drawn from the papers of his chronicler, a Cervantes-figure who proves to be one of the novel's narrators and has been sent to the galleys because, as an innocent man, he is dangerous. When Guzmán becomes alarmed at the king's having the heretical ideas written down, Felipe indicates that heresy maintains a healthy debate within the Church. He even exempts thoughtful heretics from extermination—as long as they do not threaten his political power. As it turns out, Fray Toribio burns the papers, using the rays of the sun, which plays such a decisive background role in the work, through a magnifying glass.

Toribio and Julián are two subversive ecclesiastical figures within the palace. Julián is the true painter of the picture in the chapel which torments El Señor so much, although it reputedly was brought from elsewhere. It is disturbing because, as Renaissance paintings do, it places Christ in a setting contemporary to the painter, thus indicating that revelation continues, or perhaps more accurately, must be reapplied to the changing circumstances of the world. It serves as the basis of El Señor's frequent hallucinations, in which Christ and those listening to him confront him with the sexuality that means there is more to the gospel than the sterility of asceticism. The painting is later reflected up the stairs which symbolize travel in time, and is last seen in a church in the jungles of Yucatán, where the Indians, told of Christ as the God of love, misunderstand and fornicate before the altar.

In the palace the painting has been replaced by Hiernoymus Bosch's *Garden of Earthly Delights,* adapted to El Señor's circumstances, perhaps by his imagination. He views it with the head supposedly severed from one of the three youths, who had been a leader of the Adamite rebellion in Flanders. The youth, however, abandoned that identity at the point of execution, and the head is that of Bosch.

Fray Toribio is something of a compendium of Copernicus and Galileo. As court astronomer he might have been expected merely to keep charts of the movements of the heavenly bodies for purposes of Spain's well-known obsession with astrology at this period, but he has discovered that the earth is not motionless—recall Felipe's "immovable world" principle—but travels among the other heavenly bodies. "Earth is in the heavens," he says, to which Julián remarks, "Hell is on earth" (p. 297). Moreover, he develops a metaphysics in which there emerges a new sort of coherence capable of replacing that of El Señor's mortiferous system. Mentioning Pythagoras, he states, "One [circle] impels another, one sphere affects another, indeed the entire universe, without a single imaginable fissure, without a single rupture in the chain of cause and effect; each is related to the other so that beginning with the revolution of each planet all phenomena are explainable" (p. 299). Julián concludes that an infinite universe can have no center, administering still another blow to El Señor's concept of *Terra nostra*.

The scene has been set from the beginning for every imaginable sort of assault on it. Even in the hunt with which the narration concerning Spain begins, El Señor notes that the peasants are restless and grumbling, and that events in the ritual hunt have begun to happen automatically, without his having given the signal. When the Pilgrim returns with his story of the New World and its possibilities, however, the situation becomes nearly uncontrollable. Felipe orders that it not be written down so that it will not become real, and even decrees its nonexistence. In this he is not far wrong, for at this point the New World has only been dreamed by a youth whose adventures in turn were dreamed by his two brothers, in a motif apparently derived by Fuentes from Indian mythology, in which Vishnu, in his sleep on the surface of the primordial ocean, " 'dreams' the world; when he awakes it disappears."[3]

Guzmán repeatedly warns El Señor that the world outside the palace is being turned upside down, that money has become a powerful god. This fact is brought to the fore with the bankruptcy of the royal treasury and the necessity of bringing in a Jewish *converso* moneylender from Seville. There is a great deal of pastiche in *Terra nostra*, and this case serves as an example of how it is used. The moneylender turns out to be the father of the nun Inés, who is later to travel to Mexico and become Sor Juana Inés de la Cruz. Her father's reward for saving El Señor in his debt is to be named Comendador de Calatrava. Inés is one of the women seduced by Don Juan, who kills her father in a duel and later is seemingly turned into a stone statue, in a variation on Tirso de Molina's *El burlador de Sevilla*. Fuentes seems to want to underscore the fact that his version of *Terra Nostra* is a literary one.

Before dying, the old moneylender has declared that, while his motivation is money, his god is reason. Furthermore, in the course of the confusion in the palace, scant attention is paid to the fact that the Reformation is taking place. Far more astounding to El Señor is the news that deeply influences the Reformation: that mass printing is now available. Felipe, whose character is based mainly on that of the bureaucrat Philip II, believes that only what is written is real, and the point is not lost on him that now reality is available to anyone—including the new reality being constructed out of the ideologies of money, reason, and freedom of conscience.

The youth born as Juan Agrippa has assumed the identity of Don Juan when the latter is unable to fulfill his destiny in one lifetime because he has died in a duel. Thus, the youth carries out deeds in accordance with the character of the other until converted into a stone statue. This youth is the son of the first El Señor and Elizabeth, who is known as La Señora, although she fails to recognize him when he is brought to the palace. She is somewhat adept at witchcraft and feels that her burial of a mandrake in the sand of her room is what has brought Juan to the beach. The situation is far more complex than that, of course, for he also arrives from the Paris of 1999 as Polo Febo, as do the other two, since all three have on the clothes Polo Febo is wearing as he plunges into the Seine. He also arrives from a trek through Europe with his two brothers and Ludovico, having been thrown off a boat into the surf.

He is taken by La Señora into the darkness of her room, a darkness matched by that of her occult practices. The allusion to the sun hero Odysseus in the power of Calypso seems fairly obvious, and far more so in the case of the youth who comes to be known as the Idiot Prince with the Mad Lady in her carriage. For a time Juan is La Señora's lover, but he escapes to convert the sexual stirrings of the nuns lodged in the palace into action. Celestina tells him, "I want you to break down the order of this place" (p. 251); as Fray Julián realizes at the same time, "Perfect order is the forerunner of perfect horror" (p. 253). Thus, we have the spectacle of a solar hero deliberately spreading chaos, but doing so in the name of a different order, the dynamic order of life. This is Trickster at work, assaulting the barriers so that his work as creator may be accomplished on the ruins. Inés has been taken to El Señor by Guzmán, and has contracted the king's venereal disease. Her sexual union with Don Juan purifies her of that disease, for he is viewed as the incorruptible liberator of love, whose eventual destiny is to merge with Celestina into the androgyne. While frankly described as

201

satanic in his destructiveness, he is at the same time a Christ-figure, appearing in that guise before the Mother Superior at her devotions. She sees his face in that of the Christ of the painting by Fray Julián.

Throughout the work stress is laid on the concept that what is circular is eternal. This is a denial of Felipe's doctrine of living as if one were dead until the point at which "eternal glory" is entered, so that heaven's beauty might stand out all the more. For example, the various strains of ancient thought encountered by Ludovico in his travels through the medieval world with the three boys indicate that only that which, at the end of its cycle, returns from diversity back to unity in order to begin again is eternal. Ludovico is first seen by the reader in Polo Febo's Paris, as a green-eyed flagellant with a deathly complexion, proclaiming, somewhat paradoxically, "one single principle: that of pleasure" (p. 29). He is never quite in the mainstream of the ideology Fuentes develops throughout the work. Instead he seems to be an eclectic extremist (if such a thing were possible), gathering in heterodoxies from all quarters and using them to burst open the consciousness of the people so that new forms of life may emerge. He fiercely proclaims his atheism, yet he and Celestina both sign the note saying the baby is to be given a name meaning "Grace is from Yahweh." His ideas in some form are communicated to the boys, so that one of them becomes the militant leader of the Adamites, whose central notion is that of sex as Adam might have known it before the experience of guilt.[4] This concept is incorporated into the Third Age as described at the end of the text, but the idea of purifying oneself through sexual excess is not. Generally speaking, Ludovico's thinking consists of a compendium of the free-floating heresies of sixteenth-century Europe.

Ludovico has served as man of words to the boys, who are to be men of action, and when his exploration of the wisdom of the Mediterranean world is done he closes his eyes, vowing to see no more until the day of the Apocalypse. Significantly, he opens his eyes later to read *La Celestina, Don Quixote,* and *El burlador de Sevilla,* which reveal to him the essence of Spanish reality and its destiny. Presumably because Celestina proclaims the principle of love for pleasure's sake, Don Quixote lives for the reality of the world above the given, and Don Juan lives for pleasure.

The work of the youths takes place in Spain because that nation is in the greatest need of renewal, having rejected the unity of the three "peoples of the book," the Christians, Jews, and Muslims, this according to Valerio Camillo in Venice. Earlier Ludovico has been told by a Jewish scholar in Toledo that "all faiths are nourished by a common wisdom" (p. 519). The fact is that at one time Spanish royalty did recognize the unique opportunity possessed by Spain in having great scholars from all three faiths within her borders. Alfonso X, rightly called the Wise, brought them together in Toledo to work in peace and intellectual cross-fertilization, preserving and dealing with manuscripts of the ancient world. Out of this tradition came the great Moses Maimonides. It was not to last, however, for in the same year of 1492 the zeal for uniformity of faith caused the final defeat of the Moors, who were forced to be converted, and the expulsion of the Jews who had not declared themselves Christian (although economic factors were very important as well). In *Terra nostra* the expulsion is by order of El Señor. In it the product of the *convivencia* of the three great cultures and faiths is a character known as Miguel de la Vida. The Chronicler, also named Miguel, sees him eating an orange, which reminds him, no doubt, of the sun, for he perceives him as "the hero," and the narrator comments that "he was able to mistake, in that split second, the appearance of the sun and that of this boy, naked and alone." Later he sees him as "born with the sun, twin of the sun" (p. 237).

The chronicler Miguel writes poems about the youth Miguel, imagining his relationship to La Señora, although without knowing that they are in fact lovers. Julián is aware of this fact, and urges her to have a child by Miguel in order to bring about renewal in Spain. The symbolism is clear: Spain is being ruined by her dependence upon a decadent bloodline and ideology, and must return to the best she has known. It does not take place in that time, but the child born of her earlier becomes Don Juan to stir up the palace and Mexico and eventually merge into Polo Febo's identity. As for Miguel, he engages in homosexual relations with a kitchen boy and is burned at the stake by El Señor.

Before his death he is thrown into a cell with the Chronicler, and reveals that he has lived with Jewish, Moorish, and Christian communities, each time having his name translated into the appropriate language, for Michael in Hebrew and Mihail in Arabic mean "Who is to be compared with God?" and the rest of the name alludes to the solar hero's associations with life. A mandrake born at the stake where he is burned is the one used by La Señora to call back her son. When Juan is defeated by El Señor before his work can be completed, the mandrake becomes the homunculus behind the royal mummy, screaming, "Death to intelligence!" (p. 743). It is partly his unfulfilled destiny that the three youths are called upon to complete.

In some of the earlier books we have considered, there appeared the theme of the hero as "being lived" in some negative sense. Here the hero, both in his unified form as Polo Febo and in his triple identity, is generally unaware of what he is to accomplish in a given setting, and often unaware even of his own identity. The youths are more mindless than any of those heroes we have encountered previously, and a far cry from the mad but feverishly conscious, questioning Erdosain or the overly literate Oliveira. Fuentes has gone back to the hero as collective ego or solar archetype and caused him to live the pattern of renewal decreed by the will of mankind. The youths, as they appear ready for their assault on the palace, are called forth by three women and given form by those women's desires. As was mentioned, La Señora feels she has virtually created Johannes Agrippa (which is true in a sense, but not as she construes the case) as her lover. The Mad Lady, even in her funeral carriage after he is rescued, forms another youth into the image of her dead husband, and he becomes the Idiot Prince. The last is retrieved from the beach by Celestina, who brings him to the palace as the Pilgrim, for the express purpose of telling the story of his New World voyage, which may only be dreamed by the other two youths as he tells it. In this the women represent Eve as the desire for the perpetuation of life, and more specifically her desperate hope that has given birth to the Redeemer.

Nevertheless, the women are only the immediate cause of the youths' arrival. In their origins they go back to three men, all of whom died sacrificial deaths under Tiberius Caesar, and who, in a sense united in the person of the last of them to die, were sent into the waters to be reborn as three again in a later time. Tiberius has murdered his relative Agrippa, a pretender to his throne, and the legend has grown up that the young man is alive, although the reality is that his place has been taken by a clever slave named Clemens. Jesus of Nazareth has been crucified in this era and is also said to be alive. Then a poor fisherman appears unannounced in Caesar's supposedly impregnable palace on Capri, having found a way up the rock cliffs in order to present a large fish he has caught to Tiberius. Realizing that this means he can be reached and assassinated, the emperor treats the man with his usual senseless cruelty. As a result the fisherman shows Clemens the way to the palace, and there he strangles Caesar.

Previously Tiberius, hearing of Jesus' crucifixion and the fact that his disciples have declared that "his kingdom of slaves will be eternal" (p. 692), decides that the cross should become a symbol of dispersion after the unity achieved by Rome is broken up. If he had three sons, he says, he would divide the empire among them, requiring that each of them divide his share among three sons, and so on. He would like them to copulate with wolves and have children with crosses on their backs as the symbol of the slave who rules. "They would be my heirs, but in a different time, in a time of defeat and dispersion" (p. 695). Now a slave, bearing the identity of the murdered royal pretender, has killed him. The fish, symbol of the slave-king who died on a cross, has shown the way.

Clemens is condemned to die by being thrown from a cliff into the sea, and one is reminded once more of Icarus' ascent to the heights only to plunge to his death not many miles from Capri. Before the execution the Chronicler Teodoro carves a cross into his back. The slave, now bearing all three identities, is to be born as three men, each of a wolf, "to contemplate the dispersion of the Empire of Rome," which of course turns out to be a form of the Holy Roman Empire of Charles V. Nine will be born of those three, twenty-seven of those nine, and so forth, until—"since everyone will be Caesar, let no one be." As a joke he curses the slave with an extra toe on each foot, saying, "Let the sons of Agrippa, who shall bear the cross on their back, be called by the Hebrew name Yehohannan, which means 'Grace is from Yahweh'" (p. 698).

205

The three are born, all sons of that heir of Tiberius known as El Señor, and all of wolves in a sense, one literally, one of La Señora, who defends the child's life "like a she-wolf" (p. 659), and the other of Celestina. Each has on his back the cross that indicates the sacrificial death of a slave, and each has six toes on each foot, not as a joke now, but because hexadigitalism signifies the renewal of a dynasty. El Señor, aware that they are all his brothers, sons of his father, realizes they are usurpers of his throne. He calls them the founders and, thinking at first that there are only two of them, he recalls that the birth of twins announces the end of a dynasty. Earlier his father, in anguish, has recalled the prophecy and realized that he has engendered the slaves who are to usurp his kingdom. When the youths arrive on the beach, Julián sees a vision in which they are repeated to infinity. They are, of course, in those tens of millions of commoners who have fought through the past several centuries for the principles of life and freedom.

The boy known as Johannes Agrippa is the first to be born, to La Señora in a place apart so that the scandal will not become known. He is brought back to the palace—not yet the Escorial—and cared for, appropriately, by the court jester, the official trickster-figure. Since the jester knows the secret and attempts to use it for purposes of blackmail, he is poisoned by the first El Señor and the baby is discovered. Following the slaughter of the celebrants, Ludovico and Celestina escape the palace with the baby, hidden in a cartload of corpses. Once again the image is that of new life contained within death, the representative of Being surrounded by nonbeing. This scene will be repeated in a sense, for Johannes Agrippa, who is then also Polo Febo, will be reborn with Celestina as the androgyne in a world in which the rest of humanity is dead.

The second child is born to Celestina in Toledo, and the third to a wolf, aided by the eleven-year-old girl to whom Celestina is to pass on her identity. Celestina and Ludovico separate, he taking the boys on their twenty-year excursion around the Mediterranean world. Ludovico feels that he must remove the temptation of the woman from them, for if she were present they might re-live the myth of the two brothers, even though they are three. In Egypt, in fact, Ludovico meets a woman with the marks of Celestina, who warns him that if he fails to leave with the boys they must inevitably repeat the myth of Set and Horus. They move from Egypt to Palestine, into a community in which wisdom is sought without love, women, or money. This is a journey in time as well as in space, for Ludovico follows instructions given by Pliny, and after ten years in the community he is told by a ship's captain that the Romans did away with it long before their time.

In Venice, Ludovico, on the basis of his experience with the Jewish scholars of Toledo, is employed by Valerio Camillo, in whose "metaphysical theater" Ludovico is able to see the destinies of the boys: one as a stone statue, one dead, but one as Prometheus, although with his arm rather than his liver being eaten by a bird. In the meantime the boys have read the messages in the bottles which have come into their possession and have learned that each of them is to carry out his adventures as the other two dream him. This too will avoid the fratricidal conflict of the founders. As he comes to understand the principle involved, the born rebel Ludovico engages in a bit of secret plotting. The boys are to meet Celestina on the Cabo de los Desastres, which means "Cape of Disasters." The etymology of "disaster," which involves the undoing of a star, makes the location more significant. If each has gone on to complete the dream adventure assigned to him, he will fulfill his destiny only in dreams and not in history, as is the case with the heroes of mythology. Ludovico determines to cut the dreaming short so that they may confront El Señor in history.

The four continue their travels, Ludovico and one boy awake at all times, and the other two in coffins dreaming the other's adventures. At this stage Ludovico has his eyes closed, for only in this way can he fully open those of memory. The principle behind this, evidently, is that Utopia is not to be sought in space, but in time. Fuentes even makes it clear that Paris 1999 is not to be taken too literally; his characters are acting in an exalted, mythic spacetime complex which is far more universal. They pass through the experience in Flanders in which one of the youths becomes the leader of the Adamite sect, Felipe crushes the rebellion, and Ludovico speaks to him in the cathedral. Here the rebellious youth, about to be beheaded, is released from that dream identity so that Hieronymus Bosch may be executed instead.

After other adventures, among them one in which a youth aids Don Quixote in freeing the galley slaves, the four travelers keep their appointment with Celestina at the beach. She has now changed identities; the archetypal woman is now incarnate in the girl who at age eleven had the memory of the other passed on to her. The older woman, now bereft of that memory, has gone on to become the vicious old hag of Fernando de Rojas' great work. At this point Ludovico is concerned with making everyone believe the youths have completed the "sacred cycle" of their dreams. Pedro is present with his boat, and it should be noted that he has never attempted the trip to the New World which is supposed to be the basis of the Pilgrim's adventure there. The sleeping boys are placed in the water with their bottles, and wash up onto the beach one by one to be taken away by La Señora, the Mad Lady, and Celestina. St. Elmo's fire plays on the main mast of the boat, for it speaks of Castor and Pollux, the brothers who are the exception of the myth of the warring brothers in that their love is so great that they refuse to be separated even in death. Celestina calls them "salvation of sailors and castaways . . ., guardians of St. Elmo's fire" (p. 594).

Like Odysseus, then, the youths have spent twenty years traveling around the Mediterranean, to land, apparently shipwrecked, on a beach in order to meet a woman on a predetermined date and confront, as if usurpers, the true usurper of the kingdom, just as Odysseus enters his own palace as if a stranger to confront the Suitors. "This conflict" between hero and king, says W. T. H. Jackson, "provides the motivation of all Western epics,"[5] for the conflict on which Western literature is based is essentially a conflict between static and dynamic forces. The youths will not achieve full success in this place and time, but only later. One of them, shaped by the mindlessness of the Mad Lady into the form of the Idiot Prince, is only able to release the Jewish and Moorish prisoners he is expected to torture and kill. In a grotesque parody of the sacred wedding, he is married to the uncouth dwarf Barbarica, and El Señor has the two of them sent with the old hag Celestina (who may be the youth's mother but remembers nothing) to an asylum for those who have given up on life, to spend the rest of their days in bed. This, then, is the youth who is seen to be dead.

Johannes Agrippa's case has been discussed. Taking on the identity of Don Juan, he awakens the women of the palace, including Inés and La Señora, to their sexuality. The latter eventually returns to England to become, in one of Fuentes' best jokes in the novel, the Virgin Queen Elizabeth, scourge of El Señor's Spain. Having become a stone statue only in appearance in order to dream the Pilgrim's New World adventures, and having killed Inés' father, mad over money and power, he is condemned by El Señor to make love until death with Inés in a room full of mirrors. The effect of this is to repeat to infinity the act by which the hero of the pleasure principle liberates the woman devoted to perpetual abstinence. They escape, however, by substituting the squire Catalinón and the servant girl Lolilla for themselves, and travel to America with Guzmán to oppose his extension of El Señor's empire of non-being, each in the most appropriate way.

The Pilgrim is brought in by Celestina after much of the foregoing has taken place. In one apocalyptic night the foundations of El Señor's necropolis are under attack in various ways, from Don Juan's escapades through La Señora's attempts to build a composite ruler to Fray Toribio's revelations of his discoveries in cosmology. When the Pilgrim arrives he finds that in the stone of the palace a place has been carefully hollowed out and a stalk of wheat is beginning to grow, an indication that life has, after all, begun to win over death at the Center. The absolute Center is the chapel with thirty now-mutilated cadavers, and here the hero of life must be taken to tell his story of a New World. The youths are reunited, but only so that two of them may dream the adventure as the Pilgrim recounts it, the Idiot Prince in the coffin of the first El Señor and Don Juan in the form of a stone statue. Thus, the story truly is in a sense only the dream of a dreamed youth, but as Guzmán learns later, the details are true. And to underscore his theory that such dreaming can produce material reality, Fuentes has one of the boys wash onto the beach with a mask from the New World.

Ludovico, as a blind flutist who plays strange melodies

from the New World as the tale is told, must first bring the Pilgrim to life, "to lift his face as if in search of a sun banished from these royal dungeons" (p. 346). The youth tells of the call to adventure issued by Pedro, and of his refusal of the call, certain that it would be a voyage into death. Finally convinced, he embarks on the voyage with the older man, finding that, in the style of the hero undergoing transformation, he has lost his identity. There is a tremendous battle between a whale identified as Leviathan, ancient symbol of primordial chaos (and the equivalent of El Escorial as serpent), and a swordfish, which wins only by stabbing the sea monster in the eye with its sword and going to the bottom with it to die, as the Pilgrim is later to make certain of El Señor's defeat by drowning the falcon that symbolizes him as he himself drowns in the sea. There is also an allusion here to Odysseus' experience with Polyphemus, for in this adventure he too loses his identity, calling himself Noman to confuse the giant who represents chaos after wounding him by driving a stake into his eye. Polyphemus, moreover, is fundamentally a sea monster in his origins, for his father is Poseidon. In wounding him Odysseus marks himself for a great deal of difficulty, for he eventually reveals his name to Polyphemus and is pursued by Poseidon from then on, as the Pilgrim will be pursued by El Señor.

Poseidon seems to be present implicitly in *Terra nostra* as well, for following the battle the boat is sucked into a whirlpool—reminiscent of Charybdis—which spirals both downward and upward. The men are saved by lashing themselves to one of the objects they perceive as rising rather than sinking, the ship's wheel. The mast, being linear, sinks, and the point would appear to be that, since what is circular is eternal, those attached to the circular form are reborn. The whirlpool is "the tomb of the waters" (p. 364), and on reaching shore in the New World Eden the Pilgrim says, "I thought I had returned to life" (p. 367). The effect of Fuentes' handling of the voyage is to underscore the idea that one does not go to this New World in space, but by dying and being reborn as the hero.

However, the New World is Paradise Lost to the extent that the Pilgrim as Adam must lose his innocence in learning of his own murderous side and participate in the story of the two

210

brothers. He and Pedro are confronted by Indians, who quickly kill the old man, seemingly because he has attempted to take possession of the land but in truth because he has not been expected. Pilgrim, who has brought along a mirror and a pair of scissors, shows the latter and is immediately recognized as Quetzalcóatl returned. The scissors apparently represent the two brothers in the form of a double sacrificial knife. In his series of adventures the Pilgrim learns that while Quetzalcóatl has come to bring civilization and enlightenment and put an end to human sacrifice, his shadow side, Smoking Mirror, is ever ready to supplant him and reestablish that sacrifice, in a situation analogous to the one encountered by Pantaleón Pantoja in the jungles of Peru.

Some scholars have taken the name Quetzalcóatl to mean "the admirable twin."[6] Eventually the Pilgrim descends to the underworld and is told by its lords that he is in fact Quetzalcóatl in what he remembers and Smoking Mirror in what he does not. Typically, his quest for identity has taken him to Hades, and, as Jung would have it, he must learn of his shadow side and accept it as a part of himself. In one painting, described by David Maclagan, Quetzalcóatl, god of life, is shown back to back with Mictlantecuhtli, the skeletal god of the dead. They are "the conjoint lords of the time-span of human life (represented by the twenty day-signs on either side of them)."[7]

From the beginning of his voyage the Pilgrim associates himself with Venus, which alludes to an alternative ending to the myth in which Quetzalcóatl departs from Mexico to the east. In it he sets himself afire on the eastern shore and becomes Venus. Thus, the Pilgrim, who at first sees the planet as the sailor's guide, comes to see himself in it, as "twin star of the dusk and the dawn" (p. 402). The reader must not assume, however, that only one of the pre-Columbian meanings is in view, for Fuentes is highly eclectic in his use of mythology, and varies the details of Mexican religion to suit his novelistic purposes. As the Pilgrim stands on a temple, he offers his "love-drenched body" to Venus (p. 408), which appears to bring the Classical European vision of Aphrodite as goddess of love onto the scene. When he emerges from the underworld, reproducing the deed of Quetzalcóatl in bringing the bones of the dead to life, the Pilgrim finds that Venus' emergence coincides with his. Yet even Venus has its dark and deadly aspect, for the Aztecs saw not only Quetzalcóatl in that planet, but had a demonic version of it known as Tlauixcalpantecuhtli (Maclagan, p. 26).

After encountering his deadly double in several forms, the Pilgrim is told that there is life only "if two opposites confront each other in battle" (p. 467). This is an important thought, for in the ideology of the novel the replacement of the two struggling brothers by three who dream each other transfers the struggle to another level, on which male and female unite in a love struggle to realize the *hieros gamos* and produce a new cosmos.

Pilgrim also experiences several forms of the Meeting with the Goddess in the New World. At a burning temple she is metamorphosed from a spider into a woman, the point being that in universal symbolism Woman is the moon, weaver of destiny. More specifically, in Aztec mythology the first woman is charged with weaving. This woman is also Pilgrim's mother and sister, which is to say an anima-figure, his own feminine aspect. As such, she is his guide, for she too is Venus, and although he is later frightened into a well by a spider, he is led through the jungle by its thread. The woman is described in terms of the Earth Mother, which in Aztec mythology is Tezcatlipoca. In his sexual union with her, for which he senses he was born, he says, "We were one person" (p. 407), and yet this is only an anticipation of the sacred marriage in which Celestina and he, in the person of Polo Febo, will become the androgyne. He must still pass through many ordeals, defeating his brother, Smoking Mirror, finding that he himself has become that god of death, sacrificing himself and demanding his people's sacrificial death for him, and finally being exiled again—as Quetzalcóatl is—for his attempt to make love to his sister. This cannot be accomplished, she tells him, until their times coincide again. Like the periodic correspondence of solar and lunar cycles that makes Odysseus' and Penelope's reunion inevitable, that signifies Polo Febo's date with Celestina in Paris on the final day of the millennium.

In the course of his travels the Pilgrim finds and is given the mask that appears frequently in the course of the narrative.

It is not only a mask, which should enable a person to assume the identity of an archetypal figure, but also a map of the jungle. The mask/map is made of feathers and dead ants, the former recognizable as those of the *quetzal* bird alluded to in the name of the Mexican hero-god. The ants recall Tiberius' remark that in a dream he has seen a snake, with all its strength, overcome by ants; they had defeated it by sheer force of numbers. Felipe's "stone serpent," the Escorial, is ultimately overcome by the vast numbers of those who will bear the double identity of slave and king, even though multitudes die in the process. It is also possible that the center of the mask is not made of ants, but of spiders, which, like the female figures of the novel, are timeless (p. 717), and of course are also the weavers of destiny. Pilgrim is to keep the mask with him, for it will lead him back to the woman. In fact, two of them appear in Polo Febo's apartment, and he and Celestina wear them as they unite, fulfilling the destiny of Quetzalcóatl, bearer of light and life, and that of Tezcatlipoca, maker of destiny.

Upon leaving Tenochtitlán, the Pilgrim embarks upon the lagoon and soon finds himself in another whirlpool, going in all directions simultaneously. As he emerges he feels that Venus is near enough to be touched, and he climbs the mast to do so. This is Quetzalcóatl ascending to his destiny as the star, having become a victim of the enmity of the traditional two brothers. The Pilgrim, in contrast, is knocked from the mast into the water by St. Elmo's fire, for his destiny is not that of Quetzalcóatl but that of one of the loving brothers who guard that fire. He has returned to tell his story supported by the other two youths. In another sense he has never left, but only been thrown into the water upon his arrival from the trip through Europe with his brothers and Ludovico.

He has failed at something sought even in Aztec mythology as construed by Fuentes, for, while Smoking Mirror tells him that from the beginning there were only two brothers, the white and the red, the other version has it that there was a third, black brother, who was willing to sacrifice himself and thus become the sun for a time. If the three should become one, the Pilgrim is told, "we shall become one with our opposite—mother, woman, earth—who is also one being and who awaits

213

only our oneness to receive us in her arms" (p. 389). One is inclined to suspect that Fuentes was provided with the unique approach he has taken in this novel by the discovery of such mythic tradition. The philosophical—as opposed to mythic—foundation of its approach, nevertheless, is drawn largely from the Hebraic thought with which Ludovico comes into contact in Toledo. This is not surprising since there Spain's *three* peoples of the Book came to their flowering together and could have fulfilled their great creative potential if one of them had not set itself against the other brothers to become sole founder of the new nation.

The old scholar, basing his discourse on the Sephiroth, tells Ludovico that whatever exists fully does so three times, for three is the promise of unity: in it everything ends in order to begin again. "It combines the active with the passive, it unites the feminine principle with the masculine," for "three is the creative number" (pp. 528-29). Two is the number of conflict in traditional symbolism, and three is that of the resolution of conflict. Therefore when Tiberius, seemingly by chance, hits on the number three for his descendants who are to engineer Rome's final dispersion, he also assures that such dispersion will finally end in a new unity, and that without the conflict inherent in the traditional pair of rival founding brothers.

One of the Wise Old Man's key doctrines has to do with the number's not only bringing harmony out of conflict but bringing masculine and feminine together. One possible reason for the pastiche in the work may be that Fuentes, operating within the same fictional medium as his contemporaries, wants to fulfill what they have been searching for. This would account for the appearance of characters from several other Spanish American novels in Polo Febo's apartment just before the end, playing a game involving the cynical exploitation of brother by brother. It has become clear that the inability to overcome barriers between male and female characters—whether expressed by the term "solitude" or some other—prevents the establishment of the relationship out of which renewal might grow. *Rayuela* begins with the words, "Would I find La Maga?" and ends with the despair of Oliveira's failure to meet his goddess. *Terra nostra*, on the other hand, returns to the opening of

214

Rayuela and emerges with a different outcome. Polo Febo meets Celestina at the same location where Oliveira used to meet La Maga in Paris, the Pont des Arts. In contrast to Oliveira's avoidance of planned encounters, Polo Febo has a long-standing date to meet Celestina, even though he does not know it.

The major difference consists in the fact that in *Terra nostra* destiny, not the laws of probability, is in control of the events from this point on, and destiny operates through Woman. For Fuentes in this novel, Woman is not only lunar and an incarnation of the Earth Mother (the Pilgrim arrives in Mexico on 3 Crocodile Day, when the Earth Mother is born from the waters), but bears the continuity of the human race in her memory—not as any individual woman, but as the archetypal woman. This is essential, for the solar hero of the work is kept from the enmity of the two brothers not only by appearing as three and having the temptation of woman removed from him, but by possessing neither desire nor memory. Memory is provided only by contact with the lips of Celestina, who passes it on from each of her incarnations to the next in the form of the serpent tattoo. Thus, the original Celestina known by Ludovico chooses the eleven-year-old girl who will be the appropriate bearer of the archetypal identity, and, as the child kisses her hands, she receives the marks on her lips. Here woman renews her youth as does the serpent of the tattoo. The young girl will be the one to keep the appointment with the youths on the beach, and still another will meet Polo Febo in Paris, while the older woman in each case of transfer loses the tattooes and with them the memory associated with the eternal feminine principle. The bearer of that memory in Paris in 1999 must communicate it to Polo Febo, who is quite unaware of his destiny as he is lived by the solar archetype.

The devil tells Celestina to pass on her identity, for woman is quite generally associated with the devil throughout the work, and La Señora more than the others, perhaps because she, as Queen Elizabeth of England, is to be the "devil" who will do much to break down El Señor's deranged version of a theocracy. Ludovico says that woman, forbidden to say mass, "thus became Satan's priestess, and through her Satan regains his androgynous nature and becomes the hermaphrodite imagined by

the Eremites and seen in the Hebrew Cabala" (p. 330). This is
not the Satan of orthodox Christian theology, who is consistently depicted as the embodiment of evil and the destroyer of good.
This is Satan as the force that breaks into the false structures
which, constructed in the name of God, reflect only death and
decay. He destroys them and frees their constituent elements to
be reassembled in a manner that will be productive of life. In being viewed as underlying the hermaphroditic image he approaches Tillich's definition of love as the dynamic reunion of
that which is separated. Once again Fuentes avoids at all costs
slipping into any semblance of the polarizations of
manichaeism. For him and his characters God and Satan are not
absolute opposites, but cooperate in the tearing down of an old,
invalid order and the building of a new one. In fact, as Satan
speaks to Celestina out of the fire, he tells her of the "androgynous character of the first divinity" (p. 524).

So both the Divinity and Satan are hermaphroditic in their
origins, and the latter regains that nature as woman unites with
him. Furthermore, according to a beautiful tradition in the
Hebrew Zohar, heard by Ludovico, each human is created as a
male-female being by God, who then separates that being into
two to be born onto earth. If each lives a life in harmony with
God, they will find one another and be reunited. Seemingly
underlying this type of thought is the concept that unity can
grow only out of some kind of union of male and female
elements. This may symbolize either the fertility-producing
union of heaven and earth, or the periodic union of sun and
moon. At the opening of *Terra nostra* there is an interplay of the
phrases "sun king" and "moon queen" (p. 11).

Both are in view as Polo Febo and Celestina unite in the
last seconds of the millennium. The act has been anticipated in
many ways throughout the text. In the doctrine of the
Adamites, the essence of which becomes reality with the advent
of the Third Age, there is a desire to transform "each carnal
coupling into a redeeming communion" (p. 87). "Communion" is
a word almost never uttered in these eight novels, as the theme
of the banquet that plays such a prominent role in *The Odyssey*
is either absent or parodied, and no other form of communion
functions any better. As the Pilgrim awakens on the beach to be

216

taken to the palace, he thinks that Celestina, dressed as a page, "was . . . a new hermaphroditic figure" (p. 102), which she will be at their final meeting. His anticipatory union with the Butterfly Lady in the jungle, which he learns is only to be fulfilled entirely when their youth coincides once more, recalls the existence of an androgynous figure of Mexican mythology known as Gucumatz.

Polo Febo has come to this experience by way of two violent encounters with the forces of nonbeing. In this case the term is preferable to "death" because Guzmán and the Mexican bureaucrat, while they have brought death to the New World, have first drained the quality of life from it. The Pilgrim is last seen in Spain in a scene in which he has been released by Guzmán so that the latter may make a sport of hunting him as if he were a deer. In the final scenes the Pilgrim's arm is partially torn off by one of the hounds, and as he struggles to gain the waters of rebirth the falcon—which has come to symbolize both El Señor and Guzmán in their war against life—finishes tearing it off. According to the image in Valerio Camillo's theater, this is equivalent to the eating of the fire-bearer Prometheus' liver. The Pilgrim manages to drown the falcon as he himself drowns, so that the struggle between Being and nothingness in Spain ends inconclusively. As the narrator says, "In the obscured heaven you seek the light of your star, Venus, the sailor's guide, and in the depth of the sea, St. Elmo's fire, flame of inseparable brothers" (p. 650).

In Mexico at the end of the twentieth century the hero is seen as a guerrilla in Yucatán, the source of the nation's spiritual life, in a last stand against the forces of "sphere of influence" politics in the form of a North American takeover. His brother has invited the North Americans to salvage a seemingly hopeless situation. The Smoking Mirror is now a television monitor in his office, and the scissors have now become the single blade of a letter opener with which Pilgrim, in the role of Quetzalcóatl once more, again slays his negative counterpart. The blade is single perhaps because with this act he will return to absolute primordial unity as the three brothers have become one to unite with the goddess.

The battle between life and death reaches its climax as

several times and places coincide in a single instant in Paris at the end of the year 1999. Thousands of babies are born, but they and their parents are taken directly to the place where mankind is being systematically eliminated. At the end, when Polo Febo feels only he is left, Celestina appears and insists that they make love before midnight. He fails to understand, for the continuity of memory is borne on her lips, and she must communicate it to him. As she enters he recalls the words "I will sing of the sun" (p. 773). Maclagan says, "In the most recent of the Hopi cosmogonic myths, after Spider-Woman has created the First Twins, she creates all the forms of life on earth, including men, and animates them by covering them and singing the Creation Song over them" (*Creation Myths,* p. 30). That is a reversal of the situation here, as the song to Phoebus Apollo leads to the formation of the androgyne who is primordial unity, the first being of the new creation. On the first morning of the millennium and of the Third Age of Mankind, "a cold sun shone" (p. 778). The date is January 1, 2000, near enough to December 25, birthday of the sun in Mithraism. We have passed from the novel whose hero bears the name of the losing brother of Roman history, through *Tres tristes tigres,* which ends in silence on the last night of the year, to one in which all that is sought in the other novels is fulfilled on one St. Sylvester's Eve.

The question that remains is what sort of reality the reader is left with. Fuentes deliberately removes the most important events of his tale several levels away from the one on which the reader lives. The Pilgrim's voyage to the New World "was dreamed by a dreamed youth" (p. 597), and even within those two dreams he wonders if he truly arrived on land or only dreamed the adventures within the whirlpool. Or the experiences beyond his taking the old man's place in the basket of pearls may have been dreamed by him there, and there are dreams even within those dreams. Yet having led his reader to such dizzying heights of total fictionality, Fuentes offers the fact that (1) the mask appears on the beach (although not in the possession of the right youth); (2) a shriveled body in a basket of pearls turns up in twentieth-century Yucatán; and (3) Polo Febo, who believes he only read the totality of the rest of the

218

work, appears with one arm missing, and Celestina informs him that he lived it in reality. The point in all this is that reality is constructed by the individual out of the raw materials of that individual's observations. As Charles Olson states it, "We have our picture of the world and that's the creation" (quoted in Maclagan, p. 90). In *Terra nostra*, then, it becomes a battle of wills over whose vision of reality will prevail, and presumably El Señor would be disturbed over the publication of the novel, believing as he does that only what is written is real.

Fuentes is not averse to using Shakespeare's technique of placing key truths in the mouths of fools and lunatics. The Mad Lady says, "One must force reality, subject it to one's imagination, extend it beyond its ridiculous limits" (p. 70). El Señor, while resisting her mad trickster-desire to remove the barriers, nevertheless adopts her technique when he decrees that the New World does not exist. It becomes a reality only because millions of other wills decree that it must. One of the novel's refrains is that what is thought is, and what is, is thought, so that Valerio Camillo's theater serves as a practical device to recombine times, places, and events in such a way that a more desirable outcome for history may be achieved. For him the most absolute memory is the memory of what could have been—which would seem to be a key to the composition of this novel.

The reader may have a faint suspicion at this juncture that Jorge Luis Borges' "El jardín de senderos que se bifurcan" has nested in the text, and Borges does seem to be speaking in the opening words of the book as well: "Incredible the first animal who dreamt of another animal," for that recalls his story "Los ruines circulares." Both he and Fuentes are engaging the epistemological questions which are being raised so insistently in the twentieth century. Whereas Borges enjoys playing with the concepts involved, Fuentes takes full advantage of them to create a cosmos of desire, conceived in the imagination and brought into existence by the will.

The text purports to be the work of two narrators, for, just as El Señor believes only in what is written, the Chronicler "only believed in the poetic reality of what he had written," in a struggle to impose "his invented words as the only valid reality" (p. 238). The old Jewish scholar tells Ludovico, "There is no word that is not the bearer of imminent renovation" (p. 538). Writing this book, then, is not so much an exercise in entertainment as an attempt at re-creating the world by the Word. As Don Juan and Inés leave for the New World with Guzmán, the painter Julián tells the Chronicler Miguel, "Up to now . . . that is what I know" (p. 652). So the creator of the subversive painting that forces Christ to be viewed in a new context of time and space is also the narrator of the tale as a whole up to the departure. Then it is the task of Don Miguel, Fuentes' version of Cervantes, to complete the story. Julian, upon concluding, has warned his hearers not to "hold any faith in the simple and deceitful chronologies that are written about this epoch in an attempt to establish the logic of a perishable and linear history; true history is circular and eternal" (p. 652). Julián wants the Chronicler to complete "this novella" (p. 655), and he does so, writing it as he works simultaneously on the book about the mad knight aided by one of the youths, who, as the first hero to know himself read, is forced to create himself in his own imagination. The knight begins to conquer reality by a mad reading of himself, and this in turn transforms the world into the world of his book. The Chronicler says, "I shall create an open book where the reader will know he is read and the author will know he is written" (p. 669), which he gives us to understand is the way in which this book will be completed.

It should be noted in passing that Fuentes can be a very careful technician, so that in the portion ostensibly written by Cervantes that author's style is occasionally employed, as for example in his description of El Señor's dining surrounded by the corpses of a number of saints, a very quixotic act: "In these and other delightful Christian conversations was spent the dinner" (p. 703).

The author seemingly intends his novel to serve as something of a culmination of the quest embodied in the Spanish American novel of the twentieth century, the book in which all the obstacles against which Oliveira, Colonel Aureliano Buendía, and Pantaleón Pantoja have struggled in vain might finally be overcome. Gabriel García Márquez has said, "I believe that what we are composing . . . is just one novel,"[8] and

Fuentes has repeatedly stated the same opinion. If creation is always by the word in one sense or another—the world as the script of a divine utterance—and the complex of words known as the novel represents the experience of the people, perhaps some renewal is at hand. If in *Terra nostra* the reader knows he is read, that must mean that the only way in which renewal can be accomplished in a world in which nonbeing threatens to predominate is by the sheer force of human will to bring the desired cosmos into existence. Ultimately it is the reader who is challenged to be the hero.

X

Conclusion

It may be that the monomyth can be created and sustained only by a truly primitive mentality. *The Odyssey* may already be impossible in the age of Socrates, an analytical age in which the gods were believed in but things did not always work out as they should. Alcibiades certainly had the supreme incarnation of the Wise Old Man archetype as his teacher, but he became a traitor rather than a hero, and Socrates was put to death for his pains, even while Alexander the Great, another pupil in that great philosophical tradition, molded his career according to the monomyth pattern. One is not allowed to become too analytical in the presence of the hero story, for, powerful as it is, it is fragile. Plato, even while using myths to illustrate some of his points, dismissed them as old wives' tales, and the label has stuck through the centuries to our own day. Plato wanted no poets in his Republic, for a poet, whose title means "maker" or "creator," tends to live in a world of his own fabrication. Thus, poets are unfit to govern the other world, that of Euclid, Pythagoras, and Pericles, the world of solid facts. What, then, is the reader to make of Fuentes, Mexican ambassador to France, who creates a whole new world out of words and carefully bypasses the Greece of Pericles in the pedagogical travels of Ludovico and his heroes?

The fact is that there is little of interest for this new *Terra nostra* in classical Greece, because the latter has no place for a truly optimistic vision of the hero. In the Age of Pericles, heroes appeared on stage, but not in the context of their astounding successes. Oedipus is a great hero in renewing his cosmos by overcoming the dreaded Sphinx, but only the disasters that came later were viewed on stage by the Greeks of 450 B.C. Their *Oedipus the King* begins in the midst of the pollution of their society by its erstwhile hero, just before he becomes the equivalent of the sacrificial goat offered to Dionysus. Their focus is on entropy, not any cosmogonic process, on chaos rather than cosmos, a goat-man rather than the proud surrogate of the sun. To be sure, the catharsis experience prepares the audience for a new temporal cycle, but the renewal itself is not stressed.

In the solar myth, rationality must always be preserved, lest a lunar capriciousness prevail once more and lunatics with a penchant for human sacrifice control society. *Pantaleón y las visitadoras* is not the only Spanish American novel in which this occurs. Demetrio Aguilera Malta's *Siete lunas y siete serpientes* has the devouring, castrating White Goddess running amok in the Ecuadorian jungle with no untainted Logos-figure to check her. There must be rationality, then, but its central purpose is eventually to unite with the relational component of the universe. Not coincidentally, Odysseus' special protector is Athena, a relational being born of the Logos principle in the supreme god Zeus. She is Mount Olympus' embodiment of civilization, which in the mortal world consists of persons bound together voluntarily to make reasonable decisions together and to defend their way of life when necessary. Only when Odysseus engages in aggressive, bloody warfare in slaughtering the Suitors—necessary as that may be—does the pure Logos-figure Apollo became visibly active. Even then Penelope is set to weaving, for the moon must weave the destiny of Odysseus and his foes; or, stated another way, Logos dare not do his work without the active aid of Eros. If he does, we have another *Pedro Páramo*.

Furthermore, rationality does not imply rationalism. The age that attempts to force reality into rigidly rationalistic structures tends to be cold and pessimistic. Scholars speak of "the cold winds of Rationalism" that swept across Europe in the eighteenth century, when life was beautiful for those who could afford it but behavior was according to rigidly prescribed norms. Without the warmth of Eros as the principle of creative relationships, even the solar-related reason has no warmth. But it is difficult to live where Eros is too powerful and wields the bloody knife of human sacrifice, as in the Mexico portrayed by Fuentes, where the successive suns have only a weak and tenuous existence, and thousands of victims must be slaughtered to give them strength. "Mexico," in fact, is taken to mean "land of the navel of the moon," and at the center of that navel that ordinarily symbolizes the beginnings of life is the gory sacrificial pyramid.

The truth must lie somewhere between Tollan and Versailles, the latter the center of the land of "le Roi Soleil" during the Age of Reason. The modern novel fairly begs for a healthy balance and fruitful union between masculine and feminine forces. We have considered *Cien años de soledad*, in which Eros never has a genuine opportunity to express itself, and the vacuum created by its absence, which García Márquez calls solitude, ruins any chance for renewal. We have also seen Pantaleón's experiment with the side of Eros involving prostitution, which is to say, Eros attacked and exploited by the aggressive side of Logos, without any activation of the reasonable side of the one or the relational side of the other. Prostitution is nonbeing's substitute for the sacred marriage in a world of inverted values, and the result, not surprisingly, is human sacrifice.

As Logos-dependence grows in Western culture, the hero moves steadily down Northrop Frye's scale from divine to ironic, in large measure because he is unable to engage properly in what Campbell terms that final adventure, the marriage to the Queen Goddess of the world. Ironically, he hits his nadir in Spain's Golden Age, in the form of the anti-hero of the picaresque novel, whose call to adventure is issued by his belly. The *pícaro's* relationships with women tend to be tenuous at best. The joker in the deck, literally, is the ironic hero known as Trickster, and the great zero that he traces as he rides his Wheel of Fortune may be the one out of which creation emerges.

Many an ironic hero of literature has become successful in his or her influence on the reading public. The picaresque novels were written for this purpose, often with a lengthy sermon from the mouth of the reformed *pícaro* following each episode.

Cabrera Infante's Carrollian heroes too are ironic, but the book itself constitutes the raising of one of them from the dead by another. What we witness in part as we read the Spanish American novels of this century is the transformation of the ironic hero, the non-hero, gradually into a positive trickster. Cortázar's Oliveira, for example, becomes more and more oriented in this direction; his gazing up at the big tent pole at the center of the sky is a fitting addition to Trickster's musings. He even resembles the Oglalas' Iktomi, the spider, as he weaves himself a crazy mandala to avoid being killed by his brother.

The process culminates in Fuentes' Juan Agrippa, playing the role of the devil in Felipe's blasphemous theocracy by taking on the identity of the Trickster of Seville. Part Christ, part Satan, part king, part slave, he is Proteus the shape-shifter as the *massa confusa* out of which the desire of humanity will finally fashion a new being. Mankind has gone through several stages in its vision of the way in which a person gains identity. The pre-modern feels that one becomes "real" by reliving the hero's archetypal deeds. From the Renaissance on one breaks new ground and becomes real by being the first to accomplish something important. Now in the modern world Erdosain and others feel they are "being lived" by forces beyond their control or even their understanding. Finally, Fuentes' heroes are moved and manipulated, are lived, but by a modified version of the archetype.

It seems, then, that there is a new primitivism, thrust upon us, paradoxically, by the very vanguard of scientific thinking. The pleasant surprise is that the new cosmos is orderly after all, but in a radically different way than that which had seemed so reasonable to Isaac Newton and his contemporaries. Probably Sir James Jeans best expressed the radical change early in the century when he said, "The stream of knowledge is heading towards a non-mechanical reality; the universe begins to look more like a great thought than like a great machine."[1] With that prophetic statement as backdrop perhaps we should again consider the much more recent statement of John Wheeler, to the effect that physical reality consists of nothing more solid than a combination of our observations and our imagination. Fuentes' attempt to present a world forced into better channels by the will of millions of the oppressed represents an attempt to inform the public that the directions taken by mankind in the future really do depend upon human will.

Where in this unsettling mass of revelations is the portal to be entered by the hero in search of the realm of Being? Furthermore, where does Being fit into a universe ruled by the laws of probability? Apparently the task of mankind now is to write a new cosmogony while keeping the new cosmology in mind. If thought is strictly dependent upon language, then language is a necessary component in the formulation of reality by one's imagination out of the raw material of one's observations, and once again language is the basis of creation. In *Gravity's Rainbow* Thomas Pynchon has taken careful note of what he calls the alphabetical nature of molecules, and Guillermo Cabrera Infante has provided the reader with a linguistic trickster who began to change the names of things, thus beginning to put the fragments of the broken cosmos back together. Where there is no creative language there is no umbilical connection to the womb of the universe. *Pedro Páramo* is the only one of these eight novels that does not openly stress the importance of language, and, having razed what Heidegger calls the House of Being, it languishes in murmurs.

In Carlos Fuentes' creation by the Word, the principle is that what is thought is, and what is is thought. His villain, El Señor, is wounded by his own reality principle, for, believing that only what is *written* is real, he cannot deny the existence of a Third Age of Mankind, for it has been written by his own Chronicler and court painter within the very walls of the necropolis. *Terra nostra* is a cosmos of the imagination plastered between the pillars of observation, and that is reality. Taken as a whole, these eight novels, and that larger group of which they are representative, may be viewed as the raw materials out of which Fuentes has attempted to construct a highly ambitious cosmos.

The human race has always had a heroic cast in its willingness and ability to work with the materials at hand, even the fragments of a shattered cosmos. It remains to be seen what will come next in the highly active and creative novel of Latin America.

Notes

Chapter I. Introduction

1. Quoted in Jaime Alazraki, *Versiones, inversiones, reversiones*, p. 19. Translation mine.

2. Lord Raglan, *The Hero: A Study in Tradition, Myth and Drama*, pp. 179-80.

Chapter II. Roberto Arlt, *Los siete locos* (Seven Madmen)

1. Roberto Arlt, *Los siete locos*, p. 29. Translations are mine. Subsequent references will be noted in the text.

2. Paul Radin, *The Trickster*, p. 91.

3. Quoted by Kerényi in Radin, pp. 184-85.

4. Theodore H. Gaster, *Myth, Legend and Custom in the Old Testament*, I, 306-7. Biblical quotations are from the *New International Version* (Grand Rapids: Zoudervan Bible Publishers, 1978). Further references will be indicated in the text as *"NIV."*

5. "Stars: Where Life Begins," *Time*, Dec. 27, 1976, p. 29.

6. *The True Believer*, p. 156.

7. *Ultimo round*, p. 48.

8. *The Hero*, p. 203.

9. Heyemeyohsts Storm, *Seven Arrows*, pp. 343-44.

Chapter III. *Los pasos perdidos* (The Lost Steps)

1. Quoted in Mircea Eliade, *The Myth of the Eternal Return*, p. 121.

2. Paul Radin, *The Trickster*, p. 101.

3. Alejo Carpentier, Los pasos perdidos, p. 78. Translations are mine. Subsequent references will be noted in the text.

4. David Maclagan, *Creation Myths*, p. 25.

5. "Archetypal Patterns in Four Novels of Alejo Carpentier," p. 131.

6. Sir William Smith, *Smaller Classical Dictionary*, p. 270.

7. *The Hero*, p. 258.

8. Quoted in P. L. Travers, "The World of the Hero," *Parabola* 1, no. 1 (Winter 1976), p. 42.

9. Quoted in Dorothy Norman, *The Hero*, p. 81.

Chapter IV. Juan Rulfo, *Pedro Páramo*

1. Margaret Nancy Lester, "The Function of the Journey-and-Return Story in Representative Latin American Novels," doctoral dissertation, University of Colorado, 1973, p. 88.

2. Adrian Thatcher, *The Ontology of Paul Tillich*, p. 44.

3. Quoted in José C. González Boixo, *Claves narratives de Juan Rulfo*, p. 101.

4. Juan Rulfo, *Pedro Páramo*, p. 16. Translations are mine. Subsequent references will be noted in the text.

5. Sir William Smith, *Smaller Classical Dictionary*, p. 136.

6. Luis Harss and Barbara Dohmann, *Into the Mainstream*, p. 250.

Chapter V. Julio Cortázar, *Rayuela* (*Hopscotch*)

1. David Maclagan, *Creation Myths*, p. 7.

2. Shambaracharya, quoted in Dorothy Norman, *The Hero*, p. xiv.

3. *The Myth of the Birth of the Hero*, p. 68.

4. Radin, *The Trickster*, p. 184.

5. Julio Cortázar, *Rayuela*, p. 13. Subsequent references will be noted in the text. Translations are mine.

6. *The Myth of the Eternal Return*, p. 64.

7. "The Hodja," *Parabola* 1, no. 4, p. 86.

8. Quoted in Joel Greenberg, "Einstein: The Gourmet of Creativity," *Science News* 115 (March 31, 1979), p. 217.

9. "Through the Looking-Glass: Aspects of Cortázar's Epiphanies of Reality," *Bulletin of Hispanic Studies* 54 (1977), p. 133.

10. *Julio Cortázar*, p. 106.

11. *The Hero with a Thousand Faces*, p. 169.

12. Eugene R. Skinner, review of *Cobra*, *Hispania* 57 (Sept. 1974), p. 606.

Chapter VI. Gabriel García Márquez, *Cien años de soledad* (*One Hundred Years of Solitude*)

1. Information gained in the coastal region of Colombia.

2. Robert Lewis Sims, *The Evolution of Myth in García Márquez*, p. 113.

3. Gabriel García Márquez, *Cien años de soledad*, p. 97. Translations are mine. Subsequent references will be noted in the text.

4. Germán de Granda, "Un afortunado fitónimo bantú: Macondo," *Thesaurus* 26, no. 3 (Sept.-Dec. 1971), pp. 485-94.

5. *The Masks of God: Oriental Mythology*, p. 298.

6. Information of Ms. Dominga Bolaño, Cartagena, Colombia.

7. *The White Goddess*, p. 179.

8. Sir William Smith, *Smaller Classical Dictionary*, p. 24.

9. P. 375.

10. Quoted by Jaime Mejía in *Los claves del mito en Gabriel García Márquez*, p. 71.

11. "The Function of the Journey-and-Return Story," p. 217.

12. Quoted in Lester, p. 219.

13. *The Masks of God: Occidental Mythology*, p. 113.

Chapter VII. Guillermo Cabrera Infante, *Tres tristes tigres* (*Three Trapped Tigers*)

1. *La nueva novela hispanoamericana*, pp. 19-20.

2. Robert Henri Cousineau, *Humanism and Ethics*, p. 29.

3. *Tres tristes tigres*, p. 9. Translations are mine. Subsequent references will be noted in the text.

4. *The Myth of the Eternal Return*, p. 85.

5. R. D. Laing, in *The Divided Self*, writes of a patient whose " 'schizophrenic' role was the only refuge he knew from being entirely engulfed by the woman who was inside him, and always seemed to be coming out of him," p. 73.

6. Interview with Emir Rodríguez Monegal, "Las fuentes de la narración," *Mundo Nuevo* 25 (July 1968), p. 57.

7. See my "Mirrors and Metamorphosis: Lewis Carroll's Presence in *Tres tristes tigres*," *Hispania* 62 (May-Sept. 1979), pp. 297-303.

8. Lewis Carroll, *The Annotated Alice*, ed. Martin Gardner, pp. 13-14.

9. *Time: Rhythm and Repose*, p. 13.

10. *The Masks of God: Primitive Mythology*, p. 454.

11. An alternative version of her burial appears as "Meta-final" in *Alacrán Azul* 1, no. 1 (1970), p. 18.

12. *The Courage to Be*, p. 177.

13. "Cantando las 40," supplement to *Imagen* 42 (February 1-15, 1969), n. pag.

14. *The White Goddess*, p. 461.

15. "The World of the Hero," *Parabola* 1, no. 1 (Winter 1976), p. 42.

Chapter VIII. Mario Vargas Llosa, *Pantaleón y las visitadoras* (*Captain Pantoja and the Special Service*)

1. Lord Raglan, *The Hero*, pp. 179-80.

2. Mario Vargas Llosa, *Pantaleón y las visitadoras*, p. 217. Quotations are from the translation by Gregory Kolovakos and Ronald Christ, *Captain Pantoja and the Special Service;* this reference p. 168. Further references will be noted in the text.

3. *The Ontology of Paul Tillich*, p. 66.

4. *The Hero with a Thousand Faces*, p. 108.

5. Paul Radin, *The Trickster*, p. 184.

6. Sir William Smith, *Smaller Classical Dictionary*, p. 210.

7. "Mario Vargas Llosa: The Necessary Scapegoat," *Mario Vargas Llosa: A Collection of Critical Essays*, p. 189.

Chapter IX. Carlos Fuentes, *Terra nostra*

1. *Myth and Reality*, p. 140.

2. Carlos Fuentes, *Terra nostra*, p. 740. Quotations are from the translation by Margaret Sayers Peden; this quote p. 735. Subsequent references will be noted in the text.

3. Marie-Louise von Franz, *Time: Rhythm and Repose*, p. 70.

4. See "Adamites (Adamiani)," *The New Schaff-Herzog Encyclopedia of Religious Knowledge*, I, 37-38.

5. *The Hero and the King*, p. 7.

6. David Adams Leeming, "The World of the Hero," *Parabola* 1, no. 1 (Winter 1976), p. 21.

7. *Creation Myths*, p. 42.

8. Quoted in Margaret Nancy Lester, "The Function of the Journey-and-Return Story," p. 106.

Chapter X. Conclusion

1 . Quoted in Arthur Koestler, *The Roots of Coincidence*, p. 58.

Bibliography

Primary Sources

Arlt, Roberto. *Los siete locos*. Buenos Aires: Editorial Losada, 1958. Translation—*Seven Madmen*. Translated by Naomi Lindstrom. Boston: David R. Godine Publishing Co., to appear 1984.

Cabrera Infante, Guillermo. "Meta-final." *Alacráun Azul* 1, no. 1 (1970), pp. 18-22.

_____. "Cantando las 40." Supplement to *Imagen* 42 (February 1-15, 1969), n. pag.

_____. *Tres tristes tigres*. Barcelona: Seix Barral, 1965. Translation: *Three Trapped Tigers*. Translated by Donald Gardner and Suzanne Jill Levine in collaboration with the author. New York: Harper and Row, 1971.

Carpentier, Alejo. *Concierto barroco*. Mexico City, Buenos Aires and Madrid: Siglo Veintiuno Editores, 1974.

_____. *Ecué-Yamba-O*. Buenos Aires: Editorial Xanadu, 1968.

_____. *Los pasos perdidos*. Mexico City: Compañía General de Ediciones, 1959. Translation: *The Lost Steps*. Translated by Harriet de Onís. New York: Knopf, 1956.

Cortázar, Julio. *Rayuela*. Buenos Aires: Editorial Sudamericana, 1963. Translation: *Hopscotch*. Translated by Gregory Rabassa. New York: Random House, 1966.

_____. *Ultimo round*. Mexico City: Siglo Veintiuno Editores, 1970.

Fuentes, Carlos, *Terra nostra*. Mexico City: Joaquín Mortiz, 1975. Translation: *Terra Nostra*. Translated by Margaret Sayers Peden. New York: Farrar, Straus and Giroux, 1976.

García Márquez, Gabriel. *Cien años de soledad*. Buenos Aires: Editorial Sudamericana, 1967. Translation: *One Hundred Years of Solitude*. Translated by Gregory Rabassa. New York and Evanston: Harper and Row, 1970.

Lezama Lima, José. *Paradiso*. Mexico City: Biblioteca Era, 1968. Translation: *Paradiso*. Translated by Gregory Rabassa. New York: Farrar, Straus and Giroux, 1974.

Rulfo, Juan. *Pedro Páramo*. Mexico City: Fondo de Cultura Económica, 1955. Translation: *Pedro Páramo*. Translated by Lysander Kemp. New York: Grove Press, 1959.

Vargas Llosa, Mario. *Pantaleón y las visitadoras*. Barcelona: Seix Barral, 1973. Translation: *Captain Pantoja and the Special Service*. Translated by Gregory Kolovakos and Ronald Christ. New York: Harper and Row, 1978.

Secondary Sources

Alazraki, Jaime. *Versiones, inversiones, reversiones: El espejo como modelo estructural del relato en los cuentos de Borges*. Madrid: Editorial Gredos, 1977.

Alegría, Fernando. *Historia de la novela hispanoamericana*. Mexico City: Ediciones de Andrea, 1974.

Arnau, Carmen. *El mundo mítico de Gabriel García Márquez*. Barcelona: Ediciones Peninsular, 1971.

Bettelheim, Bruno. The Uses of Enchantment: The Meaning and Importance of Fairy Tales. New York: Alfred A. Knopf, 1976.

Bruns, J. Edgar. *God as Woman, Woman as God*. New York, Paramus and Toronto: Paulist Press, 1973.

Brushwood, John S. *Genteel Barbarism: New Readings of Nineteenth-Century Spanish American Novels*. Lincoln and London: University of Missouri, 1981.

_____. *Mexico in its Novel: A Nation's Search for Identity*. Austin and London: University of Texas, 1966.

_____. *The Spanish American Novel: A Twentieth-Century Survey*. Austin and London: University of Texas, 1975.

Campbell, Joseph. *The Hero with a Thousand Faces*. Cleveland and New York: World Publishing Co., 1956.

_____. *The Masks of God*. New York: Viking Press. *Primitive Mythology*, 1959; *Oriental Mythology*, 1962; *Creative Mythology*, 1968; *Occidental Mythology*, 1970.

Cano Gaviria, Ricardo. *El buitre y el Ave Fénix: Conversaciones con Mario Vargas Llosa*. Barcelona: Editorial Anagrama, 1972.

Carpentier, Alejo. *Tientos y diferencias*. Montevideo: ARCA Editorial, 1967.

Carroll, Lewis. *The Annotated Alice.* Edited by Martin Gardner. New York: Bramhall House, 1960.

Cirlot, J. E. *A Dictionary of Symbols.* Trans. Jack Sage. New York: Philosophical Library, 1962.

Cousineau, Robert Henri. *Humanism and Ethics: An Introduction to Heidegger's Letter on Humanism.* Louvain and Paris: Neuwelaerts, 1972.

Díez del Corral, Luis. *La función del mito clásico en la literatura contemporánea.* Madrid: Editorial Gredos, 1957.

Donoso, José. *The Boom in Spanish American Literature: A Personal History.* New York: Center for Inter-American Relations, 1977.

Dorfman, Ariel. *Imaginación y violencia en América.* Santiago de Chile: Editorial Universitaria, 1970.

Durán, Gloria. *The Archetypes of Carlos Fuentes: From Witch to Androgyne.* Hamden, Conn.: Archon Books, 1980.

Eliade, Mircea. *Myth and Reality.* New York and Evanston: Harper and Row, 1963.

_____. *The Myth of the Eternal Return, or Cosmos and History.* Translated by Willard R. Trask. Princeton: Princeton University Press, 1954.

_____. *The Two and the One.* Trans. J. M. Cohen. New York and Evanston: Harper, 1969.

Eyzaguirre, Luis B. *El héroe en la novela hispanoamericana del siglo XX.* Santiago de Chile: Editorial Universitaria, 1973.

Frazer, Sir James George. *The New Golden Bough.* Ed. Theodore H. Gaster. New York: Mentor Books, 1964.

Freeman, George Ronald. *Paradise and Fall in Rulfo's Pedro Páramo: Archetype and Structural Unity.* Cuernavaca: Centro Intercultural de Documentación, 1970.

Frye, Northrop. *Anatomy of Criticism.* Princeton: Princeton University Press, 1957.

Fuentes, Carlos. *La nueva novela hispanoamericana.* Mexico City: Joaquín Mortiz, 1969.

Gallagher, D. P. *Modern Latin American Literature.* London, Oxford, and New York: Oxford University, 1973.

Gaster, Theodore H. *Myth, Legend and Custom in the Old Testament.* Two volumes. New York: Harper and Row, 1969.

_____. *The Oldest Stories in the World.* Boston: Beacon Press, 1958.

Giacomán, Helmy F. and José Miguel Oviedo. *Homenaje a Mario Vargas Llosa.* New York: Las Américas Publishing Co., 1971.

González Boixo, José C., ed. *Claves narrativas de Juan Rulfo.* León (?): Colegio Universitario de León, 1980.

González Echevarría, Roberto. *Alejo Carpentier: The Pilgrim at Home.* Ithaca and London: Cornell University Press, 1977.

Granda, Germán de. "Un afortunado fitónimo bantú: Macondo." *Thesaurus* (Boletín del Instituto Caro y Cuervo, Bogotá) 26, no. 3 (Sept.-Dec. 1971), pp. 485-94.

Graves, Robert. *The White Goddess.* New York: Farrar, Straus and Giroux, 1966.

Greenberg, Joel. "Einstein: The Gourmet of Creativity." *Science News* 115 (March 31, 1979), pp. 216-17.

Guerra-Cunningham, Lucía. "La aventura del héroe como representante de la visión del mundo en *Alsino* de Pedro Prado." *Hispania* 66, no. 1 (March 1983), pp. 32-39.

Guibert, Rita. *Seven Voices.* Trans. Frances Partridge. New York: Alfred A. Knopf, 1973.

Harding, M. Esther. *Woman's Mysteries Ancient and Modern: A Psychological Interpretation of the Feminine Principle as Portrayed in Myth, Story and Dreams.* New York: G. P. Putnam's Sons, 1971.

Harss, Luis and Barbara Dohmann. *Into the Mainstream: Conversations with Latin American Writers.* New York: Harper and Row, 1967.

Heisenberg, Werner. *Natural Law and the Structure of Matter.* London: Rebel Press, 1970.

_____. *Physics and Beyond: Encounters and Conversations.* Translated by Arnold J. Pomerans. New York, Evanston, and London: Harper and Row, 1971.

Hoffer, Eric. *The True Believer.* New York: Time, Inc., 1963.

Huizinga, Johan. *Homo Ludens: A Study of the Play Element in Culture.* Boston: Beacon Press, 1955.

Jara, René and Jaime Mejía. *Las claves del mito en Gabriel García Márquez.* Valparaíso: Ediciones Universitarias de Valparaíso, 1972.

Jaynes, Julian. *The Origin of Consciousness in the Breakdown of the Bicameral Mind.* Boston: Houghton Mifflin, 1976.

Jiménez, Reynaldo L. *Guillermo Cabrera Infante y Tres tristes tigres.* Miami: Ediciones Universal, 1976.

Jitrik, Noé. *El no existente caballero: La idea de personaje y su evolución en la narrativa hispanoamericana.* Buenos Aires: Asociación Editorial La Aurora, 1975.

Jung, Carl G. *Man and His Symbols*. Garden City: Doubleday and Co., 1964.

_____. *Modern Man in Search of a Soul*. Translated by W. S. Dell and Cary F. Baynes. New York: Harcourt, 1933.

_____. *Two Essays in Analytical Psychology*. London: Routledge and Kegan Paul, 1953.

Koestler, Arthur. *The Roots of Coincidence*. New York: Vintage Press, 1973.

Laing, R. D. *The Divided Self: An Existential Study in Sanity and Madness*. Harmondsworth, England: Penguin, 1960.

Landeira Coracides, Carmen J. "El mito en tres metanovelas latinoamericanas." Dissertation, Arizona State University, 1972.

Leeming, David Adams. "The Hodja." *Parabola* 4, no. 1 (February 1979), pp. 84-89. This entire issue deals with the trickster-figure.

Lester, Margaret Nancy. "The Function of the Journey-and-Return Story in Representative Latin American Novels." Dissertation, University of Colorado, 1973.

Levi-Strauss, Claude. *The Savage Mind*. Chicago: University of Chicago Press, 1966.

Levy, Isaac Jack and Juan Loveluck, eds. *Simposio Carlos Fuentes: Actas*. Columbia: University of South Carolina Press, 1980.

Maclagan, David, *Creation Myths: Man's Introduction to the World*. London: Thames and Hudson, 1977.

Márquez Rodríguez, Alexis. *La obra narrativa de Alejo Carpentier*. Caracas: Universidad Central de Venezuela, 1970.

Martínez, Olga Aída. "Héroes en la novelística hispanoamericana del siglo XX." Chapter in *Figuras literarias hispanoamericanas*. Mexico City: R. Costa-Amic, 1972.

Martínez, Pedro Simón, ed. *Sobre García Márquez*. Montevideo: Biblioteca de Marcha, 1971.

Mejía Duque, Jaime. *Mito y realidad en Gabriel García Márquez*. Bogotá: Editorial La Oveja Negra, n.d.

Menton, Seymour. *La narrativa de la Revolución cubana*. Madrid: Playor, 1978.

Müller-Burgh, Klaus. *Alejo Carpentier: Estudio biográfico-crítico*. New York: Casa de las Américas, 1972.

"Mundos de Juan Rulfo, Los." Special issue of *Inti: Revista de Literatura Hispánica*. Nos. 13-14 (Spring-Fall 1981).

New Larousse Encyclopedia of Mythology. London, New York, Sydney, and Toronto: Hamlyn, 1959.

New Schaff-Herzog Encyclopedia of Religious Knowledge. Grand Rapids: Baker Book House, 1977.

Norman, Dorothy, *The Hero: Myth/Image/Symbol.* New York and Cleveland: World Publishing Co., 1969.

Nueva Narrativa Hispanoamericana. Journal published from January 1971 to January 1974.

Ortega, Julio. *Guillermo Cabrera Infante.* Madrid: Editorial Fundamentos, 1974.

_____. *Relato de la Utopía: Notas sobre narrativa cubana de la Revolución.* Barcelona: La Gaya Ciencia, 1973.

Palermo, Zulma *et al. Historia y mito en la obra de Alejo Carpentier.* Buenos Aires: Fernando García Cambeiro, 1972.

Paz, Octavio. *Corriente alterna.* Mexico City: Siglo XXI Editores, 1967.

Peden, Margaret Sayers. "The Destruction of Myth in *Cien años de soledad.* Dissertation, Ohio State University, 1972.

_____. "A Reader's Guide to *Terra nostra." Review* 31 (Jan.-April 1982), pp. 42-48.

Picón Garfield, Evelyn. *Julio Cortázar.* New York: Frederick Ungar Publishing Co., 1975.

Porrata, Francisco E. and Fausto Avendaño, eds. *Explicación de Cien años de soledad.* San José, Costa Rica: Editorial Texto, 1976.

Radin, Paul. *The Trickster: A Study in American Indian Mythology.* New York: Schocken Books, 1972.

Raglan, Lord. *The Hero: A Study in Tradition, Myth and Drama.* New York: Oxford University Press, 1937.

Rank, Otto. *The Myth of the Birth of the Hero: A Psychological Interpretation of Mythology.* Translated by F. Robbins and Smith Ely Jelliffe. New York: Robert Brunner, 1952.

Reedy, Daniel. "Through the Looking-Glass: Aspects of Cortázar's Epiphanies of Reality." *Bulletin of Hispanic Studies* 54 (1977), pp. 125-34.

Riggs, Denis W. "La presencia del mito en las novelas *Pedro Páramo y Cien años de soledad." Mérida: Revista de la Universidad de Yucatán* 18, no. 104 (1976), pp. 13-28.

Rodríguez Monegal, Emir. "Las fuentes de la narración." *Mundo Nuevo* 25 (July 1968), pp. 41-58.

Rossman, Charles and Alan Warren Friedman, eds. *Mario Vargas Llosa: A Collection of Critical Essays.* Austin and London: University of Texas Press, 1978.

Roy, Joaquín. *Julio Cortázar ante su sociedad.* Barcelona: Ediciones Península, 1974.

Sarduy, Severo. *Escrito sobre un cuerpo: Ensayos de crítica.* Buenos Aires: Editorial Sudamericana, 1969.

Seznec, J. *The Survival of the Pagan Gods.* New York: Harper, 1961.

Schwab, Gustav. *Gods and Heroes: Myths and Epics of Ancient Greece.* New York: Pantheon Books, 1946.

Siemens, William L. "Mirrors and Metamorphosis: Lewis Carroll's Presence in *Tres tristes tigres.*" *Hispania* 62 (May-Sept. 1979), pp. 297-303.

Sims, Robert Lewis. *The Evolution of Myth in Gabriel García Márquez: From La hojarasca to Cien años de soledad.* Miami: Ediciones Universal, 1981.

_____. "The Use of Myth in Claude Simon and Gabriel García Márquez." Dissertation, University of Wisconsin, 1973.

Skinner, Eugene R. "Archetypal Patterns in Four Novels of Alejo Carpentier." Dissertation, University of Kansas, 1968.

_____. Review of Severo Sarduy, *Cobra. Hispania* 57 (Sept. 1974), pp. 406-7.

Sommers, Joseph. *After the Storm: Landmarks of the Modern Mexican Novel.* Albuquerque: University of New Mexico Press, 1968.

Souza, Raymond D. *Major Cuban Novelists: Innovation and Tradition.* Columbia and London: University of Missouri Press, 1976.

Smith, Sir William. *Smaller Classical Dictionary.* New York: E. P. Dutton, 1958.

"Stars: Where Life Begins." *Time,* Dec. 27, 1976, pp. 29-33.

Storm, Heyemeyohsts. *Seven Arrows.* New York: Ballantine Books, 1972.

Thatcher, Adrian. *The Ontology of Paul Tillich.* Oxford: Oxford University Press, 1978.

Thompson, Stith. *The Folktale.* Berkeley, Los Angeles, and London: University of California Press, 1977.

Thomsen, Dietrick. "Is Modern Physics for Real?" *Science News* 109 (May 22, 1976), pp. 332-33.

Tillich, Paul. *The Courage to Be.* New Haven and London: Yale University Press, 1952.

Travers, P. L. "The World of the Hero." *Parabola* 1, no. 1 (Winter 1976), pp. 42-47. This entire issue is dedicated to the hero theme.

Vargas Llosa, Mario. *García Márquez: Historia de un deicidio.* Barcelona: Barral Editores, 1971.

Villegas, Juan. *La estructura mítica del héroe en la novela del siglo XX.* Barcelona: Editorial Planeta, 1973.

Von Franz, Marie Louise. *Time: Rhythm and Repose.* London: Thames and Hudson, 1978.

Wandenberg, Mercedes F. de. "El héroe novelesco en García Márquez." Chapter in *Lectura de García Márquez.* Manuel Corrales Pascual, ed. Quito: Centro de Publicaciones de la Pontífica Universidad Católica del Ecuador, 1975.

Wheelwright, Philip. *Metaphor and Reality.* Bloomington: Indiana University Press, 1962.

Williams, Raymond L. *La novela colombiana contemporánea.* Bogotá: Plaza y Janés, 1976.

Index

Aaron, 187
Abyss, 198
Achilles, 50
"Acoso, El," 35
Across the River and Into the Trees, 148
Actaeon, 125
Adam, 17, 55, 69, 169, 211
Adamites, 195, 200, 203, 208, 217
Adonis, 78
Afro-Cuban folklore, 145, 154, 168
Aguilera Malta, Demetrio, 224
Alchemy, 42, 116
Alcibiades, 223
Alexander the Great, 223
Alfonso X, The Wise, 204
Ammon, 67
Anaxarete, 125
Androgyne, 51, 176, 202, 207, 213, 216-19
Andromeda, 67
Angst, 13, 36
Anima, 124, 213
Antichrist, 110, 118, 167, 170
Antimatter, 160
Aphrodite, 78-79, 93, 212
Apocalypse, 15, 50, 52, 57, 75, 83, 123, 142, 151, 153, 156, 161, 163-64, 166, 171, 175, 182, 184-85, 192, 194, 203, 210
Apocalypse, The (New Testament), 6, 13, 24, 32, 43, 60, 62, 68, 75, 128, 129-30, 142-43, 163-67, 171, 197
Apollo, 40, 41, 177, 193, 224
Arcadia, 110, 122
Argives, 175
Argo Navis, 40, 41
Argonauts, 1
Aristotle, 199
Ark (of Noah), 185
Arlt, Roberto, 2, *12-34,* 75, 189
Armageddon, 194
Arnaldos, Count, 152
Artemis, 122, 125
Astrology, 19, 21, 40, 45-46, 101, 169, 200
Athaliah, 95
Athena, 16, 18, 84, 88, 195, 224
Atonement with the father, 40, 63
Attis, 111
Augustine, St., 57, 180
Augustus Caesar, 18
Aurelian (Roman Emperor), 117
Aztecs, 2, 213-14

Babel, Tower of, 106, 166, 167, 169
Babylon, 21, 75, 85, 128-30, 165-66
Bach, Johann Sebastian, 154
Bantu language, 112
Barrios, Eduardo, 12
Batista, Fulgencio, 140, 164, 167

241

Beckett, Samuel, 95
Beethoven, Ludwig van, 35, 40
Being, realm of, 23, 34, 36, 37, 42, 53, 61, 64, 73-77, 81, 101, 102, 108, 113, 124, 132, 136-37, 138, 155, 157, 165-66, 168, 172, 188-89, 190, 194, 197-99, 207, 218, 227
Beowulf, 6
Berenice, locks of, 40 41
Blake, William, 167
Bloom, Leopold, 86
Boar, 78, 196
Boon, 53, 64, 68, 71, 76, 77, 81, 92, 105, 115, 135, 139, 149, 161
Borges, Jorge Luis, 1, 220
Bosch, Hieronymus, 200, 209
Boustrophedon, 168
Breton, André, 59
Buddha, Gautama, 2, 82, 100, 111
Bull of Heaven, 3, 48
Buñuel, Luis, 68
Burlador de Sevilla, El, 201, 203

Cabrera Infante, Guillermo, 35, 138-72, 191, 226, 227
Caerdmon. See Cerridwen
Cain, 17
Calf, 79, 123
Call to adventure, 3, 21, 37, 41, 62, 63, 73, 74, 77, 114-15, 188, 211, 225
Call to adventure, refusal of, 63, 175, 195, 211
Calypso, 8, 47, 48, 58, 77, 89, 173, 175-76, 202
Campbell, Joseph, 15
Camus, Albert, 17
Captain Pantoja and the Special Service. See Pantaleón y las visitadoras
Carlotta, 198
Carpe diem, 166

Carpentier, Alejo, 35-61, 75, 84, 89, 106, 112, 123, 130, 160, 176
Carroll, Lewis, 149, 152-53, 161-62, 165, 171, 191, 226
Castor and Pollux, 209
Castrating female, 184, 224
Castro, Fidel, 156, 164, 167
Catharsis, 224
Centaur, 81, 162
Celestina, 202
Celestina, La, 203
Center, 36, 41, 57, 74, 76, 84, 87, 88, 91, 93, 94, 96, 98-101, 104-8, 111, 121, 132, 135-36, 139, 158, 198, 210
Cepheus, 67
Cerridwen (or Caerdmon), 128
Cervantes Saavedra, Miguel de, 7, 199, 221
Charles V, 195, 206
Charon, 81, 149
Charybdis, 211
Christ. See Jesus Christ
Cien años de soledad, 33, 66, 67, 77, 109-37, 138, 157, 189, 221, 225
Circe, 48, 58, 62, 125, 143, 176
City of God, 57
Cocteau, Jean, 181
Collective unconscious, 2
Communion. See Hospitality and communion
Communism, 20
Concierto barroco, 50
Contraries, 92, 153-54
Copernicus, 200
Cortázar, Julio, 23, 82-108, 124, 135, 226
Cosmogonic myth, 54
Costumbrismo, 10
Courtly love, 66
Crete, 104
Cronus, 62-63

Cruz, Sor Juana Inés de la, 201
Cumpleaños, 140
Cybele, 31

David, 5, 169
Dehumanization, 30
Delilah, 175, 182-83
Demeter, 78
Demetrius, 20
Devil, 112, 180, 194, 216, 226
Devouring female, 146, 174, 176, 182-83
Diaz, Porfirio, 2
Diderot, 90
Diomedes, 195
Dionysus, 51, 163, 177-80, 188, 224
Dogon tribe, 82
Don Juan Tenorio, 192-93, 201-2, 204, 210
Don Quixote, 4, 7, 8, 26, 71, 185, 203, 209
Don Quijote de la Mancha, 7, 9, 140, 151, 203
Doña Bárbara, 42
Doppelgänger. See Double
Dos Passos, John, 10
Dostoyevsky, Fyodor, 19
Double, 95, 96, 142
Dove, 84-85, 123

Earth mother, 47, 54, 56, 69, 78, 90-92, 106, 111, 114, 122, 128, 159, 160, 163, 213, 214, 216
Ecué-Yamba-O, 35
Eden, Garden of, 3, 39, 43, 57, 65, 69, 107, 130-31, 178, 183, 211
Edison, Thomas, 23
Edwards Bello, Jorge, 32
Ekué, *145-47*
Einstein, Albert, 91
Elizabeth I, 210
Emerson, Ralph Waldo, 18

Enantiodromia, 36, 69
Enkidu, 116
Enlightenment, 89
Entropy, 23, 39, 135-36, 161, 189, 224
Epic of Gilgamesh, The, 3, 56, 140
Eremites, 217
Eribó, 168
Eroica, 35
Eros, 88, 90-91, 93-94, 115, 127, 188-89, 224-25
Escorial, 196, 207, 211, 214
Eternal return, 169
Euclid, 97, 155, 223
Eumaeus, 49
Euridice, 95
Euthyphro, 9
Eve, 3, 17, 69, 182-83, 205
Existentialism, 17, 28, 64, 75, 103
Eyre, Jane, 86

Falcon, 196, 211, 218
Fall, 17, 39, 69, 102, 166, 167, 169
Fascism, 20
Father, search for, 62
Faulkner, William, 10
Fernández de Lizardi, José Joaquín, 9
Folle de Chaillot, La, 32
Ford, Henry, 23
Founding as creation, 56, 112
Freud, Sigmund, 163
Frye, Northrop, 25
Fuentes, Carlos, 1, 11, 46, 55, 85, 140, 155, 189, *190-222,* 226, 227
"Funerales de la Mamá Grande, Los," 69

Galahad, Sir, 1
Galileo, 200
Gallegos, Romulo, 42
Gamboa, Federico, 32

García Márquez, Gabriel, 44, 67, 69, 82, *109-37*, 221, 225
Garcilaso de la Vega, Inca, 177
Garden of Earthly Delights, 200
Genesis, 43-45, 50, 55, 58, 60, 79-80, 119, 185
George, St., 181
Gide, André, 10, 19
Gilgamesh, 3, 6, 48, 57, 116, 133, 176
Giraudoux, Jean, 32
Goddess, meeting with, 3, 31, 47, 54, 77, 80, 88, 95, 96, 105, 114, 123, 160-61, 182, 213, 215
Golden Age, 7, 102, 110, 185
Golden Bough, 87
Golden Fleece, 1
Gorgon, 46, 48
Gravity's Rainbow, 15, 62, 82, 189, 227
Great Time, The, 44
Great Whore of the Apocalypse, 129, 142, 166
Gucumatz, 218

Habana para un Infante difunto, La, 35
Hades, 25, 51, 62, 67-68, 72, 78-79, 81, 92, 95, 105, 117, 121, 125, 128, 133-34, 143, 149, 157, 159, 161, 168, 176, 180, 196, 212
Haydn, Franz Josef, 90
Hannibal, 20
Harmony of the spheres, 52-54, 61, 93, 112-13, 155
Heaven, 81, 104, 105, 197
Heidegger, Martin, 138, 172
Heisenberg, Werner, 52-53
Hell, 65, 67, 72, 79, 159, 171, 180, 197, 200
Hemingway, Ernest, 148, 159
Heracles, 195

Heraclitus, 103
Hermano asno, El, 3, 12
Hermaphrodite. *See* Androgyne
Hermes, 107, 125, 149
Hernández, José, 10
Hesiod, 62
Hierophany, 86, 108
Hieros gamos (sacred marriage), 2, 6, 10, 31-32, 45, 46, 51, 53, 54, 58, 69, 70, 74, 80, 89, 93, 107, 108, 112, 125, 128-30, 136, 157-58, 161, 184, 189, 190-91, 194, 209, 213, 225
Higgins, Dick, 138
Hitchcock, Alfred, 149
Hitler, Adolph, 20, 22, 23, 25
Hoffer, Eric, 22
Holdfast, 15, 16, 74, 75, 76, 77, 88, 102, 126, 153, 174, 197
Holy Grail, 1, 7, 59
Holy Roman Empire, 206
Homer, 5, 41, 48, 183
Homosexuality, 162-63
Hopis, 96, 219
Hopscotch. See *Rayuela*
Horace, 84
Horus, 208
Hosea, 13, 32, 130
Hospitality and communion, 2, 5, 6, 33, 126, 131, 217
Humor, 151-52
Hybris, 20, 54, 124
Hydra, 40, 46

Icarus, 99, 146, 161, 206
Iktomi, 98, 226
Immortality, 3, 6, 36, 126, 132, 134, 140, 151, 154, 157, 170, 179
Incest, 110, 127-29, 131
Initiation, 13, 17, 19, 33, 35, 37, 56
Invisibility, 121

Iphis, 125
Isaac, 63
Isaacs, Jorge, 10
Ishtar, 3, 6, 48, 84, 176
Ixion, 81

Jacob, 63
Janusian thinking, 91
"Jardín de senderos que se bifur-
    can, El," 220
Jason, 41
Jaynes, Julian, 16
Jerusalem, 129-30
Jesus Christ, 2, 5, 6, 14, 33, 45,
    69, 73, 110, 111, 118-20, 157,
    167, 169, 170, 189, 190, 192,
    193, 200, 203, 206, 221, 226
Johannine writings, 6, 119, 157,
    167
John the Apostle, 62
John the Baptist, 192
Joseph (husband of Mary), 110
Joyce, James, 10, 152
Jung, Carl, 2, 21, 27, 28, 31, 163

K, Joseph, 1
Kafka, Franz, 10
Kierkegaard, Søren, 13, 103
Krishnamurti, 32
Ku Klux Klan, 22, 24
Kung, Hans, 35

Labyrinth, 87, 88, 95, 104
Laertes, 59, 80
Lafcadio, 19, 20, 86
Laing, R. D., 14
Lancelot, 7
Lawrence, St., 197
Lenin, 20, 22
Lesbos, Isle of, 162
Leviathan, 127, 180, 211
Lezama Lima, José, 33, 36, 79, 82,
    126, 167

Logos, 88, 90, 92, 93, 177, 188-89,
    224, 225
Los de abajo, 1
Lost Steps, The. See Los pasos
    perdidos
Lot, wife of, 43
Loyola, Ignatius of, 20
Lunar character of goddess, 57,
    58, 66, 67, 72, 78, 89, 93, 122,
    124, 128, 176, 178, 182, 184,
    213

Machine Infernale, La, 181
Macías, Demetrio, 1
Mallarmé, Stéphane, 12
Man of action vs. man of words,
    5, 22, 82, 97, 203
Mandala, 95, 98, 103-4, 106,
    107, 156, 158, 226
Manichaeism, 194, 217
María, 10
Mars, 195
Martín Fierro, 10
Marvell, Andrew, 80
Marx, Karl, 22
Massa confusa, 42, 106-7, 139,
    167, 176, 226
Master of the Two Worlds, 21, 37,
    59, 124, 133, 157, 168
Maya, 29
Mayas, 2
Medusa, 46
Mercury. See Hermes
Merlin, 147
Messiah, 119, 169
Metamorphosis, 127, 177
Mexican Revolution, 2
Michael (Archangel), 6, 7, 167
Mictlantecuhtli, 212
Milton, John, 129
Mintho, 67
Mithraism, 68, 219
Mnemosyne, 151, 171

Moby Dick, 160
Moebius strip, 151
Molina, Tirso de. *See* Téllez, Gabriel
Monomyth, 10, 37, 223
Montaigne, 8, 90
Moses, 76, 187, 192
Moses Maimonides, 204
Muses, 151, 171
Music. *See* Harmony of the spheres
Mussolini, Benito, 20

Nabal (the fool), 5
Nahuatl, 144
Naming, 56, 112
Napoleon Bonaparte, 20, 173
Narcissus, 37
Naturalism, 30
Nazarín, 68
Nereids, 67
New Jerusalem, 24, 75, 130-31, 164
Newton, Isaac, 88, 226
Nietzsche, Friedrich, 19, 20, 22
Noah, 3, 12, 56, 84
Nonbeing, 74, 75, 77, 80-81, 102, 108, 125, 126-32, 136, 149, 157, 166, 189, 190, 194-97, 199, 207, 210, 218, 222, 225
Numerology, 154-56, 215

Oak as symbol of hero, 66
Odysseus, 2, 8, 10, 15, 16, 20, 24, 26, 30, 41, 45, 47, 48-49, 50, 58, 59, 62, 72, 80, 83-85, 88, 89, 92, 104, 125, 127, 143, 146, 161, 175, 179, 183, 196, 202, 209, 211, 213, 224
Odyssey, The, 2, 5, 10, 33, 37, 41, 48-49, 58, 59, 72, 83, 126, 131, 164, 217, 223

Oedipus myth, 29, 81, 123, 131, 181, 223-24
Oglala Sioux, 98, 226
Old Man and the Sea, The, 159
Olive tree, 84-85
One Hundred Years of Solitude. See *Cien años de soledad*
Ordeals, 51, 52, 60
Origin of Consciousness in the Breakdown of the Bicameral Mind, The, 16
Original sin, 69
Orphic thought, 52

Pan, 179-80
Pantaleón y las visitadoras, 30, 33, 42, 65, 116, 151, *173-89*, 212, 221, 224, 225
Paradise, 68, 72, 74, 102, 107, 110, 129, 162, 169, 185
Paradise Lost, 130, 211
Paradise Regained, 130
Paradiso (José Lezama Lima), 33, 36, 79, 126, 167, 190
Pas Perdus, Les, 59
Pasamonte, Ginés de, 7
Pasos perdidos, Los, 35-61, 75, 76, 80, 96, 102, 173
Paz, Octavio, 51, 130, 190
Pedro Páramo, 62-81, 88, 92, 93, 100, 114, 115-16, 129, 132, 157, 166, 189, 192, 197, 224, 227
Penelope, 2, 10, 16, 26, 30, 45, 47, 48, 58, 59, 60, 84-85, 88-89, 99, 127, 176, 213, 224
Pericles, 223
Periquillo Sarniento, El, 9
Persephone, 78
Phaeacians, 8
Pharoah, 76
Philip II, 194, 202
Phoebus Apollo, 219

Pícaro and picaresque novel, 9, 225

Piedra de Sol, 51, 130

Pindar, 36

Plato, 35, 42, 43, 53, 69, 92, 169, 223

Pliny, 208

Plutarch, 27

Polo Febo, 11

Polynesia, 128

Polyphemus, 2, 16, 49, 131, 176, 211

Popol Vuh, 72

Poseidon, 67, 88, 176, 211

Prometheus, 39, 50, 54, 208, 218

Prometheus Unbound, 39, 54

Prophets, Hebrew, 72

Prostitution, 24, 32, 115-16, 122-23, 128-30, 142, 173-89, 225

Proteus, 139, 167, 226

Proust, Marcel, 10

Puer aeternus, 86, 184

Pynchon, Thomas, 15, 138, 189, 227

Pythagoras, 154-56, 200, 223

Quetzalcóatl, 193-94, 212, 214, 218

Raglan, Lord, 4, 5, 20, 21, 28, 52

Raskolnikoff, 19, 20

Rationalism, 224

Rayuela, 14, 26, *82-108,* 133, 156, 161, 170, 183, 205, 215-16, 221, 226

Reformation, 201

Reino de este mundo, El, 35

Relativity theory, 91

Remus, 18

Return, refusal of, 38, 60, 105

Return, triumphant, 3, 142

Revelation, Book of. See Apocalypse

Rhea, 62

Rojas, Fernando de, 209

Romanticism, 9, 10, 41, 42, 142

Rome, 18, 24, 206

Romulus, 18

Roto, El, 32

"Ruines circulares, Los," 220

Rulfo, Juan, 62-81, 111, 136, 197, 198

Russian language, 156

Sacred wedding. See *Hieros gamos*

Sacrifice, human, 27, 79, 93, 120, 174, 179, 181, 184-88, 190, 194, 212, 213, 214, 224-25

Sagittarius, 40, 41

Samson, 175, 183

Samuel, 58

San Manuel Bueno, Mártir, 140

Sancho Panza, 8

Sanskrit, 110, 129, 134-35

Santa, 32

Sarduy, Severo, 105

Satan, 7, 203, 216-17, 226

Saul, 58

Scapegoat, 187-88

Self (Jungian concept), 94

Semele, 178

Sephiroth, 215

Serpent, 178-79, 188

Seseribó, 145-48

Set, 208

Seven Madmen. See *Siete locos, Los*

Shadow, Jungian, 27

Shakespeare, William, 220

Shamanism, 19, 113, 147

Shelley, Percy Bysshe, 54

Siete locos, Los, 2, *12-34,* 36, 40, 42, 45, 75, 82, 100, 130, 205, 219, 226

Siete lunas y siete serpientes, 224

Siger de Brabant, 140
Siglo de las luces, El, 35
Sikán, 145-48
Sirens, 59, 161, 175
Sisyphus, 49-50
Smoking Mirror, 212-14, 218
Socrates, 8, 9, 84, 179, 223
Sodom and Gomorra, 165
Solar character of hero, 8, 15, 30, 58, 68, 72, 73, 77, 86, 88-89, 109, 131, 175-76, 178, 180-84, 188, 192-222, 224
Source of power, 20, 23, 26, 36, 38, 53, 54, 60, 64-65, 68, 71, 73, 76, 100, 106, 110, 121, 142, 173, 189, 198
Sphinx, 224
Spider, 96, 98, 213-14, 219, 226
Spiral, 104
St. Elmo's Fire, 209, 214, 218
Styx, 149
Substitutionary atonement, 115, 148
Sumer, 97
Sun gods, 68
Susana, 67
Synchronicity, 87

Tammuz, 72
Tasso, 129
Teiresias, 12, 72, 92
Telemachus, 16, 80, 85
Téllez, Gabriel, 201
Terra nostra, 1, 30, 44, 46, 51, 55, 68, 85, 116, 120, 129, 140, 155, 173, 183, 189, *190-222,* 227
Tezcatlipoca, 213-14
Theseus, 95
Thomas Aquinas, St., 199
Three Trapped Tigers. See *Tres tristes tigres*
Tiberius Caesar, 190, 195, 205-7, 214, 215

Timaeus, 42
Time, 35-36, 43, 56, 114, 122, 132, 143, 191
Tlauixcalpantecuhtli, 213
Tollan, 225
Tragedy, Greek, 20
Tree of Enlightenment, 111
Tres tristes tigres, 33, 62, 116, *138-72,* 182, 183, 219
Trickster, 16, 17, 91, 97-99, 103-4, 139, 153-54, 171, 202, 207, 220, 225-27
Tristan, 86
Trotsky, Leon, 168
True Believer, The, 22
Twins, 96, 120-21, 207, 212, 219
Two brothers theme, 57-58, 80-81, 96-98, 110, 145, 185, 194, 207, 209, 211-16

Unamuno, Miguel de, 3, 140
Übermensch, 20
Ulysses. *See* Odysseus
Unified field theory, 155
Uranus, 63
Utnapishtim, 3, 56
Utopia, 208

Valentino, Rudolph, 32
Valhalla, 6
Vargas Llosa, Mario, 24, 32, 65, *173-89*
Vega, Garcilaso de la, 105
Venus (goddess). *See* Aphrodite
Venus (planet), 78, 130, 212-13, 213-14, 218
Venus of Willendorf, 163
Versailles, Palace of, 225
"Viaje a la semilla," 35, 36
Viracocha, 177
Virgin Mary, 6, 68, 110
Vishnu, 201

Vivian, 147
Voyage to the source, 3

Waiting for Godot, 85
Weaving of destiny, 58, 89, 127, 213-14
Wheel of fortune, 9, 225
White Goddess, 84, 96, 122, 169, 224
Wise old man, 21, 22, 25, 58, 72, 84, 106, 116, 132, 135, 215, 223
Womb, return to, 59

Word, creative, 54-55, 72, 73, 82, 105-8, 135-36, 138-72, 221, 227

Yahweh, 13, 32, 55, 73, 76, 130, 157
Yacuruma, 178
Yang and yin, 65, 89
Ygdrassil, 95

Zeus, 62, 93, 224
Zohar, 217

This book was set in Century Textbook by McClain Printing Company of Parsons, West Virginia.

The cover was designed by Paul Stevenson.

West Virginia University Printing Services was printer and binder.